THREE-QUARTER TIME

*The Life and Music of
the Strauss Family of Vienna*

Three-Quarter Time

The Life and Music
of the Strauss Family of Vienna

By JEROME PASTENE

ABELARD PRESS   *A*   NEW YORK

To My Mother,
In Remembrance of Vienna

LIST OF ILLUSTRATIONS

CONTENTS

BOOK III

THE END OF A DYNASTY

REFERENCE SECTION

AN INTRODUCTION

BY ARTHUR FIEDLER

THERE HAVE BEEN PREVIOUS BOOKS on the history of Johann Strauss, the "Waltz King," and the life and light music of his times. Yet this book is not a duplication of what already has been covered in this field, for until now most biographers of Johann Strauss have concerned themselves exclusively with the romantic story of his life. Here that story is by no means slighted—indeed, details are included which up to now seem to have escaped Strauss's biographers, notably the visits of the Strausses to America. Jerome Pastene has even dealt at length with other members of the family, who often come in for only a casual mention from other biographers. Indeed, in this respect "Three-Quarter Time" is not so much a history of Johann Strauss II as it is the history of light music in Vienna in the Nineteenth Century.

But the main distinctions of this book are the degree of attention which it pays to the compositions of the Strausses, the picture it draws of the development of the waltz as a concert form, and the analyses (technical and artistic) of a number of the compositions of the Strausses.

The average reader is, I think, inclined to consider the performance of a Strauss waltz a simple matter for a conductor. May I state emphatically that it is not! I have recorded more music of the Strauss family for the phonograph than has any other conductor, and still I find that I must approach each performance as seriously and as carefully as I might a Beethoven overture. In his foreword to the Eulenberg minia-ture pocket scores, Victor Keldorfer puts the matter suc-cinctly:

"The rendering of a Strauss waltz is at first sight childishly simple, and yet a book might be written on the way the com-poser and more especially his younger brother Eduard con-ducted them, down to the beginning of the century. This interpretation is still a living memory to the older Viennese people, and to the credit of the younger generation it has been handed down to them."

For all its apparent simplicity, the performance of a Strauss waltz, with its subtle and delicate use of *rubato,* is anything but simple. There are any number of ways of playing a Strauss waltz, and the confusing fact is that more than one may be in the Viennese tradition. As Mr. Pastene points out, this tradition is something which can be learned only through having played in a Viennese orchestra under Viennese con-ductors.

And since the technique of proper performance is something so subtle, almost so national, as to defy words, Mr. Pastene has rightly chosen to append to this volume a fairly complete list of phonograph recordings, by means of which he seeks to indicate the fine difference between the true Strauss per-formance and a distorted one.

Jerome Pastene himself brings a respectable equipment to his task as biographer of this period and form of music. First, and not least, is his personal enthusiasm for this music and his love for the period from which it stemmed. Second, the care involved in the preparation of this book, which was begun in 1941. Third, Mr. Pastene's personal experience with this music and the Strauss operettas on the stage gained as Theater and Music Control Officer for the Military Government of

Württemberg-Baden, Germany. Finally, Mr. Pastene's experience as a conductor and the thorough technical understanding of the Viennese waltz which he thereby acquired. For it takes a certain kind of courage for any American to venture to conduct a German or Austrian orchestra in music which they consider so particularly theirs, and a definite talent to make them accept such performances as authentic in style!

BOOK I

THE WORLD
OF THE WALTZ

THE EARLY DAYS OF JOSEF LANNER
AND JOHANN STRAUSS, SR.

THE Viennese Waltz did not, like Athena, spring into being full-grown. It had a long and tortuous pedigree, beginning with the Round Dance of the Middle Ages, and continuing through the Carmagnole of the French Revolution, and the so-called German Dances, to its immediate parent, the Länd-ler, to which it is so closely related that many waltz passages are marked *im Ländler tempo*. But precisely at what period the Ländler shed its peasant boots for the elegant slippers of the aristocratic ballroom, it is impossible to determine.

It is a popular belief that the first waltzes originated with Lanner and Strauss. Yet long before either had ·tucked his first violin beneath his chin, the waltz had made its appear-ance and had gained a certain popularity. Mozart, visiting Prague in 1787, described the people of that city as "flying about with such delight to the music of my *Figaro*, trans-formed into waltzes and quadrilles." Mozart was followed, and the primitive waltz improved, by Franz Schubert with his *Walzer, Valses Sentimentales, Vienna Belles* and *Valses Nobles*.

For practical purposes, however, yet another composer must be credited with the creation of the waltz as both a concert-and-dance form, for to none of these earlier compo-sitions can one dance the waltz as it was known on ballroom floors during the latter half of the Nineteenth Century.

This first true concert-and-dance waltz was the *Rondo Brillante* in D-flat major, Op. 65, by Karl Maria von Weber, the founder of the German Romantic School of opera. This composition, originally written for piano, is better known as the *Invitation to the Dance,* as well as by the erroneous but obviously natural title of *Invitation to the Waltz.* Written in 1819, when Johann Strauss was a lad of fourteen, it was stylistically a full fifty years ahead of its time. (The formal structure of the *Rondo,* however, is unlike that of the true Viennese Waltz.)

Invitation to the Dance is also the musical portrait of Vienna, 1814. Napoleon I, defeated by the major powers of Europe under England's aegis, was in exile at Elba; in Vienna the ruling sovereigns and political lords of Europe were gathered to settle the fate of France. King Maximilian-Josef of Bavaria, King Friedrich-Wilhelm of Prussia, Czar Alexander I of Russia and the King of Denmark led the van of famous visitors. Talleyrand and Metternich, each intent on his own political machinations and intrigues, mingled each evening with the select guests, rubbing elbows with the Countess Bernstorff, the Princesses of Hesse, Prince Lobkowitz and Prince Lichnowsky, the patrons of Beethoven, Prince Esterházy, Count Witt, and the Prince von und zu Lichtenstein. Other great Austrian families were represented: Auersberg, Colloredo and Zischy, among others. Even the new aristocracy, the aristocracy of finance, was prominently in evidence. A few names suffice — Mendelssohn, Eskeles, Pereira, Arnstein.

Led by this glittering assemblage, the population of Vienna and the one hundred thousand visitors to which it was currently playing host turned the five months' tenure of the Congress of Vienna into a paradise in waltz-time. The extravagance was shocking, the pace appalling. It ended abruptly during a ball at Prince Metternich's palace on March 7th, 1815, when the news of the little Corsican's return to France "struck the party like lightning from the sky," as de la Garde put it. The reaction of the guests was summarized by the Countess Bernstorff when she noted that "the Czar's pallor shouted what his lips would never have breathed."

But while the party lasted, it was a gay one. And it was to music such as Weber's *Invitation to the Dance* that the pace was set . . . .

FAR from the elegant palaces of Austria's great, the Leopoldstadt, situated on an island in the Danube, was at this period Vienna's most northeasterly suburb. It was a poor locality; the houses were old and shabby, and the streets, paved with cobbles which showed the wear of a hundred years, were medievally primitive. Street lighting was haphazard, often nonexistent, and sewer systems unknown. The Leopoldstadt was occupied largely by Poles and Czechs, together with a great number of Jewish artisans, many of them refugees from Russian domination.

Along the Flossgasse, a typical street, close enough to the Danube for it to cater to boatmen and carriers travelling to and fro between Southern Germany and Hungary, stood a small inn, *Zum Guten Hirten,* owned by Franz Strauss and his wife, Barbara Tollman Strauss. Here, amid the all-pervading odor of beer and the noise of brawling bargemen, their only child was born.

March 14th, 1804, dawned cold, with alternating rain and snow. The midwife at first refused to venture out in the inclement weather, arriving almost too late to lend any assistance. It was she who laid in the arms of innkeeper Franz the frail, thin body of his son, whom the Carmelites baptized Johann.

Among these sordid surroundings young Johann spent his childhood. When he was less than a year old, his father was found drowned in the Danube. There were rumors of suicide, but these were never verified. His mother, unable to continue operating the inn by herself, married another innkeeper, a man named Golder.

Johann was fortunate in having a stepfather who received him as his own child. He encouraged him in all his childish amusements, and it was he who first noted Johann's constant preoccupation with rhythm and melody. The child would take a stick and beat it in three-quarter time, as though it were a baton. Often, too, he would pretend to fiddle, using one stick for a bow and another for a violin, tucking one end beneath his chin, and fingering the other in rapt imitation of the vagrant fiddlers whom he sometimes saw in the *Guten Hirten*.

It was his kindly stepfather who gave him, on his name day, a cheap Bavarian fiddle. The tone was dry, thin and wiry, and might have well discouraged a less determined youngster. Legend has it, amusingly but probably inaccurately, that he at times poured beer into the body of the instrument to make the tone more mellow.

On his own initiative, and with some irregular and not always helpful advice from the strolling players who frequented the inn, he taught himself to play. When we recall that it was his warm tone and virtuosity which first established Johann in Vienna, his early and almost formless beginnings as a violinist are all the more amazing.

The love of music which he had known before now became an all-enveloping and all-consuming passion, allowing him no time for study. He brought his violin to school, and plucked on it absently during classes. His teachers despaired of him; his reports grew progressively worse. There was no cure. His stepfather, anxious that young Johann acquire at least the

rudiments of a sound education, tried every form of persuasion and compulsion, to no avail.

At last, one of the boy's teachers, hearing him play, went to
the parents and pointed out to them his remarkable talent. A
few close friends did the same. Emboldened by their support,
Johann had the temerity to tell his parents that he wished to
become a musician. They were horrified; their conception of
a musician was bounded by the itinerant "dinner musicians,"
those poor, bedraggled vagrants who wandered from *Wirtshaus* to *Wirtshaus*, offering a day's fiddling in exchange for a
dish of food and a pallet on which to sleep. A "dinner musician" was of the social level of the prostitute; this was not
the career for their Johann. His parents somehow never en-
visioned the possibility that their son might become a great
and successful composer like Beethoven or Haydn or Mozart.
And so he was apprenticed to a bookbinder.

Lichtscheidl, the bookbinder, was not an unkindly man, but
his patience was sorely tried by the unruliness of his new ap-
prentice. Johann would go into tantrums of the wildest sort,
throwing his tools on the floor, scattering the books literally
as leaves before a storm. In desperation, Lichtscheidl would
beat him and then lock him in the woodshed. His wife, a more
understanding creature, waited until he had stamped off in
fury to let the boy free.

There seemed to be one solution to this intolerable situation. One warm summer afternoon, his violin beneath his
arm, Johann slipped away from his master's shop and headed
for the Kahlenberg, that mountain which looks down so be-
nignly upon Vienna. A casino was located on the summit, and
there Johann hoped to gain a few coppers by his fiddling. Out
past Döbling and Grinzing he went. As he mounted the slope,
the valley of the Danube spread out further and further below him, a vast panorama of orchards, meadows, woodlands

and farmland. Fascinated by this enchanting vista, so different from the drab colors of his native Leopoldstadt, he came to a halt. Stretching himself on the grass in the last warm glow of the setting sun, he looked past Vienna along the course of the Danube towards Hungary. Weariness and a sort of contentment gradually benumbed him, and in this idyllic setting he fell asleep.

By fortunate coincidence, he was found there some hours later by the violinist Polyshanski. Intrigued by the sight of a young boy so peacefully asleep in the country with a violin beside him, he awakened the lad, who recounted his misfortunes. Polyshanski took Johann to his own home for the night, and returned him to his parents the following morning. Their relief was unbounded, for they had feared that in a fit of self-pity and despair he might have thrown himself into the Danube. His father's mysterious and tragic death did not allow them to discount that possibility.

Johann's new protector talked at length with the parents concerning their son's future, and at last secured their permission to allow Johann to study music as a career. Polyshanski himself undertook the violin instruction which the boy greatly needed; although Johann was already proficient on his instrument, guided by a natural and most catholic musical taste, the finer points of violin technique—bowing, fingering, and such—he could not teach himself, and Polyshanski's aid was of the greatest importance.

Johann Strauss was only fifteen when he became a professional musician. His eagerness actually to engage in musical work led him to accept an offer which caused his parents some anxiety, and certainly it was not precisely the career which his tutor would have selected for him; but his headstrong nature would take no refusals or denials. He secured an appointment in the orchestra of one Michael Pamer, a conductor famed more for his capacity as a Falstaffian tippler than his ability as a sensitive musician. Nor was Pamer's audience of much better stamp at the time Johann entered his orchestra. Pamer placed his new man in the viola section, himself giving his new recruit some instruction on that instrument.

The atmosphere in which Johann now found himself gave his parents ample reason to claim that there was indeed nothing good in a musician. Pamer himself was constantly drunk, and many of his players followed the example he set. The public to whom they catered was at best that of the lower middle-class Viennese. When one remembers that Strauss's musicians of a later day were famed for their soldierly precision, one wonders whether his disgust at the unmusical exhibitions in which he was forced to take part when he played in Pamer's orchestra did not in a large degree influence him in his later insistence on smart precision.

Wholesome or not, here Strauss stayed for close to four years. Not all of his colleagues were cut from Pamer's cloth; close beside him in the orchestra sat a tall lad, whose sensitive features were surmounted by an aureole of wavy blond hair. This young man, some three years the senior of Johann Strauss, was Josef Lanner, Vienna's first famous waltz-master. Lanner remained with the orchestra only long enough to establish a close friendship with Strauss; he then left Pamer to form a trio with two brothers named Drahanek, of Bohemian origin.

Strauss kept his seat in Pamer's orchestra until he felt sufficient confidence in his abilities to seek something better. Then one day in the Prater he sought out Lanner, who was giving an open-air concert with the two Drahaneks. Lanner invited Strauss to dine with them. During the course of the dinner, Johann asked if he might join their band and develop the trio into a quartet. Lanner was more than willing, for he knew Strauss to be a fine musician, and sensed in him that spark of mutual appreciation, sympathy and understanding always so necessary to the success of any small instrumental combination.

Josef Lanner was himself a native of Vienna, for his birthplace was Oberdöbling, a suburb close to the bastions of the city proper. He was in some respects the lesser musician, for he lacked even Strauss's meager grounding in harmony and composition; yet he was an inspired composer, and, despite the accident of Weber's unique *Invitation to the Dance,* it is Lanner who was the first to make the Viennese Waltz a dance of sophisticated appeal.

Lanner and Strauss made a perfect pair. They not only became sympathetic musicians and teammates, but roommates as well, with all the close friendship which such an association brings. The curly black head of Strauss was never far from the unruly blond thatch of Lanner. Life at first was not easy for them, and making both ends meet was a serious problem, albeit one spiced liberally with humor. Matters at last became so bad that the two young men had only one shirt between them, so that one, perforce, had to stay at home when the other ventured abroad. Together with the Drahaneks, these two boys presented, in the nonchalant acceptance of their lot, a picture that was the Viennese counterpart of Rudolphe, Marcel, Colline and Schaunard, in Henri Murger's *La Vie de Bohème.*

But matters improved. Engagements began to come in with regularity, partly because the quartet was capable of music above the ordinary *Kaffeehaus* caliber, and partly because the "musical twins" were making themselves so well known in Vienna through their irresistible escapades that they were personally in demand. Their antics were endless, until every mystifying prank came to be laid at their door. Like Till Eulenspiegel, they followed one practical joke with another until the heads of the poor Viennese were spinning around like so many tops.

Business improved so much that Lanner finally augmented his forces to twelve, acquiring at last an orchestra of a sort. Johann became his leader and first violin, even taking the conductor's stand on occasion. And still the demand continued, and more music was required of Lanner. He engaged still more men, enlarging the orchestra to the point where it could occasionally be divided into two groups. Thus did Strauss at times appear as conductor during one concert, whilst Lanner, on the same evening, directed another. As the concerts increased, so did the demand for original music. Lanner had brought forth waltzes which more and more were drawing the respect of serious and competent musicians. He was doing more for the waltz than Weber had done, for Weber, a composer in other forms, had, like Ravel and his *Bolero,* merely taken a popular dance form and with one solitary composition given to it the prestige of his name. Lanner, on the other hand, had taken a scorned dance of the common people and through his genius had succeeded in starting its rise to a level worthy of respect.

Lanner's famous *Schönbrunner Waltzes* are an excellent example of his powers at their peak; these are, in fact, among the few waltzes from his pen that are at all current today. The first waltz will immediately be recognized by anyone familiar with Stravinsky's *Petrouchka,* for the Russian composer has made an almost undistorted use of it, acknowledging its source, in the Dance of the Ballerina and the Moor, in the Third Tableau:

It is not without reason that one may stress Weber's influence on both Lanner and Strauss; there is more than a superficial resemblance between this waltz and the D-flat major theme of the *Invitation to the Dance*. Weber's is the more elegant, but both are intimately related. *Schönbrunner* was first performed at Dommayer's Garden Restaurant, where Johann Strauss II was to make his debut a few years later.

The growing number of compositions demanded of Lanner was the first step in creating a rift which was to rend the "musical twins" asunder. The younger Johann once discussed the occurence: "One day it happened that Lanner fell ill and was incapable of work. Thereupon, he sent the perfectly natural message to my father: 'Strauss, see if you can think of something.'" Strauss did, and his own true Opus 1 appeared that evening on the program, with Lanner's name on the credit line. That assumption of credit which, it must be realized, was and still is the rule in much of the world's dance music, brought the first discord into the erstwhile harmonious relations of Lanner and Strauss. There was no longer the close association of the two men to counteract the poison. Lanner was married and had been living in his own home for some time. With their close intimacy broken, these little incidents which provoked ill-will grew to form a wedge which finally resulted in a break-up. Probably Strauss was the more to blame. His temper was notoriously shorter than Lanner's and while the latter may have taken advantage of his good nature, there is no ignoring that broad streak of jealousy which was evidenced not only here, but in Johann's later dealings with his sons.

The final explosion happened in the *Zum Bock* ballroom. Strauss had announced his intention of resigning, and Lanner had agreed to allow him to go his way. That evening Lanner began a farewell speech, addressed to the audience, and eulogizing Strauss. But a drink too many had loosened his tongue, and insulting innuendoes crept in. Strauss endured all his little patience permitted; then, his temper besting him, he threw himself at his friend. With their bows drawn as swords, they went at each other until separated by members of the orchestra. Their fisticuffs spread first to the players and then to the audience, as the occupants of the hall took sides. Instruments were broken; flutes were used as clubs; a violoncello exploded when someone put an incautious foot through it; a contrabass was smashed. Someone threw a chair, which crashed into the enormous mirror, a costly and featured part of the hall's decorative scheme. This brought in the police.

Strauss departed, and with him fourteen of Lanner's best men, the nucleus of the first Strauss Orchestra.

The two men who had grown up as brothers parted as enemies. Yet they still loved each other. Lanner returned home that night to write his *Trennungswalzer* (*Separation Waltz*), "celebrating" his break with Strauss, and it is significant that the word *Klage* (lament) appears in the music.

2

THE FIRST JOHANN

STRAUSS had been separated from Lanner for only a few months when he married. His bride was Anna Streim, daughter of the owner of the *Roter Hahn,* an inn where Lanner and Strauss often appeared. The origin of the Streim family has never been clear. The genealogy may be traced back to a certain Rober, who first appears as a cook at the court of Duke Albert von Sachsen-Teschen. This man was variously described as an ex-Grandee of Spain who fled his homeland after killing a Prince of the blood in a duel, and as a Gypsy of unknown origin. Decsey advances the argument that he was really a Gypsy who, to maintain the security of his new position, had invented the ingenious fiction of the "ex-Grandee," a subterfuge which would well have accounted, in the eyes of the unworldly servant class in which he found himself, for his swarthy complexion and foreign accent. As Decsey shrewdly says, this would have been a psychological necessity, for the social station of a roving Gypsy was as far below that of a court cook as the cook would have been below the Grandee of Spain. Decsey's contention is further substantiated by a legend which would have it that the Duke of Saxony-Teschen, a friend of the fugitive Grandee, offered him shelter on condition that he conceal his origin, lest in harboring him the Duke place himself in a difficult diplomatic position. Inasmuch as Duke Albert was a brother-in-law of the Emperor Josef, his power was sufficient for him to risk the anger of the King of Spain, and openly give shelter to a Grandee, if such indeed he was. Therefore, we may rightly suppose Decsey to be correct when he suggests that this legend was merely a protective myth invented by the Gypsy-turned-cook.

This Rober of uncertain origin had five children: two sons and three daughters. One son died young; the other became a painter in the service of Prince von und zu Liechtenstein. Like her brother, the eldest daughter also died at an early age. Of the remaining two, the youngest, Maria Anna, married Josef Streim, a coachman in the service of Prince Esterházy. It was not until after their marriage that Streim left Prince Esterházy's employ and bought the *Roter Hahn,* where his youngest and prettiest daughter, Anna, met and captivated dynamic Johann Strauss.

It was largely because of her that he left Lanner's orchestra. It was a matter of necessity. He needed more money; he had to marry Anna Streim, for she was with child. Actually, although they were blindly in love, the two made an ill-matched couple. Both were of a like and difficult temperament; fiery, quick to anger, obstinate and reserved. They seemed more like brother and sister than husband and wife. Their children, born in a land where fair skin and light hair predominate, had swarthy complexions which served to perpetuate the Rober legend.

The fifteen men who formed the first Strauss Orchestra had little need for preparatory rehearsal, for each knew his neighbor well. Their first public appearance together under their new leader was at the *Gasthof zu den Zwei Tauben,* where Strauss introduced his Opus 1, the *Täuberln-Walzer,* honoring in name the scene of its first hearing. The orchestra for which it was scored is interesting: four violins, one flute, two clarinets, two horns, one trumpet, and contrabass. Apparently, in leaving Lanner, Strauss was at first unable to secure either violas or cellos, with the result that his first orchestra found itself with a strangely unbalanced string section. It is a compliment to his ability that he found no difficulty in confining his scoring to the instruments available. For, as an orchestra, this first one was certainly unconventional. Apart from the missing strings, one notes the absence of oboes, bassoons, a second trumpet and all percussion.

Strauss's success was immediate. He made his debut as a musician already known in Vienna. His fracas with Lanner had resulted in publicity which brought his first appearance before his own orchestra to everyone's attention. This publicity had one unhappy result; it prevented a settlement of the differences between Lanner and Strauss.

Despite his quick and easy success and the attractive offers of rival publishers, the new Waltz King was aware of his deficiencies as a composer, and set to remedying them without delay. He took lessons in composition, counterpoint and orchestration from von Seyfried, the conductor who had been a close friend of Beethoven. Not contented with this, he included a course in theory, under Jansa. Bolstered by an ever-widening musical horizon, he threw the narrow, unimaginative traditions of dance music to the winds, writing waltzes, each of which had its individual form and design. Previously, the waltz had been held within a rigid mold which arbitrarily measured out the number of bars allowed the introduction, the first waltz phrase, its return phrase, the bridge passage to the second waltz, and so on. With Strauss, the waltz for the first time acquired freedom of motion. No longer did the couples dance solely to a metronomical rhythm which barren tunes could scarcely conceal. Now the dancers waltzed to

long melodies, new and ingenious, always fresh and almost always completely different.

Strauss's debut as orchestra leader came at a most auspicious time—during the midst of the Vienna Carnival Season,
with life at its gayest. Vienna always found time for music-
making throughout the year, but it was the annual Carnival
which brought all entertainment to a peak. Then any orchestra of the least ability was assured of engagements; an organization as well-drilled as Strauss's compact little group was
certain of a choice of good offers.

Now began a rivalry for control of the world of Viennese
light music that was not to end until Lanner's untimely death
in 1842. To Lanner's advantage was his earlier presence upon
the scene as conductor. Consequently, many of his more
blindly devoted followers could not or would not see the qualities which Johann Strauss possessed. The two men were utterly different in style. Like his waltzes, Lanner's approach as
conductor and violinist was persuasive and heavily sentimental. Strauss, on the other hand, is well characterized in the
commanding power and exuberance of his waltzes; as a violinist, his tone was more brilliant and authoritative. Lanner
was master of the slowly swelling *sforzando,* while Strauss's
violin tone and technique were not unlike those of the Magyár *Zigeuner* fiddlers. Lanner's tone recreated the human
voice, warm, throaty and persuasive. Strauss held fast to the
Hungarian tradition that a violinist should perform dance
music with the utmost sensuality and brilliance. Strauss was
unexcelled in this style, which he had learned from Polyshanski, but he could, with almost equal ease, imitate Lanner's more conservative technique, whereas Lanner was incapable of playing in the Hungarian manner. Yet Lanner's
devotees refused to recognize this.

Striving to advance himself, Lanner, in 1829, secured the

appointment to direct the concerts of the Redoutensaal, the Imperial ballroom in the Hofburg, and was honored with the title of *Königlich und Kaiserlich Hofballmusikdirektor,* which he unfortunately later forfeited as a result of having rudely addressed the Archduchess Sofia. This Johann Strauss would never have done. Born into a world several social strata lower than that of Lanner's glovemaker father, Johann Strauss was by instinct a gentleman; never obsequious, yet far too well-mannered to have been guilty of such a breach in conduct.

Countering Lanner's appointment in the Redoutensaal, in 1830 Strauss signed a contract to direct the concerts of the famous Sperlsaal, that most select of Viennese ballrooms. Engagement at the Sperlsaal was for him as great a triumph as Lanner's newly gained title. Ten years earlier he had first seen this room as a member of Pamer's orchestra; he now reëntered it as the co-ruler of Viennese dance music.

Johann Strauss, in 1830, had progressed far beyond his humble beginnings as conductor of the few men who had followed him in his dramatic departure from Lanner's employ. He now had approximately two hundred musicians under contract. The best of these formed the regular Strauss Orchestra; theirs was a steady occupation. The others were called upon from time to time to make up other orchestras when, as during the Carnival season, Strauss had signed contracts to provide music at as many as six balls a night.

He was at this time twenty-six years old. His eldest son, Johann II, was not yet five; his second son, Josef, almost three. The third child, Nelli, was still a babe in arms. Three more children were yet to be born to Anna Streim-Strauss: first a daughter, Therese, born in 1831; later, two sons. The first, Ferdinand, was born in 1834; he died when less than two years old. The last was Eduard, born a year after Ferdinand.

As a musician, Strauss at twenty-six had gained the unqualified respect and admiration not only of the musical public of Vienna, but of the leading musicians of his day, as well. Strauss had brought the Viennese waltz to a point of development hitherto unsuspected of being possible; under his hand, the waltz had emerged from caterpillar to butterfly. It now not only had enchanted the lay public with its immediately apparent melody; it had assumed an artistic stature which could withstand the probings of that great music critic, Robert Schumann, and draw from him wholehearted approval and pleasure.

3

EUROPEAN PILGRIMAGE

IN THE late 1820's, Strauss had taken his orchestra to Buda-pest. His success there had been sensational, yet it had not excited him, for he wisely recognized Hungary's vassal status under Austria's aesthetic domination. Hungarian music, which was later to play so prominent a role when national-ism began to concern the artistic world, was still of interest only to the peasantry, and Hungary turned toward Vienna for its music, just as it had in the days when the Princes Es-terházy brought Haydn back to their Magyár estates to pro-vide musical entertainment. Now, in 1834, some five years after the Budapest excursion, having scaled the heights which Austria afforded, Strauss assembled a picked orchestra and sallied forth to make his name in Berlin. This was no easy task. There has always been between Berlin and Vienna, each representative of a widely different sort of Teutonic mind, a strong feeling of jealousy and distrust. Vienna (and to some extent Munich, too) mocks the artistic efforts of North Ger-many, which it considers ponderous, while Berliners find amusement in the tastes of the Viennese, which they consid-er shallow and effervescent.

Strauss's first appearance in Berlin, before King Friedrich Wilhelm III, his Queen and the Prussian Court, in the Kön-igsstädtertheater, was something in the nature of a daring venture. The Berliners were delighted, yet also amazed, at this

JOHANN STRAUSS, SR.
Lithograph by Kriehuber in 1835, autographed by Strauss with the
notation "*K. K. Hofballmusikdirektor.*"

A BALL IN OLD VIENNA

Oil Painting by Charles Wilda. Josef Lanner on the conductor's stand, with Johann Strauss, Sr., playing first violin to his right.

slim, pale conductor whose methods as a leader and violinist were so alien to all they had previously experienced. They were fascinated by his Gypsy-like manner of playing, the violin now held high in the air, now down and almost crouched over—"playing into the well." But unlike the Viennese, who have been known to go to any extreme to maintain a first opinion, however erroneous, the Berliners melted at once before the warmth and fervor of this art from the south. The Queen of Prussia did her utmost to persuade Johann Strauss to remain in Berlin, while the Czar and Czarina of Russia, then in the Prussian capital, made him fabulous offers if he would only visit St. Petersburg and assume direction of the Court music there.

It is interesting to speculate on what developments the waltz might have taken had Strauss accepted this profitable offer. One need only compare the typical Russian concert waltz (those by Tchaikovsky from his *Nutcracker, Sleeping Beauty* or *Swan Lake* ballets, or from the *String Serenade*) to the Viennese waltz as typified by Strauss, to note the contrast of Russian weightiness to Austrian ebullience. It can almost certainly be assumed that had Strauss taken up residence in Russia he would have exercised a considerable influence on that nation's music.

But, at the same time, it is impossible to imagine what the development of Austrian music (of all types) would have been without the Strausses. That their influence was enormous is clear to anyone who considers carefully such works as the Brahms *Liebeslieder Waltzes,* or the waltzes for piano. As with these, other great masterpieces of Austrian music, such as Richard Strauss's *Rosenkavalier,* could never have come into being without the broad and solid foundation which the waltz composers of Vienna had prepared.

However, Strauss made a courteous refusal to these offers,

explaining that his contract with the management of the Sperl was unbreakable, and doubly so with the Carnival close at hand. In truth, with Strauss it was more likely a matter of personal choice than of ethics; he would not have hesitated to break any contract or other obligation which might have bound him, if he had genuinely wished to go to Russia.

The end of the Carnival Season and the Spring of 1835 found Strauss again outside Austria. It was a real tour this time; the orchestra visited Munich, Augsburg, Stuttgart, Heidelberg, Frankfurt and Wiesbaden. The next year took him still further afield: Leipzig, Halle, Magdeburg, Brunswick, Hanover, Hamburg, Bremen, Oldenburg and Düsseldorf. He even traveled beyond German-speaking frontiers to Amsterdam, The Hague, Liège, Brussels and Aix-la-Chapelle, finding opportunity to include performances in Cologne, Mainz and Würzburg as well.

It was on October 4th, 1837, that Strauss bundled twenty-eight of his best men into the mail coaches of the Vienna-Strasbourg-Paris express. Crossing the Rhine at Kehl, they gave their first concert on French soil on October 20th. As Strauss was preparing to go upon the stage, he received a note from the Prefect of Police requesting him to have a trumpeter sound a tattoo. Mystified, and reluctant to do the Prefect's bidding because he did not know what it might mean, and felt himself in a difficult situation, a stranger in a foreign land, Strauss nonetheless signaled his trumpeter to carry out the request. The tattoo was sounded, and silence fell upon the house. The Prefect, in the center box, then arose and announced the capture of the Algerian city of Constantine the day before by French troops under General Damrémont. Wild cheering broke forth. A second tattoo was played. The Prefect, with sobs racking his voice, then announced that *"le brave Général Damrémont"* had fallen in the battle. Facile tears gushed from the eyes of the obliging audience, and the ladies fluttered their handkerchiefs in well-simulated (and perhaps well-believed) grief. A third tattoo followed, and the Prefect invited the audience to join in singing *La Marseillaise*.

Then Strauss appeared. Catching the audience at a high emotional pitch, the first waltz, played in a truly Viennese manner for which even familiarization through piano editions had failed to prepare the listeners, swept them off their feet and started an avalanche of acclaim which preceded Strauss into Paris.

This advance publicity was more welcome to Strauss now than at any other time in his brilliant career. In attempting to gain renown in Paris, he was storming the central bastion of Europe's intellectual citadel. Paris was then reaching the peak of her glory, the moment when she ruled the international world. The Second Empire, a more glittering era, was aesthetically shallow; Paris never equalled during that period the wealth of artistic endeavor which she brought forth under the reign of Louis-Philippe.

Advance publicity was one assurance of success. The other was the strong attraction which Parisians felt at that time for the culture of Germany and Austria, before three bloody wars and untold Prussian indignities roused in the Gallic mind a lasting hatred for the world of the Teuton. In Louis-Philippe's Paris, German art was eagerly sought. Von Weber's opera achieved nightly successes, and while the mysteries of Schubert escaped the French, Mozart, Haydn and Beethoven ruled the firmament of composers. Foremost among the intelligentsia upholding German art were Madame de Staël, Victor Hugo, and Théophile Gautier. Germanic art itself was represented in Paris by that expatriate German, Heinrich Heine. The adulation of German culture is even reflected in the "new" section of Auteuil, where streets and avenues are named for people famous in the world of letters, and the Avenue Mozart is intersected by the rue Georges Sand, the rue Henri Heine and the rue la Fontaine.

Strauss had no cause to fear that he might be introducing to Paris an art form alien to its intellectual thought. His concern rested with more material causes. He had not counted upon the gigantic scale on which music was heard in Paris. He had forgotten that he was entering the native city of Hector Berlioz, that composer-conductor-critic who had introduced the concept of the orchestra of several hundred men. With his small band of less than thirty, Strauss found that he would have to compete against so formidable a rival as Mûsard, whose orchestra numbered close to two hundred.

On November first, Strauss gave his opening concert. He suffered agonies of nerves before his entrance. The house was sold out; no need to fret there. Rather need he concern himself with those who sat in his audience. In the hall that night were the musical great of France. Auber was on hand to hear how Strauss played his Overture to *Les Faux-Monnayeurs.* Cherubini was also present; a leading opera composer, he was an even more powerful figure by virtue of his Directorship of the *Conservatoire.* Berlioz, too, was in the hall. Strauss had reason to quail before this critical battery. However finished a musician he might be, there was no telling how a group of Parisian composers might welcome him. Some of the most biting musical witticisms ever spoken were given birth in Paris concert halls by jealous composers. It was Gounod who spoke in contemptuous terms of Franck's *D Minor Symphony* at its first performance; it was Saint-Saëns who, listening to the opening bassoon solo of Stravinsky's *Le Sacre du Printemps,* remarked acidly, "What instrument is that?" and left the hall, precipitating a first-class riot.

Strauss need not have worried. He brought the French to

his feet, composers and all, just as he had subdued his own native Viennese.

ON THE evening of November 5th, Johann Strauss led his
small band of musicians into the Palais des Tuileries, where
they had been commanded to appear before King Louis-Philippe and his Court. In the antechamber before the central
staircase, they discovered a complete company of infantry,
drawn to attention before a battery of guns and a pyramid of
cannon balls. Mounting slowly up the broad carpeted stairs,
they at last arrived in the huge ballroom which was to serve as
concert hall. There, in a central position, they encountered the
epitome of *parvenu* bad taste—a white marble statue of the
King, astride his favorite charger. The room was almost gar-
ishly illuminated by an unusual number of candelabra. A stand
had been erected for the players behind a brass rail which was
to separate them from their august audience. To this point they
were conducted by attendants in resplendent livery.

Unexpectedly, drums were heard resounding through the
corridors from a distant point of the palace, and finally the
self-styled "King of the Bourgeois" appeared, accompanied by
diplomats, courtiers and military aides.

Louis-Philippe presented an appearance as completely opposed to that suggested by his magnificent statue as was
humanly possible. He was in truth the first constitutional monarch, lacking all semblance of majesty or military dignity; actually boasting that his power rested not with the army, as in the
past, but with the new world of power represented by the
great financiers and industrialists.

Chattering with one another, diplomats and courtiers, officers and ladies took their seats on the opposite side of the
brass railing. Suddenly a young man on the King's right arose
and, scrutinizing Strauss through his lorgnette, advanced to-

{ 31 }

wards the barrier. It was Leopold, King of the Belgians, only a few years previous the Duke of Saxony-Coburg-Gotha, until the Belgians drove out the Dutch in 1830, and called him to the throne.

King Leopold saluted Strauss, and asked him, in a natural and friendly manner, "Tell me, Herr Strauss, did we not meet before in Brussels?" Utterly confused and embarrassed, and uncertain of what etiquette was correct in this *opera-buffa* court, which was neither democracy nor monarchy in its protocol, Strauss made the same deep obeisance that he would have tendered in the Hofburg's Zeremoniesaal, and remained in that position until Louis-Philippe, to save him further embarrassment, gave the signal for the music to begin.

The first half of the concert followed the scheduled program, but at the intermission the musicians found that matters were getting out of hand. The members of the court stood chatting amongst them, the brass railing with its social significance completely ignored. Louis-Philippe bore down on the hapless Johann, took both his icy hands, and said to him, "I have known you through your waltzes for a long time, Monsieur Strauss. It does me all the more pleasure that you should now do me the honor of appearing here personally." Beside himself, Strauss relinquished his violin to a stranger, who began to play it quite decently. It was the Duc d'Orleans. Later, Strauss found himself in conversation with two attractive ladies. They had been talking for some time before he suddenly realized that his two companions were none other than the Queens of France and Belgium.

After the concert, champagne was served, and Louis-Philippe eulogized Strauss and his superb orchestra. Jacob[*] re-

---

[*] H. E. Jacob, author of *Johann Strauss, Father and Son*, published by Greystone Press, New York.

marks that "the musicians had the feeling that the concert was being continued on the social plane, with everyone play-ing an appointed part, and no one word-perfect."

But in the chill light of the next morning the Court of France, for all its democratic veneer, revealed itself as not one whit different from those other courts which had preceded it. Strauss received, at his hotel, a diamond clip and two thousand francs. Precisely the same sort of honorary token had been given to another Austrian in an earlier day; Mozart was sim-ilarly recompensed when he appeared at the court of Louis XV.

But this appearance at Court had one valuable result. It heightened enormously the esteem in which Parisians held him, and subsequent concerts were even greater successes than those which had gone before. Strauss himself guaranteed their successes with some clever bargaining. He concluded a contract with his greatest rival, Mûsard, whereby the Strauss orchestra would present the first half of a concert up to the middle intermission, after which Mûsard's orchestra of two hundred men would conclude the *soirée*. Through this ingen-ious expedient, Strauss gained a contrasting chamber-music atmosphere, a highly piquant comparison with an orchestra almost ten times larger. To the credit of Strauss's players, their perfect coördination and skilled execution, resulting in a brilliant technical finish and exquisite clarity of tone, stood in sharp relief to Mûsard's expert, but not nearly so tonally balanced, orchestra.

Strauss's complete discipline over his men finds a parallel only in the great masters of the baton who came at a much later date: Muck, Toscanini, Koussevitzky, Nikisch, Mahler and Furtwängler. His word was law. In performance, he could draw from his men a precision unknown elsewhere in his day, a precision which is to be found only in a few virtuoso orchestras of our own time. It was this same complete obedience of his men to his slightest desire which made it possible for him to give concerts with an orchestra of less than thirty pieces in a city whose public was accustomed to orchestras twice that size and larger.

In the daily lives of his men, Strauss exacted and obtained the same unswerving loyalty and blind obedience. On the sixteenth of December, at a time when many of his men were thinking of a return to Vienna for Christmas, Strauss unexpectedly announced that the orchestra would leave that very evening for Rouën. He had consulted no one, nor did it matter to him that his men had engagements of a personal nature for the next few days. He issued marching orders, and, like a general, expected them to be obeyed without question or delay. They were.

After three concerts and a masked ball, he again bundled the men into a post chaise. This time the destination was Le Havre, France's greatest port, center of the coffee importing trade and home of some of the wealthiest French merchants. Here they were to play for a gala supper and ball.

This extravaganza surpassed even the Byzantine debauchery of Paris and Rouën. Half-a-hundred bottles of champagne were uncorked simultaneously. Of all those present, only Strauss contrived to remain sober. The next morning, more dead than alive, Strauss's men found themselves once more en route for Rouën. Here their leader offered them a sumptuous luncheon, rivaling the supper of the night before. The whole meal was topped off with an abundance of champagne. Strauss had heard that still more champagne was the best cure for the aftereffects of too much champagne. He found that the effects of the cure were unexaggerated.

On the twenty-third, still in Rouën, the players began to show manifest signs of homesickness. The men longed for their wives and children, for the green of a Christmas tree, for baked apples and hot roast chestnuts, for all the other delicacies and homely intimacies of the Christmas season in Vienna.

Instead of these familiar customs, on Christmas Eve there was another magnificent supper, followed by a masked ball and gambling and a great deal of champagne. This was, although the men were unprepared for it, a typical French *réveillon*. They were shocked; their sober and religious Austrian souls could not comprehend a race of people who would carouse and make merry on the eve of the Saviour's birth. The ball continued until four in the morning, and in the cold dreary dawn that followed, the orchestra found itself once more on the road to Paris.

La Ville Lumière was shivering joyfully in the midst of the Christmas Day Carnival. Pierrots and Pierrettes, Harlequins and Columbines huddled on every street corner around the little coal braziers of the cafés, which formed small pools of warmth in the bitter cold. The Left Bank had turned out in force; artists and their models, costumed in the most bizarre and fantastic fashion, were on every street. It was a true *Fête Bohèmienne,* and the exhausted musicians could only blink their eyes in shocked amazement.

From December 27th to February 28th, the Strauss Orchestra gave a concert every evening without interruption. The body-aching weariness which overcomes and benumbs a musician who undertakes such a program can never be imagined by the layman who watches from the audience. Some of these concerts were public; others were given in the exclusive quarters of the great private houses in the Faubourg St. Honoré. One of these private balls was held New Year's Eve at the home of Maurice Schlésinger, editor of the *Gazette Musicale.* The ball was in Strauss's own honor. Paganini con-

gratulated Strauss on his music and his orchestra, and particularly on his excellent technique as a violinist, a concession of
no small nature for this taciturn genius. Cherubini insisted
that Strauss fiddled *"come un' Italiano,"* the highest praise he
could think of to bestow on the Waltz King, and one which
was scarcely conceit, when one considers that the Italian school
of violin playing has always been superior to the German.
Jacques Halévy, composer of *La Juive,* paid him compliment
after compliment, while Meyerbeer made much of the modest
manner in which Strauss accepted all these honors. He received another great ovation at a ball given by Prince Apponyi of the Austrian Embassy, at which the famous poet,
Anastasius Gruen, then enjoying a mild sensation in Paris,
recited an ode in his honor. Here, too, he met and talked at
length with the Prince de Bénévent, that self-styled Talleyrand, whose Machiavellian intrigues had brought about so
many wars, griefs, political changes and upheavals; whose
machinations had kept the Congress of Vienna in a constant
state of turmoil when Strauss himself was just ten years old.

Now the hero of the French capital, Strauss permitted himself many of the liberties which had made him famous in
Vienna. At the great mid-winter ball of the *Ville de Paris,*
where he was scheduled to play alternately with Dufresne, a
leading French conductor, black domino costumes had been
laid out for both the French and Austrian musicians. It had
long been the custom for everyone, guests and musicians
alike, to dress in costume; admittance was otherwise refused.
Yet Strauss categorically refused to have anything to do with
the costumes, and forbade his men to put them on. He insisted
that this was beneath his dignity; he was a musician, not a
clown. Count Apponyi approached him and gravely explained
that to persist in his refusal would cause diplomatic repercus-
sions. Monsieur de Gasparin, Minister of the Interior, argued

that if Strauss and his men appeared in ordinary evening clothes, there would be a riot. Strauss remained adamant, and the festivities were nowise disturbed. After the initial shock of discovering that the members of their Viennese orchestra were wearing regular evening attire, a fact which provoked only mild curiosity and comment, the dancing began and the public promptly forgot the incident.

It should not be supposed that Strauss acted out of childish pique. His refusal to wear guignol clothing, even on so appropriate an occasion, was founded on a sincere respect for the value of his art and the dignity of his profession. Just as certain of his contemporaries had to teach the society of that day that a man can be both a musician and a gentleman, so did Strauss, in his own way, wage his part at every turn in the battle to bring the musician out of the servant class and into the position which he properly deserved.

Strauss never lost his desire to learn, to progress and grow. In Paris, he asked Mûsard whether he might occasionally play in the violin section of the Frenchman's orchestra. When Mûsard, amazed and immensely flattered, asked why, he explained that he wished to learn what he could about the French quadrille, that he might introduce it to Vienna. To return with full pockets was not enough; he must also bring back something novel in his field of music.

IT WAS inevitable that Strauss, seeking new worlds to conquer, should have led his little band across the Channel to English shores. It is, in fact, strange that he never made the voyage to America, for Johann the Elder was the true adventurer of the Strauss family. It remained for his famous son finally to invade the New World, which is in itself a paradox, since, of all the Strausses, it was that son who cared least for travel and was happiest close to his own hearth. Yet perhaps Johann Strauss was wise in not attempting a transatlan-tic pilgrimage; perhaps America was not yet ready for the polished elegance of the Viennese Waltz.

England was. No other moment could have been more propitious. It was the Coronation Year of England's famous sovereign, Victoria, future matriarch of a continent of royal families, who was to give her name to the way of life of a whole half-century. The great Queen Victoria who was years later to greet Johann's son, Eduard, with pleasure in fond remembrance of her Coronation days, was, in that year of grace, 1838, a shy and graceful girl who had been unexpect-edly called to rule the Kingdom of Great Britain.

Johann Strauss foresaw a flood of balls in honor of the Cor-onation, and immediately concluded a number of contracts for appearances in England. This was the act of an astute businessman, but his failure to require guarantees was not, even though no ill came of it. But when he unexpectedly an-nounced that the orchestra was to leave directly for England without returning first to Vienna, open dissension broke out. Many of his musicians pointed to the lack of guarantees as proof that the expedition might prove a fiasco; after all, they argued, the British were notoriously cold and uncertain mu-sical audiences, and they all might end up in Debtor's Prison. Some of them openly called him an adventurer, and intimated that he had no intention of ever returning to Vienna. They insinuated that his domestic ties were none too strong, and that he was contemplating taking the whole orchestra to America. In this they were not far wrong. Although Strauss never went so far as to make active plans for such an expe-dition, a stupendous undertaking in that day of difficult trav-el, there is proof that he did toy with the idea.

Strauss simply insisted that, after the success which the or-chestra had achieved in Paris and other important centers, it was quite inconceivable that they should not enjoy a warm reception in England. However insular the English might be, he refused to believe that the notices of the phenomenal success of the Strauss Orchestra had not penetrated the island kingdom. If any of the men doubted him, they were welcome to return to Vienna. As far as he was concerned, he meant to go to England, if he had to do so alone and play there in solo recital.

His persuasive powers, his determination, his faith in future successes and his never-failing personal magnetism convinced almost all of his men that the best thing to do would be to remain with him. Of his whole band of twenty-eight men, only four refused to follow him to the British Isles, and took the coach for Vienna.

4

ENGLAND: CORONATION YEAR

It was on April 11th, 1838, that Johann Strauss and his orchestra found themselves upon the packet steamer *Princess Victoria,* on their way across the Channel. Their arrival in London the following day was well-timed. It is problematical whether puritanical England would have taken to this arch-priest of the sensuous waltz at another time; only a few years before, the waltz had been denounced throughout England as shocking, vulgar and immodest (because the man placed his arm about his partner's waist!), just as the rumba was a century later. But the wave of emotion which swept through England this Coronation Year, a wave of romanticism in which a girl of sixteen summers was the central figure, served Strauss's purpose, and made it possible for him to attain a success in England which greater musicians might well have envied.

What ensued, once Strauss reached London, might well have served as a libretto for a Gilbert and Sullivan lampoon on British customs and reasoning.

On arriving, Strauss visited the Austrian Embassy, where he was received by Prince Esterházy, Ambassador to the Court of St. James. Here he received a severe lecture from Esterházy on how to conduct himself in England. He was to examine every contract minutely, to read it at least three times. There would be no chance to plead ignorance of contract stipulations because of language difficulties. He was to keep all his money on deposit with a reputable banking establishment, and not in his rooms where it might be stolen. He was, finally, to live quietly, with none of the *réveillon* antics of France, and to avoid all lawsuits. England, the Ambassador warned him, was not France; in the British Isles publicity of that nature was not conducive to a successful career. That the advice stemmed from someone so improvident that his own fortune was sequestrated some twenty years later did not alter its worth.

Strauss soon felt the full import of Esterházy's advice. First, his rooms were burgled and £97 stolen from the pocket of a coat. Then, less than a week after his arrival, he was summoned to the law courts by an enraged hotel proprietor, who claimed that Strauss had reserved a number of rooms at his establishment, and then had failed to occupy them. This was true. When the party arrived at the hotel, they found that, contrary to representations made by letter to Strauss, the hotel did not even possess a public dining room, and that they would have to take all their meals out. Such being the case, they had picked up their belongings and moved to another, more practical hotel.

In court, Strauss was obliged to have his clarinetist, Reichmann, deputize for him, his own English being inadequate to the task of explaining himself to the peruked and befrocked judge. Even Reichmann could make but little headway, and matters had practically reached an impasse when a German seated in the court volunteered as interpreter.

Then it appeared that matters were not so serious after all. Strauss should not have moved in the middle of the week. Instead, he should have given notice and waited until the weekend, as was required in England. Furthermore, if the accomodations provided were not in keeping with the promises made him, he should have brought suit against the landlord. As it was, he must now pay for the four days, from the day he moved out until the end of the week, amounting to a sum of £29, or approximately 290 gulden. Strauss was delighted with so simple a solution, until he discovered that, as loser of the suit, he must also pay its costs, amounting to £140.

He was horrified. "I cannot leave the house until I have found surety," he screamed at Reichmann. "If I do, they will put me in their Debtor's Prison!" He urged Reichmann to get out and find some means of raising the money required by the bailiff. Reichmann went to the most logical place—to Cocks, one of England's leading music publishers. Cocks willingly put up the required surety, in exchange for the publication rights to Strauss's next waltz. Nothing could have been more satisfactory to Strauss. The waltz was immediately forthcoming, and Cocks made a tidy profit from its sale. Perhaps Strauss should not have given the waltz to Cocks; he was under at least moral obligation to Haslinger. But the situation demanded prompt and drastic action, and Haslinger, his Austrian publisher, understood.

Rescued from his difficulties through this opportune intervention, Strauss found himself free to discuss contracts with managers, and arrange for his London début. This was held at the Hanover Square Rooms, on April 17th, and although it was not well attended, the audience was keenly receptive to the magic of his bow and the excellence of his orchestra, with the result that warm notices from the press and comments of those present at the concert combined to bring about a full house for the second concert.

On the morning following the début, the music critic of the *Times* said, "The pieces performed were chiefly his own waltzes, but they are done in a manner most extraordinary and altogether novel in this country. He has so completely trained his band to work with him that all separate individuality is lost, an effect is produced like that of an accurately constructed machine. The most eccentric instruments, such as bells, castanets, cracking whips, etc., are occasionally introduced, and the construction of many pieces is highly fantastic, yet never is the mechanical perfection lost for an instant. Thus the band, though small, is made to give the effect of one three times more numerous. From the immense fame which Herr Strauss has acquired in Vienna, a more numerous audience might have been expected on this occasion. The smallness of this audience is chiefly to be attributed to the very inefficient means which were taken to give the public notice of the concert, as well as the injudicious selection of an opera night."

The program that evening was as follows:—

Le Serment—Overture	AUBER
Philomenen Walzer, Op. 82	STRAUSS
Introduction and Variations for Flute	
(performed by the composer)	R. FRISCH
Les Bouquets Walzer	STRAUSS
Gabriellen Walzer, Op. 68	STRAUSS
Rondo for Oboe	BAMBERGER
Ein Strauss von Strauss Potpourri, Op. 55	STRAUSS
Musikalische Telegrafe Potpourri, Op. 106	STRAUSS

The reviewer of the *Musical World* had this to say: "The disposition of his brass band is generally novel, frequently clever, and always claims attention. Of the wood band, we cannot say so much, and the string band appears scarcely powerful enough to make its way through the other instruments."

A strange commentary, indeed, when one considers that the essence of the Strauss waltz is its emphasis on singing string tone. The truth was that Johann Strauss was compelled by the exigencies of travel to limit his orchestra to such an extent that a sufficient number of strings could not be included. And how was the critic of the *Musical World* to know that the four men who had refused to accompany Strauss to London were all from the string section? Strauss certainly had not publicized the story of his orchestra's mutiny.

In Paris, Strauss wrote a number of compositions whose titles were occasioned by the French capital itself, and the daily events within its walls. Thus, one encounters in Strauss's catalogue these compositions dating from the Paris visit: *Der Karnival in Paris Waltzes,* Op. 100, *Paris Waltzes,* Op. 101, and the *Versailles Galopp,* Op. 107.

The London visit brought forth a similar flow of titles: *Huldigung der Königin Viktoria Waltzes,* Op. 103, and the *Londoner Saison Waltzes,* Op. 112. The *Musikalischer Telegrafe Potpourri,* Op. 106, which was given its first performance at the London *première* (though no mention was made of this by any of the critics), was written during the coach trip from the Channel steamer to London.

With the second concert, which was completely sold out in advance, Strauss established himself in London as he had before in all the great cities on the Continent, and future engagements for both public and private concerts began to come in one after the other, as the leaders of English society sought to obtain the services of this peerless dance orchestra. And great balls were frequent that season; five or six gatherings of especial social glitter were held every evening of Coronation Week. And, as had happened before in the other capitals of Europe, the social élite of England admitted Johann Strauss to their acquaintance, both as musician and social equal. A feat of some consequence on the Continent in the 1830's, this was truly extraordinary in the England of that period. Yet here was Johann Strauss, son of an innkeeper from the Flossgasse, walking arm-in-arm with the Duke of Sutherland, attended by Prince Schwarzenberg and Prince Esterházy. The demand for Strauss grew to such proportions that his schedule called for a morning musicale in town, an afternoon concert out of town, and an evening performance in the city, in public or at Court.

An account of such an appearance was printed in the *Court Gazette* for Saturday, May 12th, 1838. It was the first State Ball since the young Queen's accession. "A temporary stage for Strauss's Waltz Band was fitted up on the south side of the ballroom, as the regular orchestra only afforded accommodation for eighteen musicians. The Band performed Strauss's entire new set of waltzes entitled *Hommage à la Reine d'Angleterre,* which were much admired by Her Majesty."

On Coronation Day, Strauss and his orchestra took up a position before the Reform Club, along the route which the Royal Procession was to follow. The noise was deafening, as the crash of many cannon echoed through the streets, punctuated every few minutes by the ubiquitous *God Save the Queen,* played by a military band or the Strauss orchestra.

Instead of ending the festivities, the Coronation seemed only to increase them, and Strauss and his men shuttled here and there, trying vainly to fill all the calls for their services. They played in all types of halls, sometimes in the great private houses and castles of England's nobility, as well as in public, at Almack's and Willis's Rooms and the City of London Tavern.

There was no sleep now for Strauss. Hither and yon, across the broad, green face of England, he followed the will-o'-the-wisp of fame. In France he had given eighty-six concerts in ninety days, but almost all of these were given in one city. In England, touring from city to city, he gave no fewer than seventy-two concerts in one hundred and twenty days: Birmingham and Liverpool, Manchester and Dublin, Glasgow and Brighton, Southampton and Bath, Plymouth and Edinburgh —there was no end to the madness. It became a fever with him; no woman could have enslaved him half so much. He was given up to one passion only—the mingled sounds of applause and a turning wheel. That he could withstand the exhaustion of this endless journeying is incredible, but it is even less believable that his men should have been willing to share its hardships with him. Strauss was a name which was becoming immortal in England, but the musicians remained anonymous, an unknown quantity described simply as "Strauss's Orchestra." It was a pure, fanatical devotion to their leader which impelled them to follow him so blindly.

Yet it must end. Even Strauss realized it reluctantly. His health was failing; he could not endure much more. And the men would not. During a return visit to France, bringing them closer to their homeland, open revolt occurred. A violoncellist averred that he had proof that Strauss did not intend to return to Vienna, that he had severed his home ties and was separated from his family, that he meant to desert his wife and children, and that it was for this reason that he was now mumbling to Reichmann about an insane plan to take the orchestra to America.

Nonetheless, the men were back in Halifax on October 4th, 1838. Precisely a year had passed since they left home. They were miserable from fog and cold and acute homesickness. They alternately cursed Strauss and the wet English climate, so different from their own crisp air.

On the first of November, after a solid week of rain, on roads which were flooded and, in places, washed out, they jour-

neyed to Edinburgh. They reached the Scottish capital a day
late, all ill with severe colds. A doctor examined them, pre-
scribed a homely antidote of hot claret laced with quantities
of nutmeg and ginger, and left them to perspire and recover.

All did, except Strauss. Gravely ill with influenza, he
would not rest, would not go to bed, would not give his tired
body a chance to revitalize itself. As long as his orchestra
could play, he would conduct. With a raging temperature,
he gave concerts in Hull, Leeds, Newcastle, Wakefield and
Derby. It was in this last town that an incorrect prescription,
calling for a deadly overdose of opium, almost ended his life.
Strauss noticed the mistake himself at the last moment; the
shock was so sudden that it gave him pause. He realized that
recovery was out of the question in that foggy climate, so
alien to his nature. He crossed the Channel to Calais, and
there, during a concert, collapsed. He was taken to Paris, arriving on December 9th. He asked to stay there for a month
until his strength should return and he could conduct again.
He hated above all else the thought of being brought back to
Vienna an invalid. But the doctors, urged by the musicians
who wanted to return to their native hearths, insisted on an
immediate return, and so he was placed on the Strasbourg
mailcoach which had brought him to Paris. Almost at his native city, during a stop in Linz, he walked delirious into the
freezing street in his nightgown, and fell unconscious. Two
days later, he was carried up the stairs of his home. Johann
and Josef ran up the steps ahead of the cortège, crying, "Our
Father is dying!"

5

DOMESTIC REVOLUTION

As it happened, he did not die. The practiced attentions of
two good physicians, abetted by the devoted ministrations of
his wife and the mental peace of being once more at home in
Vienna, all combined to coax his exhausted body back from
the edge of the grave. Two months brought about a partial
recovery. Still convalescent, he insisted on appearing again
before the public. Carnival time had come again, and having
missed the festivities of the previous year during his Paris sojourn, Strauss could not bear to see a second season pass in
which he was not the dominating figure. Feebly, almost me-
chanically, he led a Carnival Ball at the Sperl. It was not a
Strauss evening. The public sensed the lack of poise and confidence in its favorite, and the ball was not gay. Yet Strauss
would not give up. The following evening, he conducted a
private ball at the Russian Embassy. The first part of the
program passed reasonably well, and the orchestra began to
breathe more freely. But at the intermission he collapsed, and
Hirsch had to rush him back to his home. Here doctors examined him once more, and pronounced him to be suffering
from gravely ulcerated kidneys. They warned him that there
could be no question of his conducting again for some years.

Thus the highly mobile Strauss found himself immured in
his apartment as firmly as a prisoner within his cell. The psychological impact on this nervous man can scarcely be con-

ceived. The Hirschenhaus was a typical building of the lower middle-class. Odors of cooking, women's chatter across the central court, the cries of passing hawkers, the noisy bustle of children in all their passing moods of joy and sorrow—his own among them—all these set his nerves on edge. He grew irascible, finding constant fault with his wife, who restrained her own quick temper only through constant remembrance of his illness. She bore all his ungracious sarcasms and fits of ill-humor, and saw to it that the children bothered him as little as possible, keeping them always away from the sickroom.

Strauss himself took remarkably little interest in his sons. The children, for their part, were not sorry to avoid him. They idolized their famous father, as children will (who else in the Hirschenhaus could boast of so magnificent a parent?), but he was a stranger to them, and he did little to break down the barrier. The affection intermingled with fear which his sons felt for him was well described by Johann II:

"He allowed Pepi (Josef) and me to have music lessons, but he thought that we simply strummed like most children; yet we worked very hard and played well, though he had no idea of it. The rehearsals for his concerts were held in the house. We boys listened to every note, and afterwards played the various pieces as pianoforte duets, trying to reproduce them exactly as our father liked to have them played, for he was our ideal. We were often invited out to other people's houses, and played his compositions by heart. One day an acquaintance—it was Carl Haslinger, the music publisher—congratulated my father upon our playing (my brother and me). He was greatly surprised. 'Send the boys to me,' he said. Not knowing what to expect, we slunk into the room. After he had told us what he had heard, he commanded us to play for him. As was customary at that time, he had an upright piano and Pepi declared he could not play on it. 'What,' he said, 'you cannot play on it?

Then fetch the grand!' The grand having been brought, we played our very best, introducing all the features of the orchestration. Our father, who had listened with a beaming face, said, 'Boys, no one can play it like that!' "

Yet Strauss had no intention of allowing his sons to become professional musicians. Was it a selfish, jealous impulse? Probably, although he certainly could not know that in the end his eldest boy would eclipse his own great fame. He was willing that his children should study piano, for it was inconceivable to him that they should have no ability or interest in an art in which he excelled. But not the violin. That was the sword and shield of the professional dance musician. Without ability upon this instrument, no man could hope to become a famous leader in the world of dance music. Young Johann II had composed his first, stumbling waltz at the precocious age of six. His father foresaw, perhaps, to what this might lead, and his proscription of the violin had been emphatic.

Thus it was all the more inexplicable when, resting one day upon the couch in his room, he heard someone playing a violin in another room of the apartment. Excellent fiddling it was, too. Intrigued and vaguely disturbed, he followed the course of the sound until he stood before the door of the room shared by Johann and Josef. Unmistakably, the music was coming from within that room. Nor was what attracted him merely that someone was playing the violin with capable fingers. It was both the composition and the technique which surprised him. Had he lived a hundred years later, he would have imagined himself listening to a phonograph record of himself. It was a Johann Strauss waltz, played in unmistakable Johann Strauss style.

Silently he opened the door a trifle, and stood rigid with rage at what he saw. Before a long pier glass stood young Johann, carefully dressed in foppish imitation of his father, playing a violin with practiced fingers, watching himself all the while in the mirror and carefully imitating the rapt expression of the elder Johann, tossing his long, black hair back and forth as he swung his body to the rhythm of the music.

Johann Strauss tore the violin from his son's fingers. A few questions elicited some startling replies. Johann had been studying with Amon, Strauss's own concertmaster.

"And how did you manage to pay Amon?"

"By giving lessons myself."

"Lessons? In what?"

"Piano lessons. I teach some of the children in the building."

Strauss saw in a flash how thoroughly he had been outwitted. Livid with fury, he took the violin and locked it in a closet. The next day, Anna Strauss gave "Schani" another violin. Ironically, the new violin was from his father's own extensive collection of instruments. The boy went right on practicing, but henceforth he was careful to do so at a friend's house.

Bent on punitive measures, Strauss enrolled his son in a school where the lad was forced to busy himself with a porridge of business correspondence, bookkeeping and stenography. What a disastrous curb on his naturally artistic bent this must have been! He refused to endure it; he was unattentive, impudent, and prankish. At last he was sent home with a warning never to show his face in the school again. The father remained adamant; he engaged a private tutor, and Schani was condemned to continue his lessons within the limits of the Hirschenhaus. Fortunately, the tutor sympathized with his pupil, and Schani's life was somewhat easier.

The intractable spirits of his eldest son, the manner in which Anna Strauss sided with that son against her husband, and the incessant little quarrels among his boisterous children, made

Strauss's life thoroughly miserable. This and the menace to his fame, which he jealously foresaw in Schani's determined preoccupation with music, served to bring about a complete cure in a matter of months where his doctors had foretold a convalescence of years.

He was happy to be free of the Hirschenhaus, where the penury of his homelife stood in sharp relief against the luxury of his public life. Welcome as he was in the fashionable world, the enormous costs of maintaining and transporting his orchestra, and the exorbitant salaries of managers and agents, cut deeply into the fees which he received. Strauss never became rich; this was due as much to his inability to budget himself properly as to conditions which obliged him to pay out almost as much as came in. To keep his orchestra contented while on tour, he found it necessary to bribe them with fine wines and foods, expensive lodgings and the best in travel accomodations. The fact that he was the most famous musician in his field did not prevent those who engaged him from doing their best to reduce to an outrageous minimum the fees which they paid him. Nor did it prevent his publishers, many of them professed friends, from fleecing him mercilessly.

Poverty was only one of his domestic woes. Anna Strauss was no shrew, but neither was she the sort of placid, patient woman whom her son Johann was to find years later in Jetty Treffz. Nor did she lack cause for anger. The idol of Vienna was fair game for a barrage of feminine charms; every woman wished to make herself attractive to this handsome and charming *Musikanten,* and not all of them failed. Many rumors found their way back to Anna Strauss, rumors of flirtations and more, and she knew her fears were well-founded.

Strauss indeed had good reason to prolong his absence from Vienna, in the face of his men's determination to return. For some time previous to the Paris expedition, he had been involved in a liaison with a young and pretty Viennese girl, Emilie Trampusch. That Strauss should have fallen prey to a pretty face which could make him forget his domestic troubles is not surprising, but his choice of *petite amie* is. Famed as he was, he might have made a *sub-rosa* alliance with a daughter of the Viennese gentry, perhaps even the nobility. Yet he allowed himself to be utterly captivated by an inconsequential and uneducated little milliner from an unfashionable suburb. Was it an unconscious acknowledgement of his own humble beginnings, an admission that he was not, and had never been, truly at ease in the *haut monde* where he was so famous? Or was it a genuine love, a product of maturer years, where his union with Anna Streim had been the result of a youthful indiscretion which he regretted?

Whatever the reasons, Strauss began, with Emilie Trampusch, an affair which quickly developed into something much more permanent. He found her an apartment in the Kumpf-gasse, on the other side of the Schwedenbrücke and the Dan-ube Canal. For some time, he visited her here whenever pos-sible, while still maintaining his home in the Hirschenhaus.

There is nothing new in this story of a dual *ménage* and a double life. Strauss's affection for his wife and children was profound; he was genuinely loath to make a final and irrevo-cable break, but the situation passed beyond his control. To Anna Strauss came rumors of his new alliance, rumors which were so persistent, so detailed and so parallel that there could be no refuting them. To his former passing attachments, Anna Strauss had willingly closed an eye. There was, she knew, something of the Gypsy in her husband. Restrict him too much, and she would lose him; give him a sense of freedom and he would always return. She had learnt to be satisfied with that. But this time, it was a different matter. To establish a second household when you do not provide money enough to maintain the first properly was inexcusable in her eyes. She could ignore indignities to her own person; she could pretend that they did not exist. But she would not allow her husband to squander money on a mistress while her children were deprived of the sort of food and clothing and opportunities which she believed they deserved of their famous father.

It was her attacks and recriminations which finally drove Strauss from his home. He removed himself to the Kumpfgasse, to a miserable little apartment that was far worse than the Hirschenhaus flat. Here the children of this illicit union were born. There were four daughters—Emeline, Klementine, Marie, Therese—and one son—Johann. It was this manchild who broke the last bond between Strauss and his true family. Anna Strauss could, unreasonably, endure the existence of the daughters; the final alienation was caused by her husband's giving his name (and that of his eldest son) to this illegitimate boy.

The children came to no good in the end. The boy, Johann, was sickly, accomplished nothing in life, and died at twenty-nine. Emeline tried to become an actress, without success. The younger daughter whose illness, transmitted to the father, was the cause of his death, was so maltreated by her mother that she had to be sent to a Home for the Protection of Children. She escaped from there and returned to Vienna, where she was found by Sisters of Charity and cared for. Later she made a miserable living as a maker of artificial flowers.

True to his fine character, their half brother, Johann II, later did much to alleviate their misfortunes and reëstablish them. But theirs was, from beginning to end, a tragic story.

From this late period date Strauss's finest waltzes: *Sorgenbrecher* and the magical *Lorelei-Rhein-Klänge,* his greatest. From this period, too, come the *Donaulieder Waltzes,* Op. 127, which rank as an example of the elder Strauss's best, although considerably less well known. The melodies are more ingenious, longer flowing and more closely interwoven and interrelated, than those he commonly wrote, and there are occasional touches of genius. One of these is the delightful question-and-answer dialogue between the lower and higher strings in one of the middle waltzes. Johann II indicated his own high esteem of this work when he recalled this passage in his *Wo die Zitronen blüh'n*. Another splendid passage is the delectable use of trumpet in the coda.

This waltz marked the summit of Johann Strauss's career; it was just at this time that the throne of Johann I was shaken to its foundations. A pretender had appeared from within. . .

BOOK II

JOHANN STRAUSS II
"The Waltz King"

EMPEROR FRANZ-JOSEF I
OF AUSTRIA IN 1848

FRANZ-JOSEF AND ELIZABETH OF AUSTRIA
at the time of their marriage in 1854. (Left rear: Schönbrunn Palace;
right rear: Vienna with the Stefansdom.)

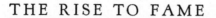

1

THE RISE TO FAME

IN THE annals of the Strauss family, the date which eclipses all others is October 15th, 1844, for on that evening Johann Strauss II dared the wrath of musical Vienna—and in those days, it seemed that the entire population was musical—to appear for the first time as an orchestral director under the aegis of a name already made world-famous by his illustrious father. Small wonder, then, that many Viennese insisted that the lad only proposed to capitalize on his father's hard-earned reputation, and that he himself possessed no musical ability. To support their contention, they pointed with conviction to the posters on which the words "Junior" and "Son" were set in admittedly small type.

Although the decision to compete against his father was a painful one for the nineteen-year-old boy to make, he had little choice. The desertion of the mother by the father, and the constantly dwindling allowance from Johann, Senior, gradually forced this upon him. Young Schani was a finished musician, far more so than his father had been at his age. In the study of the violin, he had progressed from Amon to Kohlmann, conductor of ballet at the Carl Theater. He had studied composition with Hofmann, and counterpoint with Josef Drexler, the famous ecclesiastical conductor and organist. Nor was Drexler so serious that he could not remember earlier years, when he had written the music for many of Raimund's comedies, including *Maiden from the Fairy World*, which had become a widely popular song. With so thorough and well-schooled a musical background, and possessed of the same charm, grace and creative ability as his father, there could be no choice for young Schani but the life of a musician. Every fiber in him demanded it; his father's early efforts to divert his course from its natural flow served only to set him more firmly in his determination to achieve this lifelong desire.

Yet before he could appear in public in front of an orchestra, it was necessary that he obtain a license from the Viennese magistracy "to make music for entertainment in public resorts." For a minor to obtain this license required the consent of the father. Schani knew that Johann Strauss would never give his consent. In lieu of this, he obtained warmly worded letters of recommendation from several prominent people. Even these might not have sufficed had it not happened that Drexler was a member of the committee which passed upon the application. Although the famous church musician had tried to lead the lad along the path of ecclesiastical music, even to requiring him to write a *Tu qui regis totum orbem,* which was actually performed at the Am Hof Church, he willingly assisted the boy when he sensed the fixed purpose of his mind. The ironical touch to the application was that, as evidence of his ability as a musician, he submitted the *Tu qui regis totum orbem* before the licensing board. Thus it was through ecclesiastical music that the future master of the seductive and sensuous waltz gained his right to appear in public.

Once possessed of his precious license, he began to frequent those cafés where the musicians of Vienna were wont to gather. He was hypercritical in his selection, almost unsatisfiable. From among these men he chose those he needed, changing them time and again, trying still more applicants, until at last he felt that his group, small as it was, could perform in a manner befitting the name of Johann Strauss.

Schani did his utmost to keep word of his activities from his father, but word inevitably passed from mouth to mouth. Eventually the newspapers took up the story, giving it considerable publicity. While this publicity was helpful as such, the manner in which it further estranged the two Johanns was not. Actually, there was nothing sensational in the mere appearance of a new orchestra and conductor. What did excite the unhealthy curiosity of the populace were the implications of rivalry and discord within the family.

The reports of Schani's doings agitated the elder Strauss beyond description. It seems strange that he should have been so affected by the impending début of his eldest son and namesake, but the fact is that he was so upset that he was actually ill for several days before the concert, and went so far as to express a hope that he would not live to see that day. It may be that Johann Strauss was exceptionally intuitive about his son; perhaps he had guessed what the world was later to learn: that his own personality was, after his death, to become confused and submerged in the more effulgent radiance of his son's genius.

Vienna, frustrated by an autocracy that kept every political interest and opinion but its own under rigid surveillance and check, found an outlet in taking up the sword over minor matters which, in a more politically balanced day, might never have been given a second thought. Thus the forthcoming appearance of young Johann had all Vienna up in arms, with most of the citizens divided into two distinct, vociferous and inimical camps. The one contended that he was perfectly justified in his actions, regardless of talent, since the father had treated his family shamefully and deserved retribution; the other

argued that he had no talent, that he was a young whipper-
snapper of a charlatan who ought to be given a good hiding
and sent home to bed without supper. A third group, distinctly in the minority, sat quietly through the turmoil, re-
marking simply that it mattered not at all what his name and
antecedents were, nor what the skeletons in his family closet
might be; that the only questions of musical import which entered the picture were whether he could play, and whether
he could compose.

The ringleaders of the group antipathetic to Strauss were
Carl Haslinger, the elder Strauss's publisher, and Carl Hirsch,
his life-long friend and business manager. Both Haslinger and
Hirsch had made a canvass of the important Viennese ballrooms, in an effort to secure promises that none of them
would engage Schani. They failed; Dommayer, owner of
Dommayer's Garden Restaurant, located in the fashionable
suburb of Hietzing, not far from Schönbrunn Palace, had always wanted to engage Johann Strauss the Elder to brighten
his establishment. He had never succeeded, largely due to
Strauss's obligations to the Sperl. But now opportunity offered him, if not the great man himself, at least his son and
name. Dommayer was a good businessman; he realized, long
before it happened, the furor which would be occasioned by
the announcement of Schani's début (he probably did all he
could to increase the uproar), and he understood that whatever the outcome for Strauss, only profit could come to him.
Hence the small type, of which some of the public complained,
in the posters pasted throughout the city; Dommayer counted, perhaps, on some of the more gullible being taken in by
the deception; but even more, he intentionally created the
controversy which preoccupied Vienna for days before the
concert took place.

This, then, was to be no quiet, little-heralded début. Schani was to make his formal introduction to the world of music at a resort scarcely inferior in elegance and reputation to the famous Sperlsaal, over which his father presided. Nor did it please the older man to recall that his own début had been made under less pretentious conditions, without fanfare or publicity, at a small, and far less elegant hall. There were doubtless grounds, therefore, for Strauss's annoyance with his son; unquestionably, without the Strauss name, Schani would never have obtained a first hearing at so ostentatious a restaurant.

The evening of the concert arrived, and with it so large a number of Vienna's population that it seemed as though the entire city had converged on Dommayer's. The crowd began to gather at six, and shortly afterward people were beginning to take their seats at the tables of the restaurant, although the concert was not scheduled until later. Soon all the tables were occupied, but people continued to press past the ticket window, content to take standing positions along the walls and on the dance floor itself. Every inch of floor space was accounted for, precluding any possibility of dancing, until finally it became impossible to wedge another soul into the building. Thousands of latecomers, disappointed at not finding accomodations within, stood their ground and filled the outer square as far back as the walls of the Park of Schönbrunn itself, dimly sensing, perhaps, the making of musical history.

Leading the clique which hoped to see Schani's defeat in this opening joust between father and son were Haslinger and Hirsch, and a group of their friends, who had found a table directly opposite the conductor's stand, with the intention of creating a disturbance. Joahnn, Senior, was not present; he had his own concert at the Sperl to conduct, but even without that excuse for his absence, it is doubtful that he would have put in an appearance at a time when his close friends were on hand to shout his son down. He simply claimed to be overwrought at the very thought of the concert, and again repeated his wish to die before it took place.

The crowd murmured interestedly as Johann appeared on the stage. Indeed, this young man was truly the son of Johann Strauss. Only a heavier, squarer build distinguished him from his father. Here were the same manner, the same pallor, the same burning, intense eyes. Only the motions were a little slower, a little more deliberate, without the quick nervousness which was typical of the father.

Now the important questions were to be answered. Could he play? Could he compose? Young Strauss gave the answer to the first at once, opening his program with the Overture to Auber's opera *La Muette de Portici,* at that time enjoying an incredible popularity in Vienna. For a moment, it seemed that he would not be given a cursory hearing, for the Haslinger-Hirsch combine made a furious din, but the interest of the multitude prevailed, and the orchestra was able to begin.

The Auber Overture did not meet with much approval, largely because the small group of fifteen players was unequal to a work demanding a symphonic body. Yet the musicianship of the young leader and his men was apparent, and sufficiently impressed his audience—despite the continued protests of his opponents—to permit him to introduce the first of a group of four of his own compositions, the *Gunstwerber Waltzes,* Op. 4. The audience was now greatly impressed, although the elder Strauss's faction clung with determination to their whistles, hisses and boos. Nonetheless, the waltz had to be repeated four times; the title, *Seekers of Favor,* had served its purpose well. Originally, it had been Schani's desire to call this set of waltzes *Das Mutterherz (A Mother's Heart),* but Frau Strauss, although not insensible to the fond compliment, was aware of the weapon it would place in the hands of his enemies, who would not hesitate to call attention to the significance of the title, and the rift with the father which it implied. If this young and untried Strauss was to secure a foothold in a field dominated by the great Johann, it must be through conciliatory measures, and not through open antagonism at the start. It was with a certain degree of relief that Schani found himself freed from the original title, which may have been the result of a momentary excess of sentiment. He had no desire to antagonize his father; indeed, he hoped to retain friendly relations with him, and had even written him a touchingly naïve letter, explaining his reasons for venturing into his father's profession, and asking for their continued mutual affection.

A polka, *Herzenslust*, Op. 3, followed. Again, several repeats were demanded. The *Début Quadrille*, Op. 2, followed, and finally the *Sinngedichte Waltzes*, Op. 1. This occasioned a tempest of applause. Even the elder Strauss's faction rose to its feet and cheered with the rest. The audience called for a total of nineteen encores—this was unheard of, even at a Strauss concert! Schani had conquered Vienna.

Now he showed his true, generous nature. Had this been his father, he would have dismissed his men, packed his violin and gone home. Not Schani; he signalled for yet another encore, of another and unannounced work. The audience was quite still. Then there floated out into the hall the magic opening strains of the *Lorelei-Rhein-Klänge*, the elder Johann's greatest waltz. The listeners, touched and moved as only the Viennese can be moved, shed tears and held their breaths as the last note melted *pianissimo* away into the night. When Schani ended this generous tribute to his father, the audience rose as one, and salvo after salvo of bravos echoed into the square and the park, rousing the startled birds in the trees from their sleep. Led by Haslinger, the elder man's followers, now Schani's as well, rushed upon the stage, bore the delighted conductor aloft on their shoulders, and in this fashion carried him to his home. Hirsch, hastening out of the hall to carry the fantastic news to the Sperl, came upon a small woman seated alone at a table in the fast-emptying hall, tears of joy streaming down her cheeks. It was Anna Strauss. With tears in his own eyes, Hirsch stopped to congratulate her before continuing on to the Sperl to explain to his friend that, for better or for worse, the world of music now recognized two men by the name of Johann Strauss.

The news of Schani's triumph was not such a surprise to the father as Hirsch had feared, though he did blanch when he heard the account of the nineteen encores. Nineteen! How could it be possible; it had never happened to him! But he was a good gambler; he took his losses as coolly as he had his winnings.

The following morning, the music critic Wiest wrote, "Good night, Lanner; Good evening, Father Strauss; Good morning, Son Strauss!"

Not long after the debut, a sort of reconciliation between father and son took place. Schani was eager for this, for, despite all past misunderstandings, he was both fond and proud of his father. Proud of him, at least, as a musician, if not as a man. Nor was the older man anxious to remain at swords' points with a son who threatened to outshine him. They met on the neutral ground of a Viennese public house. Anything more was impossible; neither could visit the other in his home. For this reason, much as the elder Johann might have liked it, and much as Schani might have wished to accept, he could not take the position of concertmaster and assistant conductor which his father offered him. It would, it is true, have effectively silenced much of the vicious gossip that was hurting both in equal degree. But the young man had his own career to make; having begun it so illustriously, he could not now retire to a comparatively obscure position. He went his own way, playing at the Dommayerbau, Zogernitz's and *Zum Grünen Tor,* while his father remained at the Sperlsaal, Zeisig's and the Dianasaal. They parted friends, and so they remained.

TYPICAL of the first compositions of the new Waltz King are the *Serail-Tänze Waltzes,* Op. 5. The piano edition of this early effort is now in the Library of Congress in Washington, D.C., where it forms part of an enormous collection of Straussiana. This collection is so vast that it is said to contain over ninety per cent of the total output of the Strauss family—a monumental labor. It was the life hobby of an Austrian railroad man, Paul Löwenberg, and constitutes a comprehensive picture of the glittering days of the Austro-Hungarian Empire from Lanner to Lehár. The influence of these composers can hardly be estimated by our present standards; one need only recall the remark of an official of the Hapsburg Court, "To be precise, Franz-Josef ruled until the death of Johann Strauss." For it was these composers, over whom Johann Strauss II reigned supreme, whose music united the widely divergent racial strains which constituted this conglomerate empire into a whole that reacted as of one accord, living, as it were, in a champagne-bemused world that was governed by the tempo of the Viennese Waltz. Only in the music which streamed from Vienna throughout the whole of the Nineteenth Century could the many racial minorities of the Empire find any basis for unification and agreement.

In his tragic novel, *Mayerling,* Claude Anet mentions the debt which Vienna owed her waltz composers. "In the operettas which have carried the spirit of Vienna throughout the world, everything takes place to the rhythm of the waltz, which touches the heart and caresses it without penetrating; in the third act, there is traditionally a dramatic moment: the lovers have a misunderstanding, are about to kill themselves, or separate, which is worse. But in the midst of this great quarrel, there sound the unforgettable accents of the waltz; they become more insistent, until at last they triumph and the lovers fall into each other's arms. This same waltz, sometimes gayer, sometimes sadder, gives to Viennese living its accent and its cadence."

The *Serail-Tänze* opens with an introduction for full orchestra that is a deliberate attempt to evoke the atmosphere of the Orient, and which is based on an *alla Turca* rhythm and style of figuration. Twelve bars *presto,* and then an *adagio,* followed by a 4/4 time section that might well be another *Turkish March* from Mozart's pen. (Need one mention the Mozartean opening of the *Kaiserwalzer,* with its similar reminiscences?) A short transition, and then the first waltz appears. Brisk, almost brusque, there is, as yet, neither sentiment nor romance to be heard. But these are not long in forthcoming, in a slow, sensuous theme that Strauss, with maturer perception than one expects, has fully exploited. Here is the perfumed night, the intrigue, the romance; in short, the seraglio itself. Another sentimental moment, punctuated with triangle. Finally, the conventional *reprise* to the first waltz *quasi una marcia,* and from there through the other waltzes in normal sequence, until the flashing *stretta* with its traditional climax is reached. One senses throughout the young eaglet essaying his wings. To seek here the tonal imagery and the suavity of his later works is to search too deeply; the atmospheric effects are superficial. Yet the mastery of the medium and the promise of what was to come are fully in evidence here.

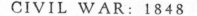

2

CIVIL WAR: 1848

1848 is a year written in blood on the pages of most European nations. In France it signalled the overthrow of the last of the Bourbons, King Louis-Philippe. There, too, a young composer and church organist named César Franck was obliged to clamber up, down and over barricades flung across the streets, in order to reach the home of his bride on their wedding day. In Germany, at the Court in Dresden, a young composer-conductor and revolutionary hothead by the name of Richard Wagner fled into exile at Weimar. In Vienna, this continental *malaise* found expression in an abortive, but nonetheless sanguinary, revolution which drove the Emperor Ferdinand from the Imperial throne, only to set up in his place the still more reactionary Franz-Josef. It was at this time that Johann I wrote his ill-starred *Radetzky March*. While he espoused the Imperial cause, his sons joined the revolutionary republicans. Eduard was still too young to leave his mother and fight his way through those tumultuous days, but both Johann II and Josef were in the front lines. Josef was a private in a student regiment, his elder brother a private in the Second Regiment of the Viennese National Guard. Johann had been obliged to enlist in this manner in order to be eligible for the position of Conductor of the regimental band, a post left vacant by Lanner's death, and highly coveted by him.

But although Schani was sympathetic to the revolutionary cause, his expression of this sentiment at its strongest took only a musical, and extremely passive, turn. He gladly wrote march after march and song after song to hearten and enliven the lives of his fellow soldiers, but the discipline and regimentation of army life affected him not at all. He ignored them as effectively as though they had not existed. He left his post to return home to compose or sleep whenever the spirit moved him; he even slept on guard duty. Only his popularity and the prominence of his position in Vienna saved him from severe punishment.

However, if he displayed no interest in active military life, he nonetheless set himself, in his music, on the side of the civilian rebels. Among his compositions of this period are some whose titles bear directly upon the world which was dying and being reborn around him: the *Freiheitslieder* (*Songs of Freedom*) *Waltzes*, Op. 52, the *Revolutionsmarsch*, Op. 54, and the *Studentenmarsch*, Op. 56.

While Schani and Pepi took their stand on the revolutionary ramparts, the elder Strauss was among the vanguard of the reactionaries. The pathetic feud between the Hirschenhaus and the Kumpfgasse, kept alive by the shallow-minded followers of both father and son, had in itself little to do with this. Strauss was unwaveringly loyal to the régime which had nursed him for so long. Like many another man reaching middle age, he fought any change in his established pattern of living. Not so Schani; like his contemporaries, the students, he did not hestitate to question the propriety of a rule which forbade parliamentary debate and freedom of thought and expression. The doctrines formulated by the American and French Revolutions found fertile soil among the young people of Vienna, and these constituted Schani's public. As his public went, so did Schani, just as the elder Strauss followed the

current of the established order which comprised his audience. In this, each was genuinely sincere and completely
expressed his personal convictions; their stands were not com-
mercially motivated. Neither was so completely cynical, although the elder man tended to be.

In August of 1848, the Imperial Austrian Army, under
one of its leading commanders, General Radetzky, met the
Italian forces in battle and scored a major victory. This occasioned great jubilation in Vienna, and Radetsky became the
hero of the day, despite the fact that he commanded Imperial
forces. (The explanation of this paradox lies in the fact that
Italy was the traditional enemy. This was not an instance of
civil war.) During this period of rejoicing, the elder Strauss
composed a march in celebration of the victory, and gave it,
as title, the general's name.

Unfortunately, delays of one sort and another prevented a
hearing of the *Radetzky March* until Winter had come.
Meanwhile, he regaled Vienna with the *Sorgenbrecher
Waltzes,* Op. 230, the *Brünner-Nationalgarde March,* Op.
231, the *Freiheitsmarsch,* Op. 226, and the *Marsch des eini-
gen Deutschlands,* Op. 227. When the *Radetzky* was finally
performed, it was in a Vienna which had been sacked, raped,
raided and burned by its own Imperial troops under Jellacic.
The *Radetzky March* branded Strauss a firm supporter of the
hated autocracy; his public cooled, and attendance at his concerts dropped rapidly; at last (could it really happen? he won-
dered) he was actually hissed!

Nothing so typifies old Vienna as the *Radetzky March*. Its
piquant melodies, recalling the musical-comedy stage—indeed, all of Austria's military music contains the spice of
operetta—are the perfect symbol of Imperial Austria's armies,
gorgeously panoplied in the ballroom, and pathetically inef-
fective on the field of battle:

The main melody has a strong dash of pepper, and something of the comic feeling of a children's march. The Trio offers effective contrast, even the hint of a waltz lilt, possibly intended as a remembrance of the Vienna which the soldiers had temporarily put behind them.

Considering discretion the better part of valor, retreating before so hostile a public, Strauss, Senior, took his men to Prague. The evening of his arrival, he was serenaded outside his hotel by the caterwauls of Bohemian students. He had forgotten that the violent hatred of the Bohemians for the Austrian government would make the people of Prague antipathetic to those who were known to be its friends. Persistent, nonetheless, he gave his concerts, building the programs with extreme care so as not to include any item which might be considered controversial, and achieving a good measure of applause, although his houses were never full. Back to Vienna went the crestfallen hero. A short stay in the still unfriendly capital, and the men set off again, this time for Germany, which Strauss hoped to find more receptive.

First to Munich, where the audience was warm, if not enthusiastic. Munich remembered the Strauss of yesteryear, free from political stigma, and, remembering that unfettered musician, applauded the man who stood before them, though most of them opposed his political leanings. But elsewhere in Germany, the reception was definitely antagonistic. Heilbronn and Heidelberg, and more particularly Frankfurt, shouted "Berlioz" at him, a suggestion that he play the *Rakocsy*

March, Hungary's national air, to which Berlioz had given world fame in his *La Damnation de Faust.* They shouted "Ber-lioz" at him, and dared him to play the *Radetzky.* He played neither. Instead, he bolted from Germany, bag, baggage and orchestra, and sought refuge in Belgium. In Brussels, for the first time in more than six months, he felt the warmth of a re-ceptive public, and could laugh and be happy once more.

Yet he wished to remove himself even further from the scenes of his recent sorrows, and so he turned once more to England, landing on April 21st, 1849. More than ten years had passed since he had last visited those shores, but the Eng-lish had not forgotten him. He was most flatteringly received by Queen Victoria and Prince Albert. The members of the Tory Party made much of him, according him every honor within reason. But their motives were, withal, political and not aesthetic. It was most apparent when he noticed that the leading members of the Liberal Party kept their distance and maintained a cool reserve. It became indisputable fact when he found threatening letters in his mail; the same sort of bigotry which had pursued him through Europe. Was there then no rest to be found in this insanely political world? The humor of the people reacted sharply upon his delicately bal-anced mind and tense nerves, and impaired his health once more.

Yet he was not without his triumphs. In one instance, the Duchesses of Cambridge, Gloucester and Mecklenburg-Stre-litz assumed the personal direction of the sale of tickets for a concert in his benefit. It was with brimming heart that Strauss thanked his good friends, whose patronage had in-sured what was possibly his greatest single success, and this at a moment when at least half his world was turned against him.

But his state of health prevented a prolonged stay. In the

midst of summer, when England was at her loveliest, he declined into a state of mental depression; his letters to Emilie and to Haslinger were gloomy; he even ventured to foretell that this was to be his last journey. He embarked for the continent at the Port of London. During his voyage down the Thames, his ship was accompanied by smaller craft, bearing some of Britain's noblest names, while the men of his orchestra sang the plaintive *So Fare Thee Well, Thy Silent House* from Raimund's *Der Alpenkönig*. It had all the character of a modern *morte d'Arthur*.

On July 15th, Strauss again gave a concert in his beloved Vienna. He played with his heart overflowing, for thousands were present, and the ovation which they gave him at his first entrance left no doubt as to the true depth of their affection for him. It was a day of rejoicing, marred only by one evil omen. As he was about to begin, his bow snapped. This upset him considerably, for he was profoundly superstitious, but the gaiety of the occasion carried him along, and he picked up another bow and began the concert.

The joy of being in Vienna once again caused him to forget his solemn vow never to dabble, even indirectly, in politics. He surely had not forgotten so soon those sorry days which impelled him to pen the melancholy *Des Wanderers Lebewohl Waltzes,* Op. 237, just before the start of his last tour. Yet with his Op. 244, he published a march which he rashly titled *Jellacic,* after the infamous Croatian general whose armies of hired Russian mercenaries had sacked revolutionary Vienna only a year before. It is amazing that Strauss could have been so completely unfeeling for his public; it is incredible that his audience should have held their peace and refrained from stoning him from the stage. But the period of storm and strife was past, and Vienna took calmly in 1849 that for which it would have lynched him in 1848.

Yet Jellacic, unlike Radetzky, was a hated figure, held in contempt by the monarchy that gave him his rank, loathed by those who had been exposed to his brutality, despised by his own troops.

Radetzky, by contrast a universally popular figure, returned from Italy after a victorious campaign. A monster banquet was planned in his honor for September 22nd. Of course, no one but the composer of the *Radetzky March* would do when it came to handling the musical part of the evening. And then, on the day of the banquet, Strauss collapsed without warning. Unknown to him and to Emilie Trampusch, one of their daughters had caught scarlet fever in school and had transmitted it to her father. First one, and then a second, doctor was called. Nothing availed. Complications in the form of an inflammation of the brain developed, and Strauss died on the twenty-seventh.

Anna Strauss had known nothing of his illness, and learned of his death only some hours after the event. A messenger brought the news, and Frau Strauss, knowing that her Johann had a horror of death amounting to a phobia, sent Josef to the house on the Kumpfgasse to see if he could decently assist Emilie in any way. A terrible sight awaited the impressionable young man when he reached his father's home. The apartment was in a state of complete disorder. Many of the furnishings had been hurriedly removed, and there was not a sheet or blanket in sight. The cold body of Johann Strauss, half-naked, lay upon slats from his bed, in the center of the room. Emilie Trampusch had packed her belongings, taken her children, and fled. It was a long time before she was heard from again.

The funeral of Johann Strauss I took place quietly, two days later.

With Johann Strauss the Elder passed the entire formative

period of the Viennese Waltz. Taking it from its humble beginnings, little more than a dance-formula in the hands of those who had preceded him, and with nothing of artistic value to guide him save the unique *Rondo* of Weber and his own endless and fertile imagination, Johann Strauss the Elder had created a new dance form which had important artistic merit. There remained only for his son to convert the dance form into an art form.

3

THE EARLY WALTZES

Although it is evident today that even the immature Schani was more spontaneously talented than his father at the peak of his career, there were many admirers of the elder Strauss who could not see this as long as the father lived. Such comparisons demand the third-dimensional measurement of time, and this yardstick was not then at hand.

Consequently, Schani's first months following his father's death were not easy. Highly sensitive man that he was, he was keenly aware of the cabals which circulated like quicksilver about Vienna. Friendly though he and his father had been during those last years, his own followers and those of his father, each opposed to the other, had prevented any public expression of this sentiment, and, after the father's death, his followers remained for a time the young man's enemies. (This was partly the result of that small-mindedness which admits of black and white, but no greys, but also it was the residual outcome of 1848.) This situation was so oppressive to him that he resorted at last to the newspapers, in an article justifying his actions and choice of profession. It was a document not unlike the letter which he had previously written his father, but without the naïveté of the earlier letter, and with a sophistication which marked the passing of the years. The appeal served to turn the tide of public opinion in his favor, and won to his side his father's partisans; from that day on, as Vienna's beloved Schani, he knew no rival.

Now, at the suggestion of Amon, his father's leaderless orchestra approached him with the request that he assume direction over it. He agreed, combining into it, as well, the best elements of his own group, and acquiring thereby an orchestra whose ability had never known an equal in its genre.

With all the rival Strauss factions now united under one hand, the press of engagements became so great that only a man of Strauss's vitality could withstand the strain. Yet, despite his popularity, one great ballroom still remained barred to him, one coveted title still beyond his reach. That ballroom was the magnificent Redoutensaal in the Hofburg; the title, that of Kaiserlich und Königlich Hofballmusikdirektor. This honor had belonged to his father; it was to have been expected that it should fall to the even more talented son upon his death, but Schani was not in the good graces of the Emperor and his Court; the role that he had played during the Revolution had not served to insure him a warm welcome into the frosty chambers of the Hofburg. Young Emperor Franz-Josef was a martinet; he had shown this trait from his earliest training. No detail was too minute for him to concern himself with; the matter of the appointment of the new Hofballmusikdirektor, a minor matter though it would seem, was not unimportant to him. He knew that eventually it must go to Strauss, that no one could compete with him in the light music of that day; yet it pleased him to inflict a punishment for Strauss's minor revolutionary role before handing over the prize.

Appeasement of the young Emperor was, therefore, a necessity. Strauss made the first essay on July 15th, 1850, during a concert at Dommayer's, when he performed the *Kaiser Franz-Josef March,* Op. 67. Then, with his Opus 96,

Schani published a piece directly dedicated to the Emperor, the *Viribus Unitis Waltzes*. If Strauss inscribed this to the Emperor, a degree of forgiveness must already have been un' officially accorded. Haughty though the Emperor was, his pride was no less intense than that of the Waltz King; Strauss would not have published a dedication which ran the risk of being refused.

He appeared for the first time in the Redoutensaal on Feb' ruary 23rd, 1852, where he conducted the first performance of his *Die Unzertrennlichen Waltzes*, Op. 108, with great success. Yet it was not until 1863, eleven years later, that he finally received the coveted title. By then, the great Johann Strauss did not need it.

ON THE evening of March 27th, 1854, the immense Zere' moniesaal of the Hofburg was brilliantly illuminated. A soft but radiant light, from hundreds of candles set in chandeliers and candelabra, streamed through the windows onto a Vienna equally decorated and illuminated. Despite the season and open windows, the temperature within the hall was more than comfortable, for the many candles and tremendous press of guests combined to give off intoxicating warmth, spiced with the scent of rare and expensive perfumes. The élite of the Austro'Hungarian nobility was present, together with royalty of other lands, for the ball was in celebration of the marriage of his Imperial Majesty, Emperor Franz'Josef, to his cousin, the young and exquisite Princess Elizabeth of Bavaria, reputed to be the most beautiful woman in Europe.

The courtship of Franz'Josef and Elizabeth is one of the rare love stories in the history of Europe's royal families.*

---

* *The reader is referred to Bertita Harding's excellent biography*, Golden Fleece.

Theirs had been a romantic courtship; theirs was destined to be a tragic marriage of misunderstanding and disenchantment. The sincere young love which these two had borne each other from the instant of their first sudden meeting in the Hapsburg summer palace at Bad Ischl was slowly soured and turned to distrust by the machinations of intriguing court officials, and, more directly, by the jealous mother of the Emperor, the Archduchess Sofia herself. It had been her intention to have her son marry Elizabeth's older, less attractive but more tract-able sister, Helena. The Archduchess, morbidly jealous of any lessening of affection in her son, and determined to retain her hold on him and, thereby, indirectly over the Empire, realized that she could achieve this ambition only if he married the plain, but completely docile, Helena, whose utter lack of spirit would not be an opposing force to the Archduchess's plans.

Helena was sent for; she departed for Bad Ischl with her mother and her fifteen-year-old sister Elizabeth, who had begged relentlessly, through the weeks of preparation for the departure, to be also permitted to visit the Austrian Court. Arriving in Ischl, they found their suite prepared in one of the wings of the summer palace. They were visited there by the Archduchess herself, who came to welcome them and ar-range for a *rendezvous* between the bride-to-be and the Em-peror. She did not fail to perceive both the extraordinary beauty and the wild wilfulness of Elizabeth, and, in arrang-ing for a luncheon on the morrow, she gave explicit instruc-tions to her sister that the young girl was not to be of the party.

When, the following noon, the impulsive girl found that she had been left to dine in her own rooms with her lady-in-waiting, she stormed out of her suite in a fine fury. The world of protocol had hitherto passed Elizabeth by; the Wittelsbach family was noted for its informality and even eccentricity;

their Bavarian castle was run along the lines of a modest manor house. She therefore felt no compunction about bursting through chambers into which she had not been invited, leaving in her wake a stream of dazed courtiers. Entering a small salon, she suddenly found herself face to face not only with her aunt, her mother and her sister, but with the Emperor himself. She understood the situation at once. Completely abashed, and yet with a freedom of spirit which Franz-Josef could not fail to note, she sank to the floor in a deep curtsy, her cheeks pink with embarrassment. The Emperor was immediately struck by her dark, exuberant, and yet patrician, beauty. He insisted that Elizabeth be seated next to him.

From that moment, the die was cast. The previous evening, Elizabeth had dined at the same table as the Emperor, but at its other end, with his younger brothers. Now the position was reversed; she sat in the place of honor, and it was her sister who found herself relegated to a place "below the salt." Furious, bitterly determined to eliminate this girl whom she rightly regarded as a disconcerting and dangerous influence, the Archduchess, nonetheless, was obliged to watch impotently while the romance flamed through its spectacular course. It reached a dramatic climax at a court ball at Ischl, to music by the Strauss Orchestra. Before the cotillion, it was customary for each gentleman to present a corsage to the partner of his choice. As the basket containing the flowers was brought to Franz-Josef, the Court watched intently, for it was generally assumed that his choice of partner would also indicate his betrothed.

The Emperor reached into the basket and scooped up not one, but an entire armful of flowers, and, heels clicking smartly on the parquet floor, strode across to where Elizabeth and Helena sat with their mother. Bowing low, he deposited the entire mass of flowers onto the lap of the enchanted Elizabeth.

The Court gasped, almost in unison. The orchestra struck up the music to the cotillion. As if in a dream, Elizabeth rose to dance....

A year passed before they married. Elizabeth was sent home with her mother and sister, as it was deemed unwise that she marry before having passed her sixteenth birthday. It was a year of impatience for the young lovers, a year which came to a happy close on the night when Johann Strauss directed his orchestra from the balcony of the Zeremoniesaal.

For so important an occasion, Strauss gave extra attention to a special composition. This was a set of waltzes, the *Ballg'-schichten*. When it was first played, the later tragedies which were to culminate in the suicide at Mayerling of the Arch-duke Rudolf, and the assassination aboard a Swiss lake steam-er of the Empress herself, were certainly undreamed of, and only the aura of this wildfire courtship was there to be re-membered.

In the short introduction to *Ballg'schichten,* there is none of the imaginative description to be found in the symphonic introductions of the later waltzes; this composition is definitely for the ballroom, and Strauss could hardly keep his dancers teetering on one foot while he made a quasi-concert of the in-troduction. This would hardly do at so august a function. Violins introduce the first waltz; here is the first clear evidence in Johann II of that style which is synonymous with the Strausses. This waltz abounds in romance and a gentle pas-sion (as our elders used to say), yet it also possesses strength, a virile directness and that elegant twist of melody that al-ways set the Strausses apart from their lesser satellites. The second is a fine instance of the exuberant tempi that so de-lighted Johann II. Light-footed and fleet, too, is the second waltz, and definitely Straussian in its catch-accent. Toward the end of the set appears a martial tune; this is followed at once by a rotating melody, which is a forerunner of the not-too-distant *Accelerationen.**

Several other compositions of interest date from this year, many of them with titles suggestive of the everyday life of the city. Sometimes these titles bear no discoverable connection to the music to which they are affixed, but occasionally they are distinctly pertinent. This is true of the *Schnellpost* (*Fast Mail*) *Polka,* Op. 159; like his brother Eduard's later *Bahn Frei* (*Free Track*) *Galopp,* it is obviously railroad music. But whereas Eduard's composition is a fairly factual approxima-tion, in musical notation, of an express train running full tilt, Johann's polka remains in the sphere of pure music. Therein lies the essential difference between the two brothers, a differ-ence as fundamental as their characters. In every way, Edi was the materialist of the family; he thought in terms of solid reali-ties, he lacked the imagination to sublimate these almost photo-graphic impressions into great music, as did his elder brother. Johann, on the other hand, was a poet, though not a dreamer and a visionary like Josef; in patterning his work on a fast-running *rapide,* he penned sounds which are his impressions of the scene; Eduard's writing, on the other hand, shows scant imagination, and little more than a straight-forward notation of the sounds of the train.

Schnellpost is a roistering piece that is Strauss at his most robust. The flashing tempo follows the rapid turning of the wheels. This is a delightful polka, an example of Strauss's most ingratiating talents. A critic once wrote, "When Strauss has been hounded to death by the too-frequent playing of the *Blue Danube,* he will be born again in some exuberant polka."

---

* *It is a lamentable tendency of latter-day conductors who have not grown up in the Strauss tradition to believe that all the waltzes in a single Strauss composition should be played in one tempo; this is com-pletely false—the tempo varies to suit the mood of each section.*

Some of Strauss's most interesting compositions of this period are those which he wrote for school dances. He was especially prodigal in his attentions to the balls of the Wiener Hoch-Schule. Strauss wrote for, and dedicated to, the medical students of this school his *Paroxysmens Waltzes,* Op. 189, the *Aesculap Polka,* Op. 130, and the *Panacea-Klänge Waltzes,* Op. 161. To the law students were dedicated the *Solon-sprüche Waltzes,* Op. 128, and the *Juristenball Tänze,* Op. 177. The engineering students were in their turn honored by the *Motoren Waltzes;* the electrical students by the *Elec-trophor Polka,* and the chemistry students by the *Explosions Polka.*

The *Paroxysmenswalzer* was first heard in the popular So-fiensaal on January 20th, 1857. The title page of the original edition of the piano arrangement depicts skeletons, test tubes, retorts, stethoscopes and other familiar medical paraphernalia. Victorian to the last degree, this is one of the many colorful piano editions which, of itself, provides a vivid picture of that bygone day.

The introduction to the *Paroxysmenswalzer,* somewhat more extended than those of the earlier works, marked *agitato,* is in 4/4 time. Apart from the clue in the marking, there is little in this section (or for that matter, in the waltzes themselves) to recall the hospital. Yet James H. Fassett, in his program notes for the Columbia Record albums of *Rediscovered Music of Johann Strauss,* contends that the fourth waltz "has a distinctly neurotic character and continues with a somewhat gayer fifth waltz." One must question the possibility of neuroticism, while admitting the unusual heavy-handedness of this section. It is doubtful that Strauss, with his peculiar psychological make-up, was at all capable of portraying neuroticism in music. Certainly no one would pretend to compare any one of his waltzes to the *Ländler* of Mahler's *Ninth Sym-*

phony, which *is* neurotic. Just as Strauss in daily life fled every aspect of life's sordid realities, even to the extent of flouting convention and fleeing Vienna because his abhorrence of death was such that he could not force himself to be present at the funeral of his beloved mother, so did he flee everything in music tending to the tragic. . . .

In the *Telegrafische Depeschen* (*Telegraph Messages*) *Waltzes,* Op. 195, one finds one of those infrequent compositions of Strauss's early period in which the composer has combined a descriptive title with descriptive music. The introduction is the most programmatic section, as always. The waltz knows but one rhythm, in 3/4 time, and this rhythm, to boot, cannot vary widely in tempo. But in his introductions, Strauss could permit himself free rein. *Telegrafische Depeschen* opens with the clicking of telegraph keys, then a few sharp chords, like miniature explosions, and the message crosses the spark gap and speeds out over the wire. It flashes through the wood winds and over the higher strings at lightning speed. A pause, the three-quarter accent appears, and the first waltz is heard. In the background, and in an occasional chord sequence, the clicking keys are heard. With the second waltz, opening in brass, the message motive returns, streaking now through the strings, and it continues to flit through the background during the course of the third waltz. Two additional waltzes, a reprise and a short *coda* conclude the work.

IT WAS during the summer of 1854, not many months after he had played the *Ballg'schichten* in the Zeremoniesaal, that Strauss went to lovely Bad Gastein, which lies, encircled on three sides by the Salzkammergut Alps, at the impassable end of a valley, the resort town rising in tiers up the steep sides of the rocky wall on either side of a foaming cataract, which comes tumbling down to split town, mountain chain and valley in two. Here he was visited by a number of Russian gentlemen. They were, they told him, certain of the directors of a new railway company which had lately built a line from St. Petersburg to Pavlovsk and Tsarskoe-Selo. Pavlovsk was then a fashionable summer resort, very much in vogue with the Russian nobility and gentry because of its proximity to Tsarskoe-Selo, a city of palaces, which was the summer home of the Russian Imperial Family and its attendants.

In an effort to increase even further the number of visitors to Pavlovsk, and thereby stimulate passenger traffic along the new line, the directors had built in Pavlovsk the Vauxhall, a large casino suitable for both concerts and dancing. Having built the most beautiful public ballroom in all Russia, they now needed the King of the Waltz to entertain Russian society. The presence at this new casino of the most famous orchestra leader of his day would unquestionably insure the success of the project. The Russians, with native prodigality, offered him a fee of such magnitude that even his deep-rooted distaste for travel could not bring him to refuse it.

There was at this time more than one Strauss Orchestra. This was the result of a demand for his music at more concerts than a single orchestra could encompass. As a result, he enlarged upon his father's idea of employing two or three orchestras. On evenings when he had booked as many as six orchestras in various halls and private ballrooms, he would make a tour of his orchestras, appearing for a short time with each of them, thus evenly distributing his favors and presence among those who clamored for the sight of him. But even this arrangement proved untenable, and after much persuasion he was able to induce first Josef and later Eduard to share the responsibility with him. But that is another story.

The Strauss family had thus become "Big Business." Strauss now controlled over two hundred musicians, a staff of librarians, assistant conductors, copyists, publicity and booking agents. He rode in the driver's seat, demanding fees which would have left his father aghast (and getting them), publishing his works on a royalty basis only, and refusing to be cheated, as his father had been before him, by outright sale of an immortal waltz for a small fee.

Leaving Josef in charge of entertainments in Vienna, Johann entrained in the early summer for St. Petersburg, at the head of a picked band of musicians. His arrival created considerable interest, but nothing to compare with a later occasion when the police were obliged to clear the square before the St. Petersburg station in order to allow him to leave the building and mount a carriage for his hotel without being mauled by well-intentioned admirers.

In Pavlovsk occurred the first of Johann Strauss's important romances. Before this, he had been drawn to many women —how could it be otherwise for this handsome and personable young man, who represented the essence of all that was romantic?—but these attachments had always proven ephemeral. Now, for the first time, Strauss fell in love. The girl was Olga Smirnitzki, daughter of a wealthy family of merchants.

He wished to marry her, but he soon realized how impossible this was. The social world of St. Petersburg was not yet the society of Vienna; the idea of a musician, no matter how exalted, marrying the daughter of one of Russia's merchant princes was a fantastic absurdity to the Russian mind. Olga was forbidden to have further communication with Johann. Their actual encounters were few, clandestine and fleeting, but messages passed steadily back and forth between the lovers, through the confidential intermediation of Olga's maid. Strauss at first begged her to marry him without delay, and, if necessary, elope with him. Olga hesitated and begged for time, and later Strauss did not press her further; he had written his mother, who urgently counseled him against this marriage.

Anna Strauss knew her Johann well. He needed a woman who could give him much love, much self-sacrifice, much patience; a woman who would watch over him, who would see that his absorption in composition would not interfere with his eating and sleeping, and (most important of all) a woman who would guard his finances and check his extravagances, for Strauss's purse was a cornucopia of largess to all. Olga Smirnitzki, beautiful, charming and well-bred though she was, would have made no wife for Johann Strauss. A perfect product of her environment, it would have been she who would have demanded attention; their marriage would have been a disaster.

Schani heeded his mother. He recalled the wisdom of her counsel in past years and knew that she had never been jealously possessive of him. He realized that her reasons must have been well-founded. Perhaps, too, he did not love Olga enough. At any rate, he bade her *auf wiederseh'n* in Pavlovsk, and returned to Vienna to consider the matter. There, freed from the enchantment of Olga and the bewitching, endless, twilit summer nights of the North, this romantic idyl slipped into the background of his memory.

But the perfume of Olga Smirnitzki lingers in the catalogue of Johann Strauss's compositions. Olga was a talented amateur musician, and her love for Schani momentarily fanned its expression. She composed a number of light pieces, two of which, the *Reise-Abenteuer Waltzes,* Op. 227, and the *Kobold Mazurka,* Op. 226, were arranged and published by Strauss as inclusions in his catalogue. There are other traces of his Russian sojourn: his farewell to that semi-oriental land, the *Abschied von St. Petersburg Waltzes,* Op. 210, and his joyous home-coming salute to Austria, the *Grüss an Wien Polka-Française,* Op. 225.

ON FEBRUARY 14th, 1860, Johann Strauss sat at sunrise before a small table in the deserted Sofiensaal. An hour before, the hall had been filled with couples stepping briskly to the tune of a polka. Now the music was over, and the men had packed their instruments and were heading homeward to bed. Strauss always enjoyed this hour of relaxation, suspended between the excitement of the concert which had gone before, and the day's work which was yet to come.

Stretched in a chair, cigarette in hand, draining the last drops of champagne from a glass, he was approached by one of the committeemen of the Technical Students' Ball, scheduled for the coming evening. The young man asked whether he had written the waltz which had been commissioned for the ball. Strauss confessed that he had not; however, there was no cause for worry—the waltz would be ready.

On the spot, he reached for the menu and traced some staves on its blank side. Then he lounged back in his chair, searching for an idea. He thought of the experiments of the technical students: currents, stresses, strains, torsions, decreasing and accelerating speeds—all these ran through his mind. Along this train of thought, a rotating melody sprang up. Beginning dreamily, it began to whirl ever faster and faster—perhaps inspired by that earlier spinning passage in *Ballg'-schichten.* Quickly, he sketched out this passage:

Everyone who has heard it once remembers it well—the distinctive *Accelerationen Waltzes,* Op. 234. This marks the flood tide of that period which may be designated as the first of three into which Strauss's career was divided. This is his formative period; those years which began with his first waltz, conceived at the age of six, continuing on through his Dommayer début to come to an end with the *Wiener Bonbons Waltzes.* It was during the second stage that Strauss produced the so-called "Great Waltzes"—works which represent Viennese dance music at its fullest flowering. Even so, it was not until the third period that Strauss completely revealed his genius. These were the years when he relinquished the directorship of his orchestra to his brothers in order to devote himself to the composition of operas and operettas, but, unfortunately, these are the works which are, all in all, least known in the Anglo-Saxon world.

Accelerationen opens with an introduction in high *tremolo* strings, under which other instruments, notably the lower strings, suggest a fragmentary melody reminiscent of the first waltz. This rises in a gradual *crescendo,* which fades suddenly at its climax in anticipation of the opening waltz. The theme of this waltz is quoted above. Starting slowly, it gathers momentum until it seems to fling itself up and out into space by virtue of its own centrifugal force. This a trait peculiar to Johann II—his melodies often have this twist, but nowhere more effectively than here. One finds in the writing for the violins in the second waltz a style used repeatedly in other works (notably the later *Morgenblätter Waltzes*), the taking of the melody out of its original, simple form, and the weaving about it of a quasi-variation figuration in eighth notes.

That Strauss was ever full of a gay and almost childlike humor is shown at every turn in his early compositions, before experience had brought him the sophistication which so illumi-

JOHANN STRAUSS II

JOSEF STRAUSS
Photograph taken shortly before his death.

nates the pages of *Die Fledermaus,* and nowhere more incisive-
ly than in the famous *Perpetuum Mobile,* in which Strauss took
a mild dig at the tendency of his day to emphasize virtuosity
to the detriment of musical content. In spirit, this work is
closely akin to a *scherzo;* certainly it deserves the name, for
few examples of a musical joke are its equal. But the *Perpetual
Motion* is a *scherzo* only in the literal sense of the word, for
in form it is the apotheosis of the dance-hall galop.

Like the *Perpetuum Mobile* which it sought to ridicule (those
of Paganini and others), Strauss's *Perpetuum Mobile* is a virtuoso piece, in which the men of the orchestra, collectively and
individually, find opportunity to demonstrate their technical
proficiency. Based entirely upon a series of quasi-variations on
a theme only eight bars long, it opens first with a galloping
rhythm in the strings, following which wood winds and strings
introduce the tune. A rollicking bit for high wood winds in-
terrupts, and then follows an hilarious bassoon solo, picked up
at once by solo piccolo, with obbligato by the bassoon. Then,
a snatch for trumpets and trombones, contrasted immediately
with the ethereal tones of bells (celesta or glockenspiel).
Flutes again, then the clarinets, and now the French horns
have their moment. The flutes return, and the whole orchestra
goes galloping off on a madcap variation which leads into that
most ridiculous and delightful of passages, a solo for tympani
over tremolo strings. The orchestra rockets off again, until it
crashes up against the tam-tam. From there, clarinets and flutes
resume the escapade, leading the orchestra into a few measures
which end the work abruptly and without warning, leaving it
hanging harmonically in mid-air, as though the composer had
tired of his efforts.

This ending is one which displeases most conductors; it is
not only too abrupt, but almost anticlimactic after some of the
wonderful ideas which have gone before. A final touch of

humor is somehow needed. It was Mengelberg's practice to effect a *da capo,* and end at the close of the variation for solo bassoon, finishing this with a downward *glissando* by that instrument. Although the writer finds no fault with this idea, his own experience has been that the average bassoonist (in Germany, at least) cannot effect a good *glissando* in that register. The writer's personal practice is to make the *da capo,* but to play only the first four measures, which establish the basic rhythm *ad libitum,* all the while having the strings play more and more softly until they are no longer to be heard.

UNDER the energetic rule of Franz-Josef, Vienna had been undergoing—with not a little protest—a major face-lifting operation. The old battlements which had encircled the Kaiserstadt (the inner city) were razed, giving place to what is today Vienna's main thoroughfare, the Ringstrasse, a spacious avenue along which a Baroque palace, an early-Gothic City Hall, a neo-Gothic church, a Grecian House of Parliament and the Renaissance Burgtheater rub elbows. Along this same avenue stand also the Hofoperntheater, the Museums of Art and Natural History, and the Academy of Fine Arts.

The Viennese citizen is, by nature, almost fanatically attached to old and familiar objects and surroundings. The old battlements, along the top of which fashionable Vienna loved to stroll, were of dated military usefulness; necessary during the days when Vienna was besieged by the Turks, they were useless in withstanding a modern army. No one knew this better than Franz-Josef, who had studied military tactics from childhood. Yet when the demolition of the battlements was announced, committees came to him from all quarters, begging that the old, familiar landmarks be allowed to stand. Two compositions by Johann Strauss commemorate this change in the familiar pattern of old Vienna. The first, written when the order for the razing of the bastions was published, was the *Demolierer Polka,* Op. 269. The second, penned when Vienna was given its beautiful new Ringstrasse, was the *Neu Wien Waltzes,* Op. 342.

4

JETTY TREFFZ

Love had, until this time, scarcely affected Schani. His one important affair of the past, the romance with Olga Smirnitzki, was now but a memory. He had known many other attachments since Olga, but these passing infatuations had not made any deep impression, to the tremendous chagrin of many an ambitious Viennese mother. This was probably the result of a combination of circumstances, not the least of which was the endless round of work which left him hardly an idle moment.

Vienna was no St. Petersburg; Johann Strauss, the "uncrowned Emperor of Austria," could have had at will his choice of any of the marriageable young ladies of Vienna's social world. Thus it was all the more confounding when Vienna learned that Strauss had suddenly married Jetty Treffz, a woman ten years his senior; a woman, moreover, who (according to the conventions of the day) lived on the fringe of respectable Viennese society.

Henrietta Treffz was born in Vienna. A beautiful voice and a profound love of music led her to study singing; in this she was assisted by grants of money from the Court of Saxony. At fifteen, she made her début in the Dresden Opera. She later traveled widely, winning great success in such antipodal capitals as lighthearted Vienna and Victorian London. A certain consonance between the names of Jenny Lind and Jetty Treffz caused her to be not infrequently compared to the

Swedish Nightingale, and, to the credit of her voice and musicianship, it can be said that *Kammersängerin* Treffz did not fare badly by these comparisons.

At forty, she retired from the stage to settle in the home of Baron Moritz Tedesco. They would have married, but Tedesco had promised at his father's deathbed to remain a Jew, and to refrain from marriage outside his religion. Therefore, making the best of a bad situation, and in defiance of moral codes, Jetty became the mistress of the man she loved, presiding over his home. She bore him two children; she was in fact, if not in name, his wife.

From the meager accounts existing, the meeting of Johann and Jetty was an instance of that rare thing, love at first sight. When longer acquaintance corroborated and strengthened their first emotions, they were frank to tell Tedesco what the change meant. Strauss told the Baron honestly that he wanted to marry Jetty, and the Baron, a man of honor, not only felt that he could not interfere with Jetty's finally obtaining the honor and position due her, but made her a settlement of such proportions that it seemed the dowry of a princess.

The marriage of Jetty and Johann in the Stefanskirche, the ancient cathedral of Vienna, was an extremely quiet one, with only a few friends, among them Haslinger, attending. Following the ceremony, Anna Strauss called the couple aside and told Johann she had a special wedding gift for them, a wedding gift which, she said, Johann himself had made. Strauss was completely mystified as his mother drew out a large box, which she unlocked, disclosing a small hoard of gold coins. Unknown to him, during his first Russian trip, his aunt (who had accompanied him) worried about his extravagance; she had taken a part of his pay each week and deposited it in a Viennese bank. The little scene was not lost on Jetty, who realized that henceforth she would have to be the brake on Schani's generosity.

The newly married couple settled first in an apartment within the city, and then moved to a villa in Hietzing, close to Schönbrunn and not far from the Dommayerbau where Strauss had begun his public life.

That perfect mirror of his life, the catalogue of his works, makes the first mention of Jetty Treffz in his Opus 271, which is dedicated to her.

THE last of the important compositions of this early period of Schani's career came shortly afterwards: the *Morgenblätter Waltzes,* Op. 279. Like the later *Feuilleton Waltzes,* Op. 293, this was dedicated to the "Concordia," an association of Viennese journalists, and was written for one of their balls. *Morgenblätter* may be translated as either *Morning Leaves* or *Morning Papers.* The latter title (in view of the group for whom it was written) would seem to be correct, but the cover of the original piano edition, showing leaves glinting under a morning sun, allows a double meaning.

Morgenblätter was played at a Concordia ball in an informal competition with the *Abendblätter Waltzes* of the visiting Frenchman, Jacques Offenbach, whose appearance in the Austrian capital was causing a minor sensation. It is a matter of record that it was Offenbach's waltzes which were more highly praised, the inspired spontaneity of Strauss's offering passing comparatively unnoticed. Strauss returned home that evening feeling a deep hurt, a hurt which rankled for years. Certainly, it was a bitter blow to find that his beloved Viennese preferred, to his own superlative set of waltzes, a composition which time has proven markedly inferior. For, in all of the Strauss output, there is no other work to match *Morgenblät-*

ter for sheer elfin lightness of step, ingenuous youthfulness and dewy freshness.

Morgenblätter is probably the most volatile of Johann's waltz compositions—it fairly skips along, with a jauntiness that is unique. But Strauss was also full master of the sensuous; he well knew when to convert that light skip into a silky glide. This was never better instanced than in the fourth waltz, where four measures of coquettish *pizzicato* chords are suddenly contrasted with four extraordinarily sensuous measures for bowed strings.

This waltz is, regardless of period, one of Strauss's best. If it lacks the majesty and the descriptive power of the great waltzes, it owns instead a freshness and a youthfulness which place it beside the later works.

ALTHOUGH few are heard today, the marches of the two Johanns are endowed with a charm and a musical worth that make them cherishable. They are typical of their day and their people, their mincing rhythms so opposed to the long, free stride of the American soldier, so perfectly delineated in the music of John Philip Sousa. Of the Johann II marches, the *Persischer*, Op. 289, is a splendid specimen. Commemorating a visit to Vienna of the Shah of Persia, it is dedicated to that potentate. The rhythm recalls the rolling gait of camel caravans crossing the Iranian sands. Another popular march is the *Egyptischer*, Op. 335, which, if its orientalism is more synthetic, nonetheless makes a good mate for the *Persischer*.

Yet neither of these equals the father's great *Radetzky,* which remains the ideal of the Austrian march.

Four opus numbers after the *Persicher* appear the *Aus dem Bergen Waltzes,* dedicated to that fearless (and fearsome) Viennese music critic, Eduard Hanslick, of whom it might be said that he played Boswell to Johannes Brahms' Dr. Johnson. Hanslick made no secret of a great admiration for Strauss's unique genius, an admiration which he shared with Brahms. Indeed, Johann Strauss was one of the few friends who was spared the gruff, sarcastic side of Brahms' nature; it was Brahms who wrote on Alice Strauss's autograph fan the first few bars of the *Blue Danube,* and beneath them the words, "unfortunately not by Johannes Brahms!" Hanslick often claimed that he had been the first to say that the later waltzes could no longer be measured as dance music; he called them variously waltz-poems and waltz-requiems.

The students of the Wiener Hoch-Schule were at this time honored by two new polkas, the *Prozesspolka,* Op. 294, which was dedicated to the law students, and first played at their ball in the Sofiensaal on January 31st, 1865, and the *Electrophor Polka,* Op. 297, dedicated to the technical students, whose ball was held in the Dianasaal on February 14th.

It is not difficult to trace a resemblance in *Electrophor* to the earlier *Telegrafische Depeschen Waltzes,* which is not surprising when one considers that both works concern themselves with electrical energy. The whirling tune that whizzes through the fiddles is clearly akin to that which dashes along in the first waltz of the earlier work.

Only nine published works separate this polka from the *Wiener Bonbons Waltzes,* Op. 307, the composition which is the best point of demarcation between Strauss's formative years and those which established him as one of the world's musical masters.

5

THE GREAT WALTZES

WHAT, precisely, was it that provoked this broadening and deepening of Johann Strauss's creative talents? Several causes contributed, of which the most important was his marriage to Jetty Treffz. Possessing extremely good business sense, she took over the management of his affairs, and at once insisted that the harassed composer-conductor devote more time to composition, less to conducting. It was under her influence that Strauss henceforth gave up leading his orchestra at dances, with the sole exception of Imperial functions, and appeared before his musicians only in concert performances.

Freed from the bondage of having to conduct pure dance music on an almost nightly basis, Strauss was able to relax. Composing at a slower rate, taking greater pains, and giving more thought to each composition, he shows consistently from this point on that apparently effortless spontaneity which results only from careful planning and revision. It would be doing Strauss an injustice to insist that all his compositions—even all the major works—are inspired. No man, however gifted, could compose a new work as regularly as Strauss was often compelled to do without occasionally straining his resources.

As he found more time for composition, Strauss began to conceive his works more in terms of absolute music, less in terms of the dancers. Thus occurred the last phenomenon of the development of the waltz in the hands of the Strausses; the great waltzes are not dance music—they are the apotheosis of the Viennese Waltz, in concert garb, and into them Strauss has distilled the essence of everything that is Vienna.

The introductions and the codas now grew longer; they developed in form, in complexity and imagination, until the waltzes proper came to assume a role hardly greater than that of their preludes and postludes. Thus, in *Tales from the Vienna Woods,* the introduction and coda together are almost as long as the waltzes, when these are played with the conventionally observed repeats. In *Wine, Women and Song,* the outer sections assume an importance greater than that of the waltzes, which are themselves not among Strauss's most inspired moments. In these "great waltzes," the couples find themselves in the awkward situation of having to stand and listen, but not dance! Writers of the period have noted that when the waltz itself began, they actually forgot to dance! However, the "great waltzes" were written for the concert hall, not the dance floor.

Here lies a point deserving of more stress. Many of these waltzes possess two conclusions, one short and in waltz time, for the dance hall, the other a return to the slow introduction as a means of rounding out the work for concert performances. When conductors, even such famous ones as Leopold Stokowski, today play these waltzes in concert, beginning with the opening *tempo di vals* (which follows the proper introduction) and concluding with the dance ending, they are not only doing an injustice to Strauss, but they are demonstrating a complete lack of understanding, not only of Strauss's intent and content, but of simple musical form.

It was perhaps Strauss's misfortune that his early steps in music, and the demands of a dancing public, gave him no opportunity to write anything that was not dance music. Even the *Perpetuum Mobile* was no exception. Yet Strauss had within him the power to write music which belongs exclusively in the concert hall. It is unlikely that he could have poured his art into the rigid molds of the sonata, the symphony or the concerto. His path would more probably have lain along the freer lines which Franz Liszt developed in his tone poems, and which Debussy later brought to fruition in his great impressionist works. Strauss, working in a stereotyped and circumscribed medium, nonetheless managed to flirt with the style of the symphonic poem. There are moments in the opening of the *Wiener Wald* when one senses the coming of the faun; there are glimpses in the swirling, swelling currents of the introduction to the *Blue Danube* which could lead to the later aquatints of the French impressionist master.

In 1856, Johann Herbeck became Director of the newly founded Wiener Männergesangverein. The establishment of this choral group was an important event in Vienna, for the Viennese have always been passionately fond of vocal music. Possessed, as a nation, of natural singing voices surpassed only by the Italians, the Austrians needed an organization which would provide a natural outlet for their love of song.

Herbeck, director of a choir of superb male voices, found himself constantly at a loss for worthwhile choral material of popular appeal. There were, of course, the great oratorios of Handel and the great choral works of Johann Sebastian Bach, but these he could use only sparingly; the lack of enthusiasm and appreciation with which Vienna received performances of the Passions by a choir conducted by Brahms was proof of this. There were, also, the choral works of Mendelssohn, Beethoven and many others, but Herbeck wanted not only lighter music as a foil to this heavy diet, but music which was in the blood of every Viennese. It was only natural, then, that he should turn to Johann Strauss, the arch melodist of the day. He asked Strauss to write the music for a choral waltz; he had the poet to set it to words. It was to be produced at a gala concert celebrating the signing of the peace treaty between Austria and Prussia which ended the short but disastrous war in which the Austrians had suffered utter defeat and humiliation, culminating in the rout of the Imperial forces at Königgrätz. The Viennese had no desire to linger over these unpleasant memories; they wanted gaiety and forgetfulness. Herbeck knew that the man to fill this prescription was Johann Strauss.

Strauss accepted the commission. He was rather intrigued by it, in fact. For one thing, Jetty had been urging him to write an operetta. He did not think himself ready for so exacting a form as yet, and saw in this request of Herbeck's a chance to try his hand at vocal music. He had lately read a poem which had piqued his fancy. As a literary effort, it was of no consequence, but he was fascinated by the mental picture conjured by the last line of the stanza:

> *Und ich sah' dich reich an Schmerzen*
> *Und ich sah' dich jung' und hold',*
> *Wo die Treue wächst im Herzen*
> *Wie im Schacht das edle Gold,*
> *An der Donau, an der schönen, blauen Donau.*

An der schönen, blauen Donau—by the beautiful, blue Danube. The words lingered with Strauss. Good son of Vienna that he was, he knew that the Danube is often green, sometimes slate grey, but never blue. Did it matter? The words somehow identified themselves with all that was Viennese, all that was Austrian. After the war with Prussia, more devastating to Austrian honor than to Austrian lands, there came a reaction which took the form of increased national fervor.

The words identified themselves in Strauss's mind with a liquidly rotating melody, based on the D major triad—the notes D, F# and A—a theme which is recognized immediately the world over, whether played by symphony orchestra, hurdy-gurdy or harmonica. How can one describe the loveliness of the many waltzes? Our hearing has been blunted by indifferent performances, but an intelligent and sensitive reading (unfortunately all too rare) can bring one again to an appreciation of its strange enchantment. In few other compositions is Strauss's power of suggestion as evident as in the introduction to the *Blue Danube*.

Here is the river itself, that moving fluid roadway, calm and broadly-flowing, imprisoned forever in terms of sound. High in the violins, in a *pianissimo tremolo*, a breeze drifts across the face of the open stream in ripplets, silvered in the sun. Underneath, the current flows on inflexibly in the horns and violoncellos. Suddenly, *forte*, a gust of wind sends a jagged blur of ripples billowing across the surface of the water. Little whirlpools appear in the opening *tempo di vals*. Then, three *pizzicato* notes descending in the contrabasses restore the calm and set the stage for the waltzes to begin.

In the waltzes themselves, Strauss made no attempt to parallel Smetana's *Moldau,* and depict the Danube wandering from its source to the Black Sea. The formal structure of the waltz forbade this. Instead, he allowed each section to suggest a different mood or setting, and what these may be each listener must decide for himself. These waltzes, almost a series of aquarelles, are too largely absolute music to possess any fixed image. Through them all runs only one common thread, suggestive perhaps of the eddies and currents which swirl around piles and shoals, and along banks and quays. Waltz follows waltz, in a pattern which leaves the listener unconscious of transition; modulations occur with a naturalness which seems inevitable; bridge passages appear to be an integral part of the musical thought, and not merely a means of sewing seams. The *reprise* rounds out the formal structure, satisfying structural demands, but it does more than that— it constitutes almost a development in sonata form. In no other single composition, save perhaps *Wiener Wald* and the *Kaiserwalzer,* did Strauss exhibit such consummate mastery of form. Here is no simple restatement of themes, but a section which almost amounts to an enlarging of the original statements, with embellishments and connecting passages as yet unheard. Now the *coda,* harking back to the hazy atmosphere of the introduction, and then a final surge to the closing measures. Listening to these last measures, and to those which form the introduction, one cannot contend that Strauss was master only of lightness and gayety. There are few compositions which contain more nostalgia; there is an endless depth of melancholy in the *coda.* It is again the "sorrow without pain" which characterized so much of Schubert's music, and which later became even more marked in Josef Strauss's works.

Herbeck engaged a poetaster of most questionable talents to write the words to the waltz. This doubtful genius penned stanzas so pathetically inane that they almost dragged the music to oblivion with them. The intent was to allude obliquely to the ever-tense political atmosphere, and the words

were set in dialogue form between the upper and lower voices
of the choir:

> *Wiener, seid froh!*
> *Oho, wieso?*
> *Ein Schimmer des Lichts. . . .*
> *Wir seh'n noch nichts. . . .*
> *Der Fasching ist da. . . .*
> *Ach so, na ja!*
> *Was hilft das Trauern*
> *Und das Bedauern?*
> *D'rum froh und heiter seid!*

> Vienna, be gay!
> And why, pray?
> A glimmer of light. . . .
> With us, it's night!
> Carnival's here. . . .
> O dear, O dear. . . .
> Well, why seek sorrow?
> There's still tomorrow,
> So laugh and be gay!

When the singers were given their parts, they rebelled,
and it took all of Herbeck's persuasion to forestall an absolute refusal on the part of his chorus to perform the waltz.
Herbeck, convinced of its effectiveness, instilled enough of
his own confidence into the chorus to cause them to devote
some effort to it. The concert took place in the hall of the
Imperial Riding School on February 13th, 1867. The waltz
was sung, and failed. Even Strauss's inspired music could not
overcome the nonsense of the poetaster; the stupid verses,
for the moment, completely blinded the audience to the grace
of a work which was, in little time, to become Austria's unofficial national anthem. It is true that it obtained one en-

core, but for a man whose Opus 1 had occasioned nineteen, this was abysmal failure.

An der schönen, blauen Donau did not remain a failure for long, but it was not Vienna which first acclaimed it; another city owns that honor. That city is Paris.

In the summer of 1867, Paris had become the Mecca of the social world. The Second Empire was then at the height of its glittering, extravagant and transient glory; three years later this house of cards was to collapse of its own folly, in the midst of the Franco-Prussian war. But little of the growing tension was noticed by those who visited Paris in '67 to attend the International Exposition.

Paris was then a true City of Light. Gas jets flared from pipe lines stretched along the edges of the roofs, outlining the buildings with a million spots of flame; the tree-lined boulevards were thronged with strolling visitors and Parisians. Celebrities were everywhere—the Prince of Wales, later King Edward VII; the Duke and Duchess of Manchester; Alexandre Dumas, fils; Hortense Schneider, then the rage of Paris in the title role of Offenbach's *La Grande-Duchesse de Gérolstein;* Henri de Rochefort, and Henri Murger, author of the anecdotes of Bohemian student life which Puccini later put to music; Prince Metternich, the Austrian Ambassador, and his fascinating wife, the Princess Pauline Metternich, confidante of the Empress Eugénie, and a host of others. Through this imposing assemblage moved Henri de Villemessant, owner and publisher of *Figaro,* the leading newspaper of Paris, one of the most enterprising journalists in history.

It was no wonder, then, that Strauss, famous though he was, was sucked into this furious maelstrom and ignored. His concerts at the Exposition were well attended, but so many other attractions competed that they did not raise him to the omnipotent position he held in Vienna.

His first success came when Princess Metternich engaged him and his orchestra to play for a mammoth ball in her Parisian palace. His triumph again seemed assured—the guests barely danced at all, they preferred to listen to Herr Strauss. But Paris, spoiled beyond belief, the most coquettish mistress man has ever known, was accustomed to sensations, and Strauss was no exception. The next day matters stood as before.

What he needed in that competitive field was a publicity manager. He found one in the likeliest man of all—Villemessant. The newspaperman chanced into the Cercle Internationale one day when Strauss was conducting. It did not take two numbers for him to perceive that here was a unique genius.

He sent for Strauss the next day, and the Waltz King did not delay in paying his respects. Thereupon began a campaign which might have made a Hollywood publicity man envious. *Figaro* ran articles daily on *"Monsieur Strauss, qui a le diable au corps."* It was not long before other papers had taken up the fashion; it suddenly became the latest and most imperious vogue in Paris to have heard Strauss and danced to his music.

And with Strauss the Parisians associated one waltz which he played constantly—*An der schönen, blauen Donau.* Thus the waltz which had begun its career as a near-failure became the tune that was on everybody's lips, in everybody's ears.

Villemessant arranged a series of suppers for Strauss, during the course of which Schani found opportunity to meet and know the most important people in Paris. In return, Strauss insisted upon giving a supper for Villemessant, his editorial staff and a number of guests. The publisher consented only on condition that Strauss allow him to furnish the wines from his own famous cellar. Following the supper, Strauss led his orchestra in a new polka, the *Figaropolka,* Op.

320. Villemessant was as delighted as a child; the following day, a piano edition of the polka was printed and distributed as a special supplement to *Figaro*.

Another ball was held at the palace of the Princess Metternich; this time, Strauss was not only the artist, but the guest of honor as well. A typically Parisian company was gathered, ranging from His Royal Highness, the Prince of Wales, to Her Grace, the "Grand Duchess of Gérolstein," Hortense Schneider.

Strauss was a *succès fou*, and nothing would do for Prince Edward but that the Waltz King voyage on to England with his orchestra. They arrived in London late in 1867, and appeared in a series of concerts at Covent Garden which ran from August 16th to October 25th; Jetty Treffz appeared at several of these concerts as soloist.

Morgenblätter, that waltz which Vienna had passed by in favor of Offenbach's less consequential *Abendblätter*, was revived to prove a particular favorite at these concerts. Other works which Strauss conducted during this series included his father's *Tanz-Signale Waltzes*, Op. 218, the *Blue Danube* in a new choral dress, to English text, and the *Erinnerung an Covent Garden Waltzes*, Op. 329. This last is particularly apt for an English audience, since it is based on popular English airs, including that hardy perennial, *The Man on the Flying Trapeze*. Thinking again to compliment the British, he wrote the *Festival Quadrille*, Op. 341, and by mischance included an American Civil War song of the Union Army, *Just Before the Battle, Mother*.

BEFORE starting out for Paris, Strauss wrote yet another choral waltz for Herbeck's men—the lilting *Künstlerleben* (*Artist's Life*) *Waltzes*, Op. 316. This was only one of a number of waltzes which Strauss in time wrote for the Vienna Men's Choral Association, including *Tales from the Vienna Woods* and *Wine, Women and Song*. *Künstlerleben* is today known solely as an orchestral waltz, the choral form having long been forgotten. It was first heard as an orchestral work at the Hesperusballtanz on February 18th, 1867, in the Dianasaal, five days after the fiasco of *An der schönen, blauen Donau*. Apparently Strauss must have been working on the two waltzes at once; it is scarcely conceivable that this masterwork, completely orchestrated, could have been done in five days, even admitting Strauss's unusual facility. For the work is clearly the product of Strauss's pen alone, even to the last of the orchestration. Strauss had on his staff a number of arrangers, and many of the minor works were completed and orchestrated by them, but it is highly improbable that any of the "great waltzes" fall into this category.

It is by no means unfortunate that the vocal parts have been eliminated from the waltzes. The truth is that melodically they are unsuited to voice; orchestrally they are complete in themselves, whether Strauss desired it or not. In consequence, a text often makes the waltzes sound like a *tour de force*.

While the programmatic implications of the Strauss waltzes are limited, one constantly encounters among the greater waltzes a perfect correlation of title to music. If there is in *Künstlerleben* no attempt to portray the life of an artist, the title is nonetheless perfectly suited to this *sans-gêne* music. One could never imagine this title applied to the rich-blooded, exotic music of *Wiener Blut*. And just as the titles bring to mind two widely varied images, so do these two sets of waltzes occasion entirely different emotional reactions in the listener. Despite the common Straussian resemblance, there is nothing to relate the impassioned, buoyant *Künstlerleben* to the lush strains of *Wiener Blut* or the intoxicated melodies of *Wein, Weib und Gesang.*

As in the *Blue Danube,* Strauss has taken the theme of the first waltz as subject matter for the introduction to *Artist's Life,* thereby achieving a sense of unity in composition which had previously not been found in the waltz. With these two works, the Viennese Waltz reached its third and final phase of growth. The first step had been brought about by Johann, Senior, and Josef Lanner; the second took place when the compositions of Johann II began to display a smoother phrasing of thought and construction, when the rhythms stretched out and became perfectly free. The last step was the fusion of introduction, waltzes and *coda* into a single work which was not the accidental assembling of parts which fitted well together, but the creation of a single musical thought, carried out from start to finish. Since the "great waltzes," of which *Kaiserwalzer* was the last, the form has remained static. This is exemplified in the *Rosenkavalier* waltzes of Richard Strauss and *La Valse* of Ravel.

LITTLE more than a year after Strauss first introduced the *Blue Danube,* he gave the Viennese another great waltz, the only one (except the *Kaiserwalzer*) which has been able to rival successfully the waltzes which have become Austria's unofficial anthem. This new set of waltzes he named *G'schichten aus dem Wiener Wald* (*Tales from the Vienna Woods*), Opus 325. Words by Hans Müller were set to it, and like its great predecessor, it was sung by the Wiener Männergesangverein, this time with marked success.

The *Wiener Wald* was dedicated to the Princess Constanze von und zu Hohenlohe-Schillingfürst, and was given its first performance on June 9th, 1868. Although he inscribed these waltzes to a member of one of Austria's greatest families, Strauss must have had the average Viennese *Bürger* in mind when writing them. They are really dedicated to each and every member of that vast army of city dwellers who, weary of a molelike grind in dusty offices throughout the week, seeks escape on Sunday from the all-confining city to the restful green and coolness of the adjacent woods.

If the *Blue Danube* is evocative of the river from which it takes its name, Strauss's *Wiener Wald* is an even more graphic description of the verdant woods which lie beyond Vienna. This is truest in the introduction, where Strauss has virtually written a tone poem. With the opening notes of the horns and clarinets, reminiscent of the pipings of shepherds amid their flocks, a cool, leafy greenness steals through the orchestra. It is like a page from Beethoven's *Pastoral Symphony*. It reaches a climax, and then follows a statement of what will later be an important waltz theme. As in the *Blue Danube,* there is a sentimental nostalgia here, but it is more pastoral and less emphatic than the emotion of the earlier work. A few notes in the horns open a wide vista of spreading landscape, over which the flute trills bird songs. Then, abruptly, appear the wild, barbaric and untamed tones of a solo zither, playing the waltz theme in its introductory guise, almost as an improvisation. The mood brightens and changes, and gives way suddenly to the full orchestra in the opening 3/4 measures which precede the first waltz.

The sweeping, upsurging beat of this waltz is irresistible. There is no need to analyze the waltzes at length; they are as well known as those of the *Blue Danube*. But it is interesting to note that the theme which Strauss had made his principal motif in the introduction to the *Wiener Wald* and which recurs in the waltzes proper is a frank and admitted plagiarism and development of one of the waltzes by Johann, Senior, *Die Schwalben.*

Vienna Woods:

Die Schwalben:

The *coda* is beautifully wrought. Especially charming is the short dialogue for strings and harp which precedes the zither solo. Here the pastoral mood is resumed, until a final sweep of the orchestra, interrupting the zither's soliloquy, brings the work to a close.

Wein, Weib und Gesang (*Wine, Women and Song*), Op. 333, was another of the waltzes which Strauss wrote for the Wiener Männergesangverein. Unlike the *Blue Danube* and the *Wiener Wald,* it proved a well-knit work in choral dress, whereas both of the earlier waltzes were built upon melodies whose long, legato lines were unsuited to the human voice and its limitations.

Strauss dedicated the waltzes to Herbeck, and gave them their first performance on February 2nd, 1869, in the Diana-saal.

The introduction proved Strauss's greatest venture into non-danceable music, insofar as his waltzes were concerned. It was only a short time after this that he interested himself in the field of operetta and opera. It may be for this reason that the waltzes which followed this composition are provided with less ambitious introductions, again with the exception of the *Kaiserwalzer.*

There is no denying that, for dancers, the introduction is a case of the tail wagging the dog. Together with the few final measures, it forms better than half the playing time for this composition when only a normal number of repeats are observed. For this reason, the work is most effective when heard in concert, for its charm lies entirely in the introduction; the waltzes themselves are second-rate Strauss.

Andante quasi religioso, the introduction begins. A call to attention in horns and wood winds, and then the strings introduce a falling cadence which leads to an exquisite theme for the violoncellos and violas:

There is a Mendelssohnian touch to this phrase; it is a true flower of the Romantic School. A passage reminiscent of an old German march style appears, and then the proclamation, *maestoso:*

> *Wer liebt nicht Wein, Weib und Gesang,*
> *Bleibt ein Narr sein Leben lang!*

> Who does not love wine, women and song,
> Remains a fool his whole life long!

Only then may the waltzes begin. A variation on what has gone before, the first opens hesitantly, slowly gaining strength until, in the twenty-seventh measure, it suddenly leaps wildly, and all the festival spirits of gayety are released.

The second waltz finds Strauss quoting once more, with

considerable modification, his father's *Die Schwalben*. Suddenly the waltz modulates into A-flat major, setting in waltz time the descending cadence which opened the introduction. Then, to deny the gentleness and sentiment of this passage, *staccato* thirds appear in the strings and wood winds, and a strongly accented bass appears to guide the dancers through the maze.

The fourth waltz varies the close of the introduction to form yet another link unifying the whole. This may not be Strauss's most inspired waltz, but it affords a revealing insight into his formal development as a composer.

And then—the orgy. *Forte,* the full orchestra reels out the final crude and drunken measures. . . .

JOHANN Strauss had been interested for a long time in the music of Richard Wagner. Strangely enough, it was Anna Strauss who was responsible for this. She was indeed a woman of unusual and unsuspected qualities. Completely untutored in music, save for what had come her way as the wife of one musician and the mother of three others, she nonetheless had unusual perception. She was among the first in Vienna to sense the significance of Wagner's music, and it was largely because of her enthusiasm that Johann II was attracted to the works of this new Prometheus. It was Johann Strauss who first performed some of the music to *Tristan und Isolde* in the Austrian capital. Wagner had wanted to stage the music drama there, but the concerted efforts of Hanslick and other rabid anti-Wagnerians had succeeded in drumming the music out of the city. Then Strauss, during a Volksgarten concert, began without introduction or announcement the prelude to *Tristan,* and the applause which greeted the close of its first Viennese performance testified to the appeal of the music.

Wagner, in turn, paid tribute to Strauss at the close of the first Bayreuth season, in 1876. Anton Seidl was conducting; Wagner was in the audience. Unexpectedly, Wagner mounted the stage, took the baton from Seidl, and conducted *Wein, Weib und Gesang.*

IT WAS a year later that death came to Frau Strauss. With her sons and daughters married, she had felt alone and neglected. She had taken to remaining in her room in the Hirschenhaus, that same room where her children had been born, and there, one day, they found her, seated in her favorite chair by the window, sleeping her last, final sleep. She had passed away quietly, with neither illness nor pain. Johann was grief-stricken, but even his sorrow lacked the depth of that which the morbidly sensitive Josef felt. Frau Strauss had idolized her Schani; Josef had worshiped his mother. He did not outlive her long; Anna Strauss died on February 13th, 1870, and Josef's death occurred a little over five months later.

Apprised of his mother's passing, Johann hurried to the Hirschenhaus. There, before her inert corpse, the horror which he had always felt for death and its mysteries overwhelmed him, and he rushed from the house and from Vienna, neither knowing nor caring where his flight led him, nor did he return until after the funeral was past. . . .

ALTHOUGH Johann Strauss wrote many waltzes and other dance pieces after his *Neu Wien,* one may say that it was at this moment that he exchanged his career as composer of dance music for that of composer of operas and operettas. It is true that some magnificent waltzes were written during this latter period, notably the *Kaiserwalzer, Frühlingstimmen, Wiener Blut* and *Wo die Zitronen blüh'n.* The *Kaiserwalzer*

and *Wiener Blut,* however, were from their inception concert works and not for the dance hall. *Frühlingstimmen* is also
a concert waltz—for piano solo, later orchestrated by Strauss.
Wo die Zitronen blüh'n is closest to the dance waltz, yet even
this was written principally with the concert hall in mind.

Strauss's origin as a composer for the lyric stage may be
traced to Offenbach's earlier visit to Vienna, and the competitive performance of his *Abendblätter* with Strauss's *Morgenblätter.* Wishing to pay Strauss a compliment, Offenbach
suggested that he try the lyric stage. Offenbach apparently
was merely being complimentary—certainly his professed
admiration for Strauss while in Vienna seeems to have
been merely political, for in his own luxurious Paris home,
as well as at his summer estate near Boulogne, the music of
the Waltz King was said to be strictly forbidden.

If the suggestion failed to strike a responsive chord in
Strauss, it was not wasted upon Jetty. With tact, but with
inflexible perserverance, she gradually steered her husband
through the preliminaries leading to the stage itself. As an
old familiar of the stage, herself an opera singer, it was only
natural that she should encourage her husband to attempt his
hand at a lyric production. Indeed, it had been mainly at her
suggestion that Strauss had given his attention to the writing
of Herbeck's choral waltzes.

Finally, when she thought the moment right, Jetty paid
a visit to Johann's study. Examining the manuscripts stacked
in piles, she selected several which showed lyric possibilities.
These she took to Maximilian Steiner, Director of the Theater-an-der-Wien. Like Jetty, he had long urged Strauss to
write operetta. He received the manuscripts and her ideas
with open arms. The *Hausdichter* (staff poet) was called in,
a hasty plot patched together, and the librettist set to writing
a book for the music.

When completed, it was put into rehearsal. When the rehearsals were completely at an end, Jetty brought Johann to the theater, where he was treated to the novel, thrilling and delightful surprise of a private performance of an operetta for which he had unwittingly written the music.

He was thoroughly impressed. He saw at once the suitability of his music to stage production. From choral-waltz to waltz-operetta, he realized, was a short step indeed. He consented to write an operetta for Steiner. With typical dynamic energy, he threw himself into the task, and composed *Die Lustigen Weiber von Wien* (*The Merry Wives of Vienna*). Steiner prepared to put the work into rehearsal, with Marie Geistinger, diva of the Theater-an-der-Wien, in the leading role. But here plans suddenly came to grief. It seemed that Johann Strauss had another actress in mind when writing the work. She was Josefine Gallmeyer. But this actress was under contract to the Carl Theater, which naturally would not consent to her leaving to bring forth the first stage work of Johann Strauss in another theater. Steiner was in despair; he begged, pleaded, cajoled and even threatened Strauss—to no avail. Strauss withdrew the operetta; it was never performed.

Only a genius as prodigal as Strauss could permit so large a work to be scrapped. Only a man who could never put to paper all the melodies which surged within him, so fast was their flow, could afford to throw away a three-hour musical production. At his wit's end, Steiner called together his staff and ordered a new libretto without delay. This was *Indigo, oder die Vierzig Räuber* (*Indigo, or the Forty Thieves*). For years, a stock Viennese joke was whether Strauss's forty thieves were not more reasonably forty librettists. A more baffling, disjointed, patchwork quilt of a libretto it would indeed have been hard to find. How Steiner, experienced in stagecraft as he was, allowed such nonsense to be set to Strauss's delicate music, no one will ever understand. Perhaps, so confident was he of Strauss, he believed that the music would support the libretto.

In a sense, it did. The *première* was held on February 10th, 1871. A year had passed since the composition of *Neu Wien*. Everyone who could beg, borrow or steal a ticket was there, and, despite the obvious defects of the libretto, the play was a success. However, Strauss and Steiner were aware of its weaknesses, and the play was reworked again and again. For the Berlin production, the editor of *Kladderadatsch* wrote a completely new story, of greater humor and merit. In Paris, further changes were made, one of which was the inclusion of the ever-demanded *Blue Danube*.

Eventually it was retitled *Tausend und Eine Nacht* (*Thousand and One Nights*). A better story, it is still rarely performed, and only a few scattered selections are generally known. Outstanding are the lovely and rhapsodic intermezzo, the interpolated song, *Launisches Glück*, and the delightful set of waltzes collected from themes of this operetta.

6

A KING FOR AMERICA

In the summer of 1872, some three thousand miles across the Atlantic, the city of Boston was staging a gigantic World's Peace Jubilee. The moving spirit of this Jubilee was Patrick Sarsfield Gilmore, a bandmaster who subscribed three hundred per cent to the American philosophy of "Bigger and Better." In earlier years he had staged other musical festivals, but nothing the size of this behemoth. John Tasker Howard, in his book, *Our American Music,* comments, "Five days were devoted to programs of colossal dimensions. Besides Gilmore, conductors of genuine ability, Zerrahn and others, helped in leading the musical forces. It proved too much for John S. Dwight, who left town to spend the week at his summer home at Nahant, where he hoped he could not hear the cannon used to mark the rhythm of the national airs. . . Besides the cannon, which were fired by electric buttons on a table in front of the conductor, one hundred real firemen in red shirts helped in the proceedings by pounding real anvils in the Anvil Chorus from *Trovatore.*"

Among the conductors of genuine ability who had been invited were Giuseppe Verdi, Franz Abt and Johann Strauss.

Strauss, by nature almost allergic to travel, would have flatly refused to consider a voyage of such length, had it not been for the concerted efforts of his intimates, led by Jetty, and the promise of so great a fee that to refuse would have been sheer lunacy.

Having finally agreed to the journey, Strauss traveled north through Germany to Bremerhaven, where he embarked, in company with Jetty and Abt, on one of the vessels of the North German Lloyd Line, sailing on the first of June, 1872. This was a small ship of some five thousand tons gross, equipped with auxiliary sails and powered by a none-too-powerful but fairly dependable steam engine. In its interior furnishings, it was a far cry from the spacious liners of our day. The passenger accomodations were located in the stern, where the motion of the vessel took greatest toll of the passengers' spirits and stomachs, and the entire recreation quarters consisted of nothing more elaborate than a large central hall, which served the combined offices of lounge, smoking room and dining hall. Around this focal point were grouped the passengers' cabins, little niches hardly large enough to hold an upper and lower berth, a wash stand (without running water) and a clothes rack. Lighting was by means of oil lamps set in gimbals; to minimize the fire hazard, these were required to be extinguished by ten-thirty every evening. Heating systems in the cabins did not exist. Social life was, consequently, at a minimum.

On the westward voyage, conviviality was not improved by heavy seas, which kept a good number of passengers in their berths. Yet Strauss, for some perverse reason, remained perfectly steady on his feet—the man who loathed travel of any sort was enjoying himself wholeheartedly. For he had found aboard ship the Band of the First Prussian Guards, also on their way to Boston. Every evening was a *Strauss-abend*; his melodies filled the social hall from right after the supper hour until curfew, to the delight of the passengers, and be it added, to his own not inconsiderable pleasure.

The voyage took almost seventeen days, the ship entering New York Harbor on June 16th. Strauss's arrival, for all his fame, was completely inconspicuous; in part this was due to the intense jealousy which New York City felt for Boston's Jubilee. The travelers set out for Boston without delay, arriving there the following day.

Whatever the neglect shown him in New York, Boston gave him a real reception. Strauss was led on a triumphal procession through the streets. On billboards, on the walls of the old Boston Music-Hall, on the Tremont Temple itself, on house fronts along Washington and Boylston Streets, he saw everywhere enormous posters, lurid with color showing him crowned and with scepter in hand, astride the world.

The posters embarrassed him. They appeared to him in the worst possible taste; they were only one of the details which made it impossible for him to understand America, then experiencing its most violent growing pains. Unable to perceive the sincere admiration behind this gaudy demonstration, because he had never encountered the like in his own world and was completely unprepared for the vigorous life into which he had suddenly been plunged, he returned to Europe retaining only the impression of a noisy, hysterical populace; of a country where the quality of everything was measured by its size and cost. To some extent, of course, he was right. The importunate demands of thousands of feminine admirers who flocked after him for locks of his hair, a demand which was satisfied only at the sacrifice of the curly, black pelt of his favorite Newfoundland, caused him to conceive of American womanhood in terms of a flighty, shallow-minded female.

The grandeur of America, its high ideals and aspirations, all went unnoticed. It could not have been otherwise; he was given no opportunity to glimpse its future, and he did not remain long enough to understand its past. But Strauss was not alone in his misunderstanding of America in a day when even voluntary ignorance of its size, content and nature was the rule, rather than the exception, in well-informed European circles.

The possible effects of unwelcome adulation upon the European visitors did not pass unnoticed among American journalists. The *Boston Post* had this to say: "If the enthusiastic girl gatherers of musical autographs could hear the amused comments on their energy and enterprise, which do overstep the bounds of maidenly modesty, they would certainly abate their enthusiasm and put away the fans and autograph albums and blank cards which they now flourish so wildly in the face of every member of the foreign bands. The poor fellows never feel safe—they are attacked on all sides by an army of feminine besiegers, and only turn in desperation from one dozen pairs of supplicating hands holding aloft the inevitable album, the pleading hand and clamorous lips, to encounter another dozen, and they finally have to surrender to Fate and American girls, wearily scribbling their names on page after page of blank paper."

Basing itself on the axiom, so popular then, and not unpopular today, that the bigger an object, the better it is, the city of Boston had erected a gigantic concert hall, capable of seating over one hundred thousand people. Built as a long rectangle, its roof supported by four parallel rows of slender pillars which soared from floor to ceiling, it can be imagined how impossible this hall proved from the standpoint of acoustics. Depending on where the listener sat, a note played on the stage would either be inaudible, or resound in echo *ad infinitum*.

When confronted with this enormous battleground, appropriately and waggishly named the Coliseum, Strauss was

JOHANN STRAUSS II
Photograph by Gurney & Son, taken in New York in 1872, after completion of his engagement at the World's Peace Jubilee.

The Memorial to Johann Strauss II in the Stadtpark in Vienna.

struck dumb. When informed of the size and disposition of the orchestra which he was to conduct, he became panic-stricken. Small wonder! For here, extracted from the *Directory of the World's Peace Jubilee,* is the manner in which the orchestra was composed:

    400 First Violins
    200 Second Violins
    100 Violas
    100 Violoncelli
    100 Contrabasses
     24 Flutes
     24 Oboes
     24 Clarinets
     24 Bassoons
     24 Trumpets
     24 Trombones
     24 French Horns
      4 Tubas
      6 Pair of Tympani
      4 Side Drums
      2 Bass Drums
      1 Monster Bass Drum (18 ft. in diameter)
      2 Triangles
    ─────
  1,087 Total Number of Instruments

Such a gargantuan array of instruments would have given pause to a Berlioz; it is hardly surprising that it struck terror into the heart of a conductor accustomed to leading an orchestra of seventy-five players.

The worst was yet to come. It developed that a high platform had been built for him, from which vantage point he was to direct the orchestra through the medium of *twenty* assistant conductors! Further, for certain choral works, *no fewer than twenty thousand* men and women had been provided! The last straw was the announcement that the entire audience, numbering one hundred thousand lusty throats, was to sing a final stanza with the chorus and orchestra.

Musically, such a concert is ludicrous, but it was not out of character with its day. Absurd though it was, it was one expression of an entire world—not merely America—in a period of transition. It was a world of dreams, of globe-girdling in eighty days, of traveling incredible distances beneath the sea, of voyages to the moon. It was the world of Jules Verne. Let us not mock it, for world of dreamers though it was, these dreamers were practical men, and they produced the way of life we know today.

Strauss was no visionary. The world of Jules Verne held no significance for him. He would have turned tail and bolted had he not actually feared for his life should he refuse to conduct. Somehow he nerved himself to the ghastly task (he never would have succeeded without Jetty and Abt) and mounted the stand.

Let Strauss himself tell the story:

"On the musicians' tribune there were twenty thousand singers; in front of them the members of the orchestra—and these were the people I was to conduct! Twenty assistant conductors had been placed at my disposal to control those gigantic masses, but I was only able to recognize those nearest to me, and although we had rehearsals, there was no possibility of giving an artistic performance, a proper production. . . .

"Now just conceive of my position, face to face with a public of one hundred thousand Americans. There I stood at the raised desk, high above all the others. How would the business start, how would it end? Suddenly a cannon shot rang out, a gentle hint for us twenty-thousand-odd to begin playing the *Blue Danube*. I gave the signal, my twenty assistant conductors followed as quickly and as well as they could, and then there broke out an unholy row such as I shall never forget. As we had begun more or less simultaneously, I concentrated my entire attention on seeing that we should finish together too! Thank Heaven I managed even that! It was all that was humanly possible. The hundred thousand mouths in the audience roared applause and I breathed a sigh of relief when I found myself in fresh air again and felt the firm ground beneath my feet."

Hilarious though the description is—and it is an accurate and unexaggerated report—there can be no doubt but that this performance was the foundation upon which Strauss built in America an undying popularity.

Perfect in its delineation of those hilarious days are the headlines from the June 19th edition of the *Boston Post,* reviewing the proceedings on "German Day."

THE PEACE JUBILEE
THE MAMMOTH COLISEUM OPENED
FOR THE THIRD SERIES OF HUB-BUB!!

GREAT DAY FOR GERMANY

HOCH LEBEN DIE KÖNIGIN EUTERPE UND DER KÖNIG GAMBRINUS!!

Teutonia Wild With Delight!

THE BAND OF THE KAISER FRANZ GRENADIERS
ENCORED TO DEATH!!!

ABT & STRAUSS AS LEADERS
Blending of Universal Discords—Music, Lager & Gibberish
ALLES!   HOCH!   HOCH!

Among the many paragraphs given to Jubilee activities on that day, there appears the following review of Johann Strauss's conducting:

"Strauss conducted his *Morning Leaves* waltz with the characteristic fire and *élan* which made him such a favorite at his first appearance. He is a remarkable little man, nervous, quick, excitable, and he throws himself heart and soul into his music. The orchestra becomes inflamed with his enthusiasm and the tone becomes warmer, the *ensemble* more perceptible, and the *tempo* quicker when each player sees that nimble bow, waving arms and flushed face of the great monarch of the ballroom."

Three days later, on the 22nd, the following paragraph appeared:

"The chorus received a generous amount of well-deserved applause, and was followed by the ELECTRIC STRAUSS and one of his waltzes, entitled *Neu Wien*, which set every head moving sidewise in response to the swinging of his baton, and every fan swinging as though guided by his hand and assisting him in leading the measures of his music. Strauss himself was conductor, performer and enthused listener all at once, using bow, fiddle, feet, every facial muscle, elbows, hips and head in conveying his wishes to the musicians. He got an *encore*, and gave a little light composition entitled the *Sängerslust Polka*."

The following day, the papers carried an advertisement for an "International Grand Jubilee Ball, at the Coliseum, Boston, Wednesday evening, June 26th, on which occasion the Grand Orchestra will be led by the celebrated Waltz-Writer, Johann Strauss, of Vienna."

The success of this mammoth ball was enormous, and the occasion was repeated again some days afterwards. Meanwhile, on the regular scheduled series of concerts, Strauss led

the Jubilee Orchestra, now reduced to a reasonable number
so as to permit performances of quality, on the afternoon of
the 27th in his *Wine, Women and Song,* the fifth number on
a program conducted by several musicians, including Abt,
and featuring the music of several nations, the Jubilee Orchestra and Chorus, the Kaiser Franz Grenadier Band, as well
as one number played by the combined bands of various regi-
ments of militia, National Guard and fire brigades stationed
in or around Boston. This super-band was led by Gilmore
himself.

The concert held on the afternoon of the 28th featured
Horace Greeley as speaker and special guest of the city of
Boston. On this occasion, Strauss took the stand twice, first
to conduct his *New Vienna,* which apparently had something
of a special success in the Hub, and later to direct the ubiquitous *Blue Danube.*

Two days later he led the first performance of a "new
Grand Concert Waltz, entitled *Jubilee Waltz,* and dedicated
to Mr. P. S. Gilmore." This composition does not appear in
the catalogue of published works; presumably Strauss considered it a mere *pièce d'occasion.* Neither is there a trace of
another waltz which was actually published in America at
this time (without opus number, and not included in his catalogue), the *Klänge aus dem Boston,* a copy of the piano edition of which was once seen by the author. This latter work
bears traces of some of the finer moments of the great waltzes,
but resembles more a potpourri of these great ideas than a
work which has homogeneity.

It was now time for Strauss to head home. He had directed
thirteen concerts in a single series at the Coliseum, as well
as two superballs; his name was now immortal in America
as it was in Europe. Still, he tarried in New York to direct
one concert before sailing. It was here that he introduced the

Manhattan Waltzes, which have also been omitted from the catalogue. It is amusing and typical of one aspect of Strauss's creative nature that this waltz closes with a remarkably *sans-gêne* arrangement in waltz-time of Foster's *Old Folks at Home!*

It has often been said of Strauss that "he was the first king America was ever willing to crown." His success was without doubt unequalled by any other visiting musician until the advent of the great Paderewski. Offers of concerts came from all over the country, but Strauss said he would not accept any further offer for all the gold in the hills of California.

It is small wonder, and it was certainly not conceit on Strauss's part, that he should have made such a statement. Compared to European standards for fees, he certainly must have felt himself a Croesus. He was already a millionaire more than once over. He returned to Europe on July 13th, an extraordinarily rich man, richer than any musician of his day, wealthier than many of the families of the Austrian nobility. Between the prodigal fees received from his Russian tours and his American expedition, he had laid by a sizable fortune. Before he left Vienna for Boston, a guarantee of one hundred thousand dollars had been deposited in his name with a European bank; when he returned he brought with him an even larger sum to add to that respectable amount. . . .

7

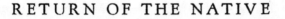

RETURN OF THE NATIVE

HE DID NOT return at once to Vienna. There was an epidemic of cholera, and he prudently remained away. Instead, he accepted an invitation to journey to Baden-Baden, where several of the crowned heads of Europe impatiently awaited his music. Strauss accepted the invitation, and then petulantly decided to do something else. He was tired, he said; he must rest. He would not go to Baden-Baden at once; he would visit Bad Schwalbach first, where he meant to take the cure. Back and forth from the Baden spa to the little town near Wiesbaden, in Hessen, flew frantic emissaries. There was no moving Strauss.

Someone finally hit upon the right argument. The Hofmusikdirektor of the Court of Baden said only a fool would let an offer of two thousand francs an evening slip through his fingers! Strauss quickly admitted the logic of this; America's fabulous fees had not so turned his head that he had forgotten Europe's more sober scale.

The party set off the following day, and proceeded as far as Heidelberg. Here Strauss, enchanted with the atmosphere of the picturesque old town, with its ruined, red stone castle glowering above it, again became obdurate. King or no King, Grand Duke or no Grand Duke, he was adamant. He had reached the Grand Duchy of Baden, hadn't he? That ought to suffice His Grace for a bit. Jetty needed all her tact and powers of persuasion; it was she who finally prevailed upon him to complete the journey, and the party then reached Baden-Baden without further delays.

Strauss had not been in the resort long before visitors saw him strolling in the parks, arm-in-arm with either the Grand Duke, or his other admirer, Kaiser Wilhelm I. He was fêted by royalty, and took with him, when he left Baden, their best wishes and two colorful and imposing Orders.

But if the decorations weighted down his coat somewhat, we may be sure that this added burden was compensated by a corresponding lightness in his wallet. Like many another tourist, he had succumbed to the temptation of the spinning wheel, and laid before it a good many of his American dollars, the sacrifice of an impassioned slave to the great god *Rouge-et-Noir...*

Strauss then paid another of his summer visits to the Vauxhall in Pavlovsk, composing there the two *Russischen Marsch-Fantasien,* Op. 352 and 353, and the *Im Russischen Dorfe Fantasie,* Op. 355, which he dedicated to the Baroness Stackelberg. Returning to Vienna, he introduced one of his most famous waltzes, the seductively sensuous *Wiener Blut,* Op. 354.

Wiener Blut is a title which defies direct translation. It is derived from the famous Viennese quotation, *"Stärkt Wiener Blut den Mut?"* (Does Vienna blood strengthen one's courage?). More properly, it can be translated as *Vienna Spirits* or *Vienna Moods.*

Those who would insist that the titles of the Strauss concert waltzes were chosen haphazardly and without thought to their relationship to the music would do well to consider this waltz, whose pulsing beat is not unlike the steady throb of a great, central artery. Indeed, it is, in musical terms, the very pulse of Vienna itself, Vienna, great and luxury-loving, a *Bürgerlich* Big Town, not yet caught up in the harrying rush of the industrial metropolis.

The *Boston Jubilee Waltzes* were described by Strauss as "Grand Concert Waltzes." This is far truer of *Wiener Blut;* while it may be danced if played in strict and rigid tempo (which is unnatural to its character), it is primarily a work written for the concert hall, and falls, as such, into the classification of those works which include Ravel's *La Valse* and the ballet waltzes of Tchaikovsky.

The work opens (clarinets and horns) with a call to attention, heralding a jubilant *allegro moderato* (mainly strings) which concludes with a typical Straussian flourish in wood winds. Then comes an *andante* in which the violins, *legato,* lead imperceptibly to one of the main waltz motifs, here sounded more broadly than it is in the waltz proper.

Following the *tempo di vals* comes the first waltz—the one forecast in the introduction:

The second half of this waltz is typically Straussian—the strong beat in the measure constantly recurring elsewhere, so as to give a momentary feeling of 2/4, rather than 3/4. It is healthy, virile music, almost denying the languor of the preceding passage. Waltz II is almost a development or variation of the opening waltz theme, and again the second half of this waltz grows out of the first. The third waltz certainly does not belong in the dance hall, but on the ballet stage, with its graceful leaps which suggest the *tutus* of a Degas painting more than the whirl of the ballroom floor, and this lack of relationship to the dance floor is soon emphasized by a sudden *ritard* and *fermata,* followed by a gradual, non-danceable acceleration of tempo, required by Strauss in his markings.

QUITE some time had passed since the writing of *Indigo,* and Strauss, newly returned to Vienna, was sought out by Steiner, who suggested another operetta. Strauss agreed, and Steiner sent him a number of librettos for examination. None of them suited Strauss. In music, his taste was instinctive and infallible, but in the selection of the books for his lyric productions, he showed lamentable judgment. He lacked the critical faculty to be able to select a good book. His poor judgment misled him on every occasion; he was still following this ill-starred intuition years later, when he turned down the wonderful libretto to *Der Bettelstudent* in favor of a book of obvious failings.

Almost despairing of finding a librettist to suit Strauss's uncertain desires, Steiner sent him Josef Braun, a medical student turned journalist. Braun had good theatrical leanings and could no doubt, had he put himself to it, have produced a book of real merit. But he allowed himself to be influenced by French *opéra-bouffe,* a field which had been exploited by Offenbach until it was well-nigh barren. Its brittle, cynical style was, in any case, ill-suited to the Viennese vein of sentiment in Strauss's music.

The libretto which Braun presented to Strauss shows that he was strongly influenced by Sardou's *Piccolino,* for it is a blatant and none-too-careful reworking of that material. The story is overly naïve:

Arthur Bryk, a young painter, encounters a peasant maid, Marie, and falls in love with her. He paints her picture posed in prayer, promises to marry her, and travels on to Rome, where he promptly forgets her in the pleasures of the city. But Marie, who has apparently taken a course in "how to get your man," assumes the garb of a Savoyard youth, and sets out after her truant lover. Finding him in Rome, she becomes a student in his class and, after the usual operetta-formula misunderstandings, succeeds in leading him to the altar.

If Strauss had been theater-wise, he would not have allowed Braun to make the hero a painter, for few characters are less romantic on the stage.

Nonetheless, when *Karneval in Rom* was first produced on March 1st, 1873, at the Theater-an-der-Wien, its success was immediate, and this lasted throughout the whole Exhibition Year. Time, however, has shown its weaknesses for what they are, and only a little of the music is known today.

1873 was an important year for Vienna, for it was then that the great International Exhibition opened. By comparison, the Paris Exposition was a puny affair; in size alone, the Vienna Exhibition covered an area five times greater.

The International Exhibition was held in the Prater. It was located mainly in one enormous building, built in the shape of a long rectangle, from the sides of which smaller rectangles projected. In the center was a dome, approximately as large as that which surmounts the Capitol in Washington. This was the so-called Industrial Palace, and about it were situated the smaller, less imposing buildings of the exhibition.

The formal opening was held on the first of May, 1873, a gusty, squally day. Despite the inclement weather, the turnout of royalty was imposing. Foremost among them in the inaugural proceedings, of course, were Their Imperial Majesties, Franz-Josef and Elizabeth of Austria, accompanied by the young Archduke Rudolf.

Hotels were packed, and rooms were at a premium. Giant

civic balls vied nightly with small, super-élite dances. There had not been so much gaiety and glamor in old Vienna since the days of the Congress.

There was Strauss at the Theater-an-der-Wien, Strauss in the Volksgarten, Strauss at the Sperl, Strauss at the Diana-saal and the Sofiensaal, Strauss at the Exhibition.

In fact, it might well have been Strauss's Exhibition; it was certainly Strauss's Vienna.

It was at this time that the first serious rift occurred between Johann and Eduard. The younger man had counted on having the Strauss Orchestra, of which he was by then officially Conductor, pressed into service for the Exhibition's regular concerts. To his chagrin, the Strauss Orchestra was not chosen; instead the Langenbach Orchestra was engaged, and Johann shared the direction of it jointly with Langenbach.

This was a bitter pill for Eduard, and one which did not alleviate the envy he had always felt for his more talented brother. To keep peace in the family, Johann arranged to have the Strauss Orchestra engaged to play alternately with the Langenbach Orchestra.

And then—the banks failed!

A week after the Exhibition opened, the shaky supports of Vienna's financial structure gave way, engulfing many prosperous Viennese citizens, and bringing about bankruptcy after bankruptcy. Those who recall the days of the Wall Street crash of 1929 can imagine the same sequence of events set fifty-six years earlier. There was one principal difference; the suicides were not jumping from skyscrapers—they were leaping into the Blue Danube.

The corridors of the Exhibition emptied of Viennese as though by magic, and only lonely foreign visitors wandered about the empty halls. Fortunately, conditions took a marked change for the better within a few weeks, as the government intervened and brought some semblance of order out of the chaos of the Vienna *Bourse,* and soon the festivities were again in full swing.

Strauss composed a set of waltzes especially to commemorate the Exhibition; this was appropriately named *Bei uns z'Haus,* Op. 361. Indeed, Vienna was At Home to the world, and Strauss was her major-domo.

Bei uns z'Haus is a gay little waltz, light and graceful, not too consequential. Originally composed as a choral waltz, the vocal parts have since been dropped.

It was at this time that Fortune extended to one of her favorite sons the great triumph of a long and glorious career. Steiner brought him a new libretto.

Its name was *Die Fledermaus....*

8

THE CULMINATION
OF AN ART

In 1873, Steiner bought the rights to a popular French play, *Le Réveillon*. After careful examination of the piece, he regretted his hasty purchase, and sought to dispose of it to the directors of the Carl Theater, but these gentlemen would have none of it. The work was too typically French, and would not suit the Viennese stage.

A *réveillon* is a gala all-night party held on Christmas Eve, no doubt a delightful French custom, but repugnant to the strict Catholicism of the Viennese, indulgent though they otherwise are.

Steiner felt that the play contained possibilities for Strauss's music, and called in Richard Genée, playwright and operetta composer, and Karl Haffner, a hack writer from the Carl Theater. A truly talented writer, Haffner's gift had been atrophied by the steady stream of banal pieces which he was required to turn out on a yearly-contract basis. It took a rejuvenation in the form of an association with Genée to let him draw from the delicate subject matter of *Le Réveillon* that mad concoction of confused identities and glorious nonsense which Steiner laid before Strauss.

When Johann Strauss wrote *Die Fledermaus*, he reached the pinnacle of his career, scaling artistic heights which he was not to duplicate for many years, until he composed *The Gypsy Baron*. Even this opera, for all its musical worth and fine libretto, fails to capture the magic aura of *Die Fleder-maus*. This comic opera takes its place among the greatest of all time; only the comic operas of Mozart, Rossini's *Barber of Seville*, Verdi's *Falstaff*, Wagner's *Die Meistersinger von Nürnberg* and Richard Strauss's *Der Rosenkavalier* are of like standard. The Mozart operas are the finest; it is equally certain that *Die Fledermaus* is, in its way, not inferior to *Der Rosenkavalier*. For Richard Strauss's opera is derivative. That is to say, it depends for many of its themes upon the waltz style developed by Johann Strauss. It is significant that little else duplicates the style and mood of *Der Rosen-kavalier*, and this in a composer whose other major works bear a distinct stylistic resemblance to one another. It is not exaggerating to say that without the precedent of *Die Fledermaus*, *Der Rosenkavalier* would not be the opera we know. As it is, it contains many dull pages which a superb libretto cannot conceal. For all its great charm, it lacks the effortless spontaneity which flows like freshly uncorked champagne in *Die Fledermaus*.

Throughout the seventy years of its history, *Die Fleder-maus* has achieved only occasional success in the Anglo-Saxon nations. This is not due to any defect in the music, or even to the superficial nature of the book, but to the blundering translations which have exaggerated its existing flaws. Typical was the Unger-Anderson script, choked with banal rhymes, which was first presented in London's Lyric Theater in December, 1911, under the title *Night Birds*. Here in America, in addition to authentic presentations at the Metropolitan during the first decade of the Twentieth Century, it has been given many second-rate performances under a variety of new titles, among the latest of which was *Champagne Sec*, in 1932.

It took the brilliantly staged 1942 New York production

by the late Max Reinhardt, paralleling, in an English libretto of great charm and wit, his 1929 production in Berlin, finally to reveal the beauty of *Die Fledermaus* to American audiences. This was *Rosalinda,* perhaps the happiest possible choice of title for English-speaking audiences, more understandable than the cryptic *The Bat.* This production, which ran to full houses for more than two years, proved conclusively to Americans the beauty of *Die Fledermaus* when properly produced. It was brought to London in 1945 as *Gay Rosalinda,* where it enjoyed a long run at the Palace Theater under the baton of Richard Tauber, who, in more youthful days, had been the toast of the Continent in the opera's leading male role of Eisenstein.

Strauss read the libretto, and was turned to fire. Never before or after in all his life did he experience the violent emotional reactions which this book produced in him. He secluded himself in the Hietzing villa, avoiding everyone except Steiner and Genée, almost refusing to eat or drink, snatching only an occasional hour of sleep, giving himself up only to the impassioned music which this intoxicating story had roused in him. In little more than a month of nights, the score was completed. Nights is indeed the word; Strauss noted down his melodies whenever and wherever they came to him, day or night, on a menu, an envelope, or the cuff of his nightshirt; but he did the actual writing and orchestrating only at night.

Die Fledermaus had its *première* on April 5th, 1874, at the Theater-an-der-Wien. It met with a cool reception, and Steiner retired it from the repertory after only sixteen performances, for at best *Die Fledermaus* only half-filled the house, whereas Madame Patti was available and would fill the theater every night that she could be induced to appear.

The lapse of time now allows us to see what Strauss and Steiner could not. There could have been no more inappropriate moment in which to produce a comic opera on such a theme. Vienna was frightfully close to total bankruptcy. Whatever the value of the measures of reconstruction undertaken after the fateful Black Friday, they had done nothing to reëstablish those thousands of fortunes, large and small, which had been engulfed in the abyss. Even among those who had suffered least, the gloomy caution caused by the calamitous day still hung heavy in the air.

Vienna was in no mood for a *réveillon*. A musical play which showed riotous extravagance and high living must, perforce, have appeared in poor taste. Vienna would have none of it, despite its inescapable melodic appeal. The time simply was not right for an opera of this character.

Die Fledermaus went to Berlin, and Berlin went to *Die Fledermaus*. The play became the thing; it was a social necessity for every Berliner to have seen it. In Paris, even though presented in a garbled version called *La Tsigane,* it was highly successful.*

Steiner was aghast. He could not understand this success; he knew that every step had been taken to insure its acceptance in Vienna, that no expense had been spared. Almost a year later, he reluctantly decided to give it another trial. The reaction left him speechless. Vienna went again and again to see *Die Fledermaus.*

It is still going....

Die Fledermaus is a kaleidoscopic assemblage of perfect numbers, fitted together with consummate artistry and spontaneous yet cunning timing. From the magnificent overture, one number of matchless charm and gaiety follows another un-

---

* Fledermaus *did not appear in Paris in the original libretto until 1904, when it was produced at the Théâtre des Variétés as* La Chauve-souris, *because of an injunction obtained in 1875 by Meilhac and Halévy.*

til the mind is whirling. For variety and prodigality of melody, only *The Marriage of Figaro* can match the rapid flow of *Die Fledermaus.*

The Overture, of itself, is a fully-formed and complete work. Strauss meant to write, as prelude, the conventional potpourri of tunes from the piece. So catholic was his taste, however, and so unerring his musical sense, that, although the overture claims nothing more than the potpourri style, it nonetheless suggests the formal structure of the sonata form. And this firm foundation is one of the foremost reasons for its undying popularity.

THE first act opens in the living room of Gabriel von Eisenstein, a Viennese financier. Off stage, the lilting tones of a high tenor voice are heard in a serenade to Rosalinde, Gabriel's wife. The voice belongs to Alfred, a member of the Vienna Opera, and a former suitor of Rosalinde. It seems that he proposes to reënter the lady's life. In order to set Alfred apart from all the other characters of an opera in which everyone, perforce, sings, Strauss wrote his part in an unusually high register; this has regrettably reacted in lending him a purity of character which his words thoroughly belie.

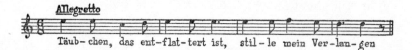

Adele, the chambermaid, appears at the close of Alfred's serenade, holding a letter from her sister, a member of the Ballet, asking her to attend a ball to be given that evening by a young Russian, Prince Orlovsky, and suggesting that she "borrow"

from her mistress a gown suitable to the occasion. From her first notes, we have a clear picture of Adele's sunny and light-hearted nature, for she enters upon a rippling cadenza of laughter, and then sings:

Da schreibt meine Schwester I-da die ist nämlich beim Bal-let

Rosalinde enters. Adele begs to have the evening free, on the pretense that she has received word that a dear old Aunt is ill and needs her. The request is denied, to the measures of a charming duet that is reminiscent, in its sophistication, of some of the duets of *The Marriage of Figaro*. Enter now Gabriel von Eisenstein and Dr. Blinde, a lawyer. Eisenstein, having committed a minor offense, has been sentenced to prison for five days. In appealing the case, Dr. Blinde, who stutters wretchedly (another parallel with *Figaro!*), has only made matters worse, increasing the penalty to eight days, as Eisenstein explains in the Trio which follows. Eisenstein's choleric character is vividly set forth in the explosive passage which he sings here:

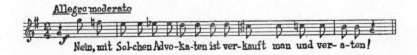

Nein, mit Sol-chen Advo-ka-ten ist ver-kauft man und ver-a-ten!

Blinde is ejected by the outraged Eisenstein, who instructs Adele to lay out his oldest clothes for his prison stay. Adele meanwhile announces Dr. Falke, a close friend of Eisenstein's.

It is around Falke that the central idea of *Die Fledermaus* revolves—indeed, he is the *Fledermaus*. The incident dates back two years to the night of a masked ball which Falke and Eisenstein attended together. Falke was dressed as a bat, Eisenstein as a butterfly. During the course of the evening, Falke drank not wisely but too well, and fell asleep while Eisenstein was wheeling him home in a wheelbarrow. As a joke, Eisenstein left him, in costume, beneath a tree in the central square, where he awakened the next morning to find himself surrounded by the townspeople, who followed him home, laughing at his discomfiture. For months, the neighboring children had called him "Dr. Fledermaus." Falke is determined to perpetrate a practical joke on Eisenstein which will square accounts. With this in mind, he now invites Eisenstein to the Orlovsky supper; it was he, and not her sister Ida, who sent Adele her invitation. Eisenstein's acceptance is given to a delightful, insouciant 2/4-time melody:

Allegro non troppo

Ein Sou-per uns heu-te winkt, wie noch gar keins da-gwe-sen,

Rosalinde recalls that Alfred, the tenor, will be calling shortly. Earlier, he had forced his way into her salon for a moment to say that he knew of Gabriel's forthcoming imprisonment, and would appear to keep her from being too lonely in her husband's absence. So Rosalinde gives Adele the evening free to visit her "sick Aunt." Eisenstein reappears in full evening dress, explaining away this odd sight by remarking that the prison governor has invited him to dine. Rosalinde bids Eisenstein *auf wiederseh'n* in a song that will be recognized as the oboe solo of the overture, in which she laments the loneliness of the coming eight days, describing with mock anguish how the sight of his empty coffee cup at breakfast will make her own drink taste bitter:

So muss al-lein ich blei-ben, acht Ta-ge oh-ne Dich!

Then, to the words, "Oh! how this grieves me!" husband and wife sing a *coda* so brazen in its deception that one biographer suggested it should bring blushes to the faces of the audience. But Strauss's music is above simple immodesty; seen through the prism of his music, the situation is only amusing, a prank in the Carnival spirit:

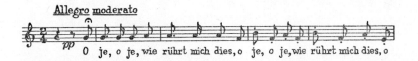

O je, o je, wie rührt mich dies, o je, o je, wie rührt mich dies, o

Husband departs, and Rosalinde admits Alfred, who enters wearing the husband's slippers and dressing gown. Rosalinde is horrified: "What *are* you doing in my husband's dressing gown? Do you wish to ruin me?" "Not at all, no thought of it!" Alfred begins to sing. "Oh! no, don't sing," cries Rosalinde, "you know I can't resist that high A!" But Alfred will not stop; he knows his advantage, and so he gaily carols the immortal drinking song:

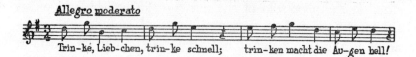

"Drink, my sweetheart, drink with me,
Wine will make your heart feel free.
When your heart beats strong and true,
All things will seem clear to you."

Then follow, borne on a melody so lazily dreaming, so sensuous that it is like a caress, the words which have since become a Viennese proverb, "....Happy he who forgets what
can't be changed."

Now the *tête-à-tête* is interrupted; Frank, the prison governor enters. Here is a situation! The lover found *en déshabillé*
in the wife's boudoir. The inevitable confusion occurs. Rosalinde cannot very well say that her husband is already on his
way to the prison. Frank mistakes Alfred for Eisenstein, and
though Alfred would at first deny it, Rosalinde quickly in-
terposes, singing her famous couplet song, in which she points
out, with dubious logic, that he can only be Eisenstein, since
he wears his dressing gown and finds himself in so intimate
a position:

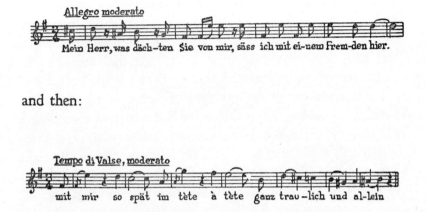

and then:

What Frank thinks of this situation is not made clear. Perhaps a cynicism evolved as prison governor leaves him unable
to be surprised by anything new. However, the facts being as
presented, Alfred must go to prison. Here Strauss introduces
one of his best marches, as Frank invites Alfred to reside for
a while in his "beautiful, airy bird cage."

Thus ends the first act, with Alfred being marched off to
prison, while Rosalinde falls fainting into a convenient chair
as the curtain descends.

Act II is set in the great ballroom of the home of Prince Orlovsky. The room is bathed in the yellow glow of candled
chandeliers. The guests are already assembled; their opening

chorus describes their anticipated pleasures of the evening. The eighteen-year-old host appears with Dr. Falke, who outlines his plan for settling accounts with Eisenstein, calling it facetiously "The Revenge of the Bat." At that moment, Eisenstein enters, and is introduced by Falke to the guests and to his host under the pseudonym of Marquis Renard. The Prince is, of course, in on the secret and aware of Eisenstein's true identity. Orlovsky tells Eisenstein that he trusts he will enjoy himself, explaining that, as host, he alone retains the right to be bored at his own parties, and will toss empty bottles at the heads of any who would also enjoy this prerogative:

This melody resolves itself into the insouciant polka in which the young *roué* explains his peculiar pleasure; *chacun à son goût*:

The role of Orlovsky was formerly played by a mezzo-soprano; Strauss scored the part for this voice because he wanted an agile voice, able to reach wide intervals in order to suggest the not-yet-fully-changed voice of an adolescent. It is easier for a woman to sing this role than a man, but the modern theater demands that the role today be sung by a male.*

Following Orlovsky's song, Adele enters, and is introduced to Eisenstein as Mlle. Olga, a young Russian lately arrived in Vienna. Eisenstein recognizes her as Adele, but becomes confused when she professes to be highly insulted at being mistaken for a chambermaid. This is Adele's famous "laughing song."

"My dear Marquis, a man such as you should really be more discerning!" Finally she breaks into the laugh cascades:

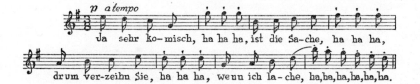

The prison governor is announced. He, too, is incognito, and poses as the Chevalier Chagrin. The two pseudo-Frenchmen experience some awkward moments as they try to con-

---

* Casting a man's role for a woman is a weakness commonly shared also by Marriage of Figaro (Cherubino) and Rosenkavalier (Octavian), but the delicate musical fabric of these two works would be so damaged by revising them for male voices that no change is ever made. Rarely is it, however, that a woman can be found to play these roles who can successfully portray them.

verse in French. Orlovsky comes to the rescue, insisting that both "Frenchmen" converse in German, so that all may understand. Meanwhile, Adele has "forgiven" Eisenstein, and they go for a stroll in the garden adjoining the ballroom.

Falke has sent a note to Rosalinde, asking her to come at once to the ball. Falke meets her and points out Eisenstein strolling in the garden with a lady on his arm. Rosalinde is furious, finding insult added to injury when she recognizes his companion as Adele, dressed in one of her mistress's gowns. ("I'll give her a prescription for her sick Aunt!") Rosalinde has come masked; she is introduced as an Hungarian countess. Eisenstein is entranced by the charming new guest, and at once abandons "Mlle. Olga." The varied reactions of Gabriel and Rosalinde during the first few moments of conversation are vividly etched. Eisenstein begins it with the words, "This posture so graceful, this waist so fine and slender!"

His masked wife (forgetting her episode with Alfred) virtuously remarks, "Oh! how vain was all my anguish! He, whom I saw in prison languish, now smiles before me, would adore me!"

But Rosalinde has not quite forgotten her own precarious position with Alfred deputizing for Eisenstein in the prison; the moment of reckoning is not many hours away, and she must find something as a hold on her husband when he learns of her own perfidy. Gabriel has long boasted of the many conquests which he has made with a watch of unusual design. If she can obtain this from him, she will have the evidence to make him forgive her own folly. Eisenstein, true to form, plays into her hands by producing the watch. Thus begins the "Watch-Duet," in which she pretends palpitations of the heart, suggesting as a cure that she count her heartbeats while he counts the seconds with his watch. Then, she asks to hold the watch while he listens to her heart. Once possessed of the watch, she pops it into the bosom of her dress, and Eisenstein is outwitted.

Rosalinde is asked to sing for the guests, and begins a song of her "homeland," the Hungarian countryside, leading into the well known Czardas:

This is a true Czardas, containing all the pulsing rhythm of the dance, from its languorous opening to its conclusion in a whirling blur of tempo.

At this point someone asks Eisenstein to recount the affair of the "Fledermaus episode," which he does with obvious delight. Falke comments darkly, "he who laughs last, laughs best."

Now begins the great *Finale* to the Second Act, in itself the greatest single lyric achievement of the Waltz King, a true Bacchanalia that owns far more intoxicating spirit and infectious gayety than can be found in a dozen Venusbergs.

All are invited to drink to "His Majesty, King Champagne the First." Jacob observes that the allegory is not casual, that "as other tonal works may be said to be governed, some by air (Weber's *Oberon* for example), others by water (*Der Fliegende Holländer, Das Rheingold*), so the governing medium of *Die Fledermaus* is champagne."

Then, as the guests have already divided themselves into couples, Orlovsky urges them to form "one great brotherhood of love."

continuing:

Orlovsky instructs them, *"Erst ein kuss, dann ein Du,"* (First a kiss, then a "thou"), and all at once, overborne by an irresistible tide, we are swept along in a flood of *Du's,* which soon extend themselves into a rich, coined word, *Duidu,*

whose meaningless but liquid syllables express the ultimate in
sensuousness and affection:

A ballet troupe enters to divert the guests. But the sated
host soon tires of this sport: "Enough, there, enough! Let
these dancers be stilled."

No one with any knowledge of Strauss's music can fail to
recognize this passage. There is no other waltz like it, save
for a few bars of *Frühlingstimmen*. It is not a dance for one
couple, it is a dance for a huge ballroom swimming with couples.* Beginning slowly, gathering pace, momentum and

---

* *Here lies the major flaw in many productions of* Die Fledermaus.
*Properly executed, this one scene demands a stage as large as that of
the Metropolitan or Covent Garden, and at least one hundred extras
waltzing in the background. No operetta company can hope to present this vital scene effectively.*

weight as it progresses, at last it seems as though everyone, even the audience, must join in the mad revel. One cannot be a mere onlooker in this scene; even in an indifferent production one is picked up, transported and carried along by the impetuous will of the music.

Eisenstein does his best to persuade Rosalinde to unmask, without success, nor does he retrieve his watch. The clock strikes six; Eisenstein must be off for prison at once. So must Frank. Both depart together, while the knowing principals chortle over the thought of their forthcoming encounter at the jail. The curtain comes down on Act II.

ACT III takes place in the central room of the prison. Frosch the warden, is seated at a table drinking applejack, an occupation in which he has been assiduously engaged for some time, if one is to judge by the color of his nose. From off-stage comes the voice of the supposed Eisenstein (Alfred) singing yet another serenade in praise of his Rosalinde. Frosch shouts to him to be quiet. The door leading to the street yawns slowly open, and Frank enters unsteadily. In his bemused state, he imagines himself still at the ball, and after accompanying his entrance to the tune of his Bird Cage March, the orchestra dreamily recalls the melodies of the second act *Finale,* as Frank calls for Ida, "Olga," and the other ladies of the gathering. He waltzes tipsily about the room, his coat off, his hat askew, while the orchestra accompanies him in a reeling parody of the *Fledermaus* waltz, with a heavy emphasis on grinding contrabasses.

At this point, the Reinhardt production introduces a superb ballet, in which Frank's bemused mind evokes the presence of some of Orlovsky's guests, mimed by a classical ballet group, who dance about him in the room, only to fly out of the doors and the windows and the wings at the end. He subsides into a chair, smoking a cigar, holding an opened newspaper before him. He drowses, the paper sinks onto his face, the cigar burns through, and nothing is heard but a resonant snore. . . .

This opening scene is one of the finest bits of pantomime ever introduced to the opera stage, and it is in no small measure responsible for sustaining the movement of the opera through this act, which is the weakest part of the opera. Yet Strauss was almost induced by his leading lady, Marie Geistinger (who had nothing to do in this scene), to cut the sequence; only the intervention of Girardi, who was to play the role, prevented him from scrapping this extraordinarily droll bit of business.

Frosch wakes Frank, for someone is at the gate. Frosch, befogged by drink, cannot make out whether there are one or two ladies. "I'm all mixed up!" he moans. But there are indeed two ladies—Olga (Adele) and Ida. Frank is delighted to see the girls, especially Olga, to whom he has taken a particular fancy. They explain that they have come to seek his help; Adele confesses that she is only a chambermaid, but tells Frank that she hopes he will help her to get a start on the stage. Frank, in turn, confesses his deception of the evening—he is not a director of a Paris theater, as they had supposed, but governor of this prison. No matter; to prove her ability, Adele sings an aria in which she demonstrates her talent for playing, turn by turn, a simple country maid, a regal queen, or a Parisian lady involved in a compromising situation:

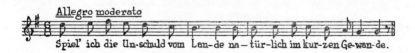

Allegro moderato

Spiel' ich die Un-schuld vom Lan-de na – tür-lich im kur-zen Ge-wan-de.

Frank promises whatever help he can give. A knock is heard, and Frosch bundles the girls into a cell until he knows who the newcomer is. It is Eisenstein. Each is equally surprised to find the other here; confusion results. Frank identifies himself as the prison governor; Eisenstein considers this a howling joke, and in turn identifies himself as Frank's unwilling guest for the coming eight days. This strikes Frank as a superb joke, for, he says, he had already arrested Herr von Eisenstein the preceding evening in his own home, as he was supping with his wife in dressing gown and slippers. "Dressing gown? What color dressing gown?" "A red one," Frank recalls. The real Eisenstein is stunned. "Oh! This Eisenstein I really must see!"

Meanwhile, Alfred has sent for Dr. Blinde, the lawyer, to get him out of jail. Blinde arrives, is intercepted by Eisenstein, who takes from him his wig, lawyer's robe and glasses, and sends him off. Rosalinde enters. Disguised as Blinde, Eisenstein then confronts his wife and Alfred. They ask his help in outwitting Eisenstein. He is furious, and they are offended by their lawyer's lack of sympathy for them. To explain how she has been wronged, Rosalinde complains of her husband's faithlessness, ending with the words, "I shall scratch his eyes out, and then I shall divorce him!" Alfred adds, "Yes, tell us how we may tweak his nose and get out of this scrape."

Livid with rage, Eisenstein unmasks himself in a manner, and to music, recalling the melodramatic Verdi-Donizetti school; this is a refreshing parody that is surprisingly effective. For although it is parody, Eisenstein reaches a certain grandeur as the angered and betrayed husband: ". . . . Yes, it is I, whom you betrayed!"

EDUARD STRAUSS,
photographed in the uniform of a military bandleader.

A scene from the Philadelphia Opera Company's production in English
of *Die Fledermaus*.

Ja, ich bin's, den ihr be — tro — gen.

Rosalinde counterattacks—she reveals herself as his masked inamorata, and produces the watch. "Oh! . . . . You! . . . . My Hungarian Countess!" Gabriel is speechless; coaxed back to good humor by the damning evidence of the watch, he laughs and, perforce, forgives. Falke arrives at this point with Orlovsky and the guests of the ball, to explain that the entire series of events was part of a prearranged plan. Adele and Ida are liberated from the cell in which they were hidden, and young Orlovsky promises Adele to get her on the stage. Thus, all confusions are swept away, as Rosalinde sings, to the melody of the Act II Champagne Song, the words, "Champagne is the one who is to blame, tra-la-la-la-la-la-la-la!" and the curtain descends with regret on this insane and lovable *réveillon*, which has swept us with it to heights of delight which no other comic opera has ever reached.

The appeal of *Die Fledermaus* is immediate. It offers no riddles, it flows steadily along on a succession of exquisite tunes which well up one after the other. It is the crowning jewel in the Golden Age of Light Opera.

Strauss was not habitually an analytical composer. He never consciously sought to make arias reflect the personalities of his various characters. Yet, unintentionally, he did so here. Hardly a note of the music given Rosalinde—feminine, flirtatious, and yet elegant *dame du monde*—could have been sung by Olga, Ida or any other lady of the play. Certainly Adele's impish laughing music suits only her sunny disposition. Nor could the choleric music given Eisenstein in his opening scene fit the character of any other player. But

Strauss's finest delineation was the accompaniment which Orlovsky receives in his opening song, based on rhythms and melodies which spring directly from the liturgical music of the Russian Orthodox Church.

9

SUCCESSES AND FAILURES

FOR the waltzes which he titled *Wo die Zitronen blüh'n*, Johann Strauss turned to Goethe and his dramatic poem *Wilhelm Meister*, which contains verses which have attracted the attention of many another musician, notably Hugo Wolf and Ambroise Thomas. It begins with the words *"Kennst Du das Land, wo die Zitronen blüh'n?"*

This is one of the loveliest—as well as one of the most unusual—of Johann Strauss's waltzes. In mood, it fits more easily into the catalogue of his brother Josef, whose works frequently reflect, in their minor tones, his somber temperament. The introduction is especially delicate and expressive. It is entirely relaxed, effortless, the mood sustained with the falling cadence of the first waltz. An uprushing phrase in the strings, given once and then immediately repeated an octave lower, will be identified as a reminiscence of the elder Strauss's string dialogues from the *Donaulieder*. Later, a brighter atmosphere is felt, only to give place once more at the close to the first waltz of the falling cadences.

The *Zitronen Waltzes* are almost unknown; the only plausible reason for this would seem to be that their strange mood, so alien in spirit to that which one commonly expects from Strauss, does not reveal their inner beauty at first hearing, so that the casual listener is likely to pass them by without becoming aware of their rewarding grace.

In 1875, Strauss began work on a new operetta, *Cagliostro in Wien.* Here was a fine story for his music; one to which it seemed he might do ample justice. But again, Strauss failed to find a Gilbert for his Sullivan, and what might have resulted in a compact play of charm and wit developed instead into a book which begins brilliantly, only to ramble and peter out miserably.

The locale of the story was colorful enough in itself. In 1874, Vienna was celebrating the hundredth anniversary of its deliverance from the Turks. Into this atmosphere of fiesta arrive an Italian charlatan and professed alchemist, Cagliostro, and his beautiful wife. Here the festival spirit gave Strauss the chance to use a brilliant palette, an opportunity which he did not waste and which has resulted in the best moment of the play. But the plot labors in the scenes which follow: Cagliostro and his wife become involved in amorous intrigues which are confusing to the audience; he is exposed in a confidence game, and alchemist and wife, with entourage, are lucky to escape the city a few steps ahead of the police. None of this amounts to anything in terms of dramatic interest, and there is no climax. Even so, Strauss's music, and the excellent performance of a cast headed by Alexander Girardi as Blasoni, Friese as Cagliostro, and Maria Geistinger as Lorenza Feliciana, the wife, saved the operetta from failure and insured it a successful run.

No biography of Strauss could be complete without a parallel mention of Alexander Girardi, one of the most spectacular and phenomenal figures to grace the Viennese stage. By trade a locksmith from Graz, he made his way into the Viennese theater, where he scored triumph after triumph. Only twenty-five when he appeared in *Cagliostro,* he was completely untutored in music, which he could not read, being obliged to learn his roles by aural memorization. This was understandably a task which tried the patience of his coaches and conductors. Yet when he had finally mastered a role, his personification of the character was so vivid and exciting, his singing so delightful, that the effort was thoroughly repaid. Girardi's voice was neither tenor nor baritone, but possessed many of the qualities of both. His parts, at first, were small but important; later longer roles came his way, until, in *Der Zigeunerbaron,* Strauss devised for him the remarkable role of Zsupan, with its tremendous potentialities for burlesque characterization.

Not even Strauss's music and the wealth of talent assembled to perform it could make of *Cagliostro* a work of enduring appeal. Today none of it is generally known save its lilting individual waltzes.

Prinz Methusalem followed *Cagliostro* in short order. Strauss had found his natural style in *Die Fledermaus;* there was no reason to abandon it in *Prinz Methusalem* for the hard, cynical manner of the French operetta stage, as exemplified by Offenbach. Because he did, the work failed in his native city, where it opened at the Carl Theater on January 3rd, 1877. In America, among a people unaware of the inconsistencies of French farce and Viennese sentiment, it has had a considerable success. It was first shown in New York City in 1883, where it scored a run of 102 performances.

Despite the Italian locale, the book is typically French, and should have been set to music by an Offenbach or a Lecocq. The setting is "somewhere in Italy," and deals with the realms of two petty sovereigns, Sigismond and Cyprian. Sigismond's army is small, his finances smaller. He therefore engages his daughter, Pulcinella, to the neighboring ruler's son, Methusalem. There then begins a libretto of cynical overtones and implications, completely lacking either in French wit and finesse or Viennese sentiment. There are many good opportunities for musical writing: the leading romantic roles are given suitably prominent positions; there is an abundance of arias and concerted numbers, but these opportunities were for a man who could write in the piquant style of French *opéra-bouffe.*

Johann Strauss was not that man.

Not the least dismayed by the failure of his latest operetta, Strauss took his orchestra on a tour through Germany in the summer of 1877, visiting Leipzig, Hamburg, Dresden, Baden-Baden and Berlin. In that capital city, he gave a concert at the Kroll Opera House, where he was scheduled to conduct a program of ten numbers. He was obliged to lead well over twenty before the enraptured audience permitted him to leave the hall. He was deeply touched; in later years he frequently spoke of that reception, and never forgot it.

From Berlin, Strauss took the orchestra to Paris. The French capital had its own Strauss in Olivier Métra, the successor to Mûsard. Métra was no match for the great waltz-master, and Strauss was soon drawing the larger audiences. Certain Parisian musical circles became enraged, and a pernicious whispering campaign was begun. The newspapers played up the incident; they reported "authoritatively" that Strauss had spoken slightingly of French music. Strauss's reply was characteristic: he devoted an entire program to the works of French composers, and donated the proceeds of the concert to a French charity. This had, as aftermath, the presentation of the ubiquitous *Croix de la Légion d'Honneur,* which was promptly packed away among an imposing array of more resplendent orders.

The idyllic peace that blessed the lives of Johann and Jetty outlived itself; Jetty began to reap the bitter harvest of past indiscretions and marriage to a man so many years her junior.

Johann was still a young man, the *beau idéal* of womanhood throughout Europe; Jetty, on the other hand, middle-aged, was now fast reaching that time of life when the gap between their years was to be most strongly felt. She found herself obliged to sit quietly by while Strauss passed from flirtation to flirtation, and sometimes to something less pardonable. That many women went out of their way to be attractive and interesting to him, seeking his company, did not lessen Jetty's anger. There were scenes in the villa at Hietzing and in the new Strauss palace on the Igelgasse. Even then, the matter might have adjusted itself had not something more startling occurred.

A son of Jetty's appeared. He was no child of the Baron Tedesco, but of a *liaison* concerning which Strauss had been totally ignorant. Even so, he had known the manner of Jetty's life before their marriage; he knew he had no cause for reproach. As it happened, this son of Jetty's was a thorough rascal. He importuned her for money, and she gave him what she had, begging only that he should not trouble Johann. But the man would not be satisfied with what was a pittance in comparison with the great Strauss fortune, and he made the fatal error of approaching Johann himself.

Strauss sent him packing, and, paradoxically, the discovery of Jetty's own indiscretion temporarily reunited the couple. And then, Strauss returned home one day to find the household in turmoil. Jetty had had a severe stroke and was unconscious. She had received a letter from her son, threatening to expose her past to public scrutiny if she did not persuade Johann to part at once with a considerable fortune. Jetty's heart gave way under this last agonizing strain. Every effort was made to effect her recovery, to no avail. The will to live had left the body of Jetty Treffz.

{ 169 }

Jetty died on April 7th, 1878. In death, her face assumed a tranquility which it had not known in life those last, tragic months. She seemed younger, even beautiful. Heartbroken, grief- and conscience-stricken, Strauss lifted her hand to leave upon it one final kiss. As he touched her already icy fingers, the old revulsion for death and its unknown secrets swept over him, and he fled to his sisters at the Hirschenhaus. Eduard was hurriedly sent for, and it was he who made all the arrangements for the funeral.

Strauss would not even remain in the city. Utterly beside himself, he took the first train from Vienna, and rode crouched upon the floor of his compartment, fleeing from he knew not what, bound he knew not where—and he stayed away until Jetty had been laid to rest. . . .

A few weeks later, he married again!

Never could there have been a worse match. Had Jetty ever wished to be revenged for the heartaches which were hers those last months, when Johann made love to other, more attractive women, she would certainly have found her wish fulfilled in this union.

Angelika Diettrich was a young singer, of minor talent in all things save the art of love-making, wherein she excelled. She had recently come to Vienna from Cologne, and had made the acquaintance of Proch, Director of Music to the Imperial Court. Through him, she was introduced to Johann Strauss, then living at the Hotel Viktoria, since he could neither bring himself to occupy the new Igelgasse palace nor return to the too-familiar locale of the villa on the Hietzingerstrasse.

Angelika, just past her twentieth birthday, met Johann Strauss, then fifty-two, sang for him, flattered him, and married him. There then began a tragi-comedy to exceed anything Strauss ever staged. Angelika (she might better have been named Diabolica) humiliated Strauss, reviled him, mocked him, deceived him and made him feel old. She made her affairs with other men a public scandal; she let everyone know that Strauss was not young enough for her. Vienna watched these goings-on with amazement and a soft, ironical chuckle, in which was mixed no little compassion for Strauss. The Waltz King himself seemed to appear older, and his music lost some of the sparkle it had known. The intolerable affair lasted five years, during which the anything-but-pure Lilli passed from one flaming flirtation to another. To Strauss, the climax of his horrors came about when one of Angelika's lovers proved to be none other than Steiner himself. In the end, it was Angelika who brought the incident to a close. One fine September evening she ran away from Schönau with her lover of the moment.

It was a nightmarish libretto, one that was best ended soon.

The toll Angelika exacted of Strauss's creative powers is evidenced in the dismal failure of his comic opera *Blindekuh*. An impossible libretto shares the blame, but this is the one Strauss score which can be called vapid and devoid of true inspiration. Never before had Strauss written such trite, banal, unworthy music. There was not one tune in the entire work which the public could take away whistling. Opening at the Theater-an-der-Wien on December 18th, 1878, *Blindekuh* played just three performances!

Then came a period of stagnation, of inactivity. For the first time in his life, Strauss was unable to compose. The fountain of melody which had always sprung effortlessly and overabundantly within him simply dried up. He no longer knew a moment's peace or contentment. Gone were the sheltered, restful years which Jetty had carefully wrapped about him. Now his life was a distillation of bitter hours. It was impossible, in such an atmosphere, to write the gay music which Vienna awaited from him. It took him almost two years to regain his footing; two years during which he had to teach himself to be wilfully blind to Angelika's promiscuity.

It was not until the first of October, 1880, that he produced at the Theater-an-der-Wien a comic opera with which to redeem himself. This was *Das Spitzentuch der Königin*. Although it did not have the success of *Die Fledermaus*, this new work was a favorite from its first performance in Vienna until long after its appearance in New York, on October 22nd, 1882, when it opened the newly-built Casino Theater with a run of 234 performances. It was again presented in 1885, and on occasions thereafter. In Vienna, and other German-speaking cities, it is still occasionally presented with success to this day.

The story is, in its basic elements, one of the best ever given Strauss. The locale is Portugal during the days of Philip II of Spain, who was then trying to gain dominion over the entire Iberian peninsula. The Portuguese prime minister, in the pay of the Spanish monarch, finds little difficulty in swaying the weak young King of Portugal, whose fondness for truffles leads him to pay too little attention to affairs of State.

Unhappy over his neglect of the country and herself, his Queen embroiders upon one of her handkerchiefs the words, "A Queen loves you, though you are no King." This she thoughtlessly leaves as a bookmark in a copy of Cervantes' *Don Quixote*. Cervantes, in exile from Spain, is Reader to the Queen, and in love with Irene, one of her ladies-in-waiting. The Prime Minister convinces the King that a *liaison* exists between the Queen and Cervantes. The latter succeeds in making his escape with his servant, Sancho Panza, while the Queen is sent to a convent. With the aid of bandits, Cervantes and Sancho Panza kidnap the Queen and Irene. The ladies then masquerade as servant maids at an inn which the King visits on a hunting trip. They serve his favorite dishes,

coax him into a mellow mood, succeed in exposing the duplic-
ity of his minister, and finally reveal themselves, with a satisfactory explanation of the true significance of the embroidery.
And, as it should, all ends happily.

The story possessed dramatic interest, and afforded many
opportunities for Strauss to make his music an integral part of
the action, as in the dancing lesson of the King, or in the scene
where a learned commission attempts, without success, to cer-
tify Cervantes as insane. But in practical showmanship the
book had too many weak spots. If painting lacks drama, so
does eating. Gourmet or gourmand, it is all the same on the
stage. Food lacks romance. Where Strauss writes music suggestive of the Queen's lace handkerchief, his music lives;
where it seeks to picture the King's epicurean delights, it fails.

BOUND to a home life of reproaches, recriminations and infidelities, Johann Strauss barricaded himself within his study
and began work on a new operetta. The book had been provided by Zell and Genée, who named it *Der Lustige Krieg*. In
writing it, Strauss found temporary solace and surcease from
domestic turmoil. The play abounds in delicious, carefree
moments. The wonderful waltz-song, *Nur für Natur*, proved
such a success that its triumph was a foretaste of the furor
which the *Merry Widow* waltzes were to occasion years later.
The theme of this song is the recurring one which predominates in the *Kiss Waltzes*, a compilation of themes from the
operetta. Yet the song, quite unrelated to the action of the
play, owes its accidental presence in the score to the insistence
of Girardi, who appeared as the Marquis Filippo Sebastiani,
nephew of the Prince of Massa e Carrara. The music to this
play is outrageously giddy and carefree—almost suspiciously
so. One can easily imagine Johann Strauss finding momentary
forgetfulness in its composition.

Der Lustige Krieg opened at the Theater-an-der-Wien on November 25th, 1881, with instantaneous success, and traveled on from city to city. In New York, it was produced at both the Thalia and Casino Theaters in 1885. At the Casino, it had a run of 69 performances. It was also presented in Stockholm, Budapest, Chicago, Detroit, Cologne, Berlin, Munich, Moscow and Philadelphia during the years of 1885 and 1886.

That *Der Lustige Krieg* should have known any success at all in Vienna was, in itself, a real tribute to Strauss. Only two weeks after the opening of the new operetta, the famous Ringtheater caught fire and burned to the ground. Charred corpses were carried from the gutted building by the hundreds. Tragedy struck so many homes that night that the entire city went into mourning. It was a painful subject of conversation in the city for months. This was on the night of the Viennese opening of *Les Contes d'Hoffman;* the tragedy started a "jinx" superstition which, for a long time, kept Offenbach's opera off the boards of many an opera house. No one went to any theater in Vienna save one—the Theater-an-der-Wien, and Strauss's operetta.

Der Lustige Krieg is one of the maddest hodgepodges of confused identities ever set to music. At the start, the story is reasonably clear; the Doge of Genoa and the Prince of Massa e Carrara have a set-to over a dancer. War is declared. Here the confusion begins; all the officers in the army of the Prince are women, under command of the Countess Violetta Lomellini. What ensues when the two armies confront each other may be imagined. Enter here a Spanish Grandee, who marries la Lomellini as proxy for someone else—enter also Balthazar Groot, a tulip grower from Holland, and his wife Else, who is jealous of Violetta. For her part, the Countess, apparently disgusted with an intrigue which even she cannot understand, proceeds to fall in love with the man she married.

It would be difficult to conjure up less plausible nonsense. In *Die Fledermaus,* less idiotic confusions are rendered credible by the befuddled state of the leading characters, but the champagne atmosphere is lacking here.

The operetta's success was the result of a good score rather than an acceptable story, for much of the music is truly inspired. Jacob wrote that "when the D major quintet, *Komm'n und Geh'n,* set like a majestic cannon, resounded at the first performance, one enthusiastic musician fell on his knees."

It was at this time that Strauss turned for a moment from the operetta stage to write one of his most popular sets of waltzes. These were the *Frühlingsstimmen* (*Voices of Spring*) *Waltzes,* Op. 410, which he dedicated to the piano virtuoso Alfred Grünfeld. Indeed, these waltzes were composed for piano solo, and were orchestrated at a later date. Despite the quick acceptance of this music throughout the world, and the appreciation expressed by Verdi, Reger, Puccini and Brahms, the Viennese long remained cold to it. Not without reason; in the first (and principal) waltz, at least, the melodic style is quite alien to Strauss. There is an insincere brilliance to these uprushing eighth-note phrases; they recall more readily the perfumed rose and poisoned dagger of the Italian Renaissance than the *Gemütlichkeit* of the Viennese. The waltzes are excellent Strauss, but they are not Viennese Strauss.

Strauss acquired the book to his ninth operetta through a series of amusing circumstances which might have supplied material for a Gilbert and Sullivan libretto.

Walzel and Genée had in readiness two new books, one of which was *Der Bettelstudent,* and the other, *Eine Nacht in*

Venedig. They had rashly permitted Karl Millöcker to be the first to examine the books. Although Millöcker had done well with his *Dubarry,* he was no Strauss, and Genée was aware that it was Strauss who should have been given first choice. But he also knew that *Eine Nacht in Venedig* was, at best, a patchwork quilt. He felt that if anyone could make it a success Strauss could. Nor did he want to cross Millöcker in belatedly giving *Bettelstudent* to Strauss.

As he feared, the latter showed strong preference for *Bettelstudent.* Genée realized that to save his face he must act quickly. He let it be understood that he hoped Strauss would select *Bettelstudent,* since Millöcker had expressed some interest in the other libretto. As he shrewdly anticipated, this suggestion was enough to swing Strauss's opinion. Without troubling to read the book, he haughtily informed the authors that he preferred *Eine Nacht in Venedig,* and expected them to put this story at his disposal. He seemed to care nothing for whatever code of ethics may have been involved. For their part, Genée and Walzel exhibited no stricken conscience over their own deception.

Millöcker's music, coupled with this excellent story, made of *Der Bettelstudent* a work which has lasted in the repertory, but it does not take much searching to find many places where Strauss would have done better. The action occurs in medieval Poland, where the Saxon Prince, August the Strong, has elected himself King. The opposite worlds of Slav and Teuton are depicted here. Had Strauss written this music in the light, rococo style of which he was capable, it might have surpassed *Die Fledermaus.* What an opportunity lay here for his touch! Polonaises, polkas and mazurkas would have delineated with finesse the Slavic atmosphere, against which his tripping waltzes and marches would have played a counterpoint as the characterization of the Teuton spirit.

But Strauss did not take *Bettelstudent*. As ever unwilling to trust his own literary good sense, he took instead a shoddy libretto which he had not examined. True, it did place its action in Italy, a country in which he had always felt spiritually at home, and there were some fair situations and an occasional interesting character. Of these, the cook Papacoda is perhaps the best—a culinary genius who measures mankind from the standpoint of macaroni. There are all the trappings of a Latin romance and imbroglio: masks, gondolas, the Carnival of Venice, handsome cavaliers and beautiful signorinas. It seemed that one needed but to tie the story together with the thread of Straussian music, and the thing was done.

The public thought otherwise. *Eine Nacht in Venedig* was finished shortly after Angelika left the Schönau villa forever. She left behind a man grateful for his deliverance. Lighthearted, he took his operetta to Berlin, where it opened at the Friedrichs-Wilhelm-Theater on October 3rd, 1883.* The audience quickly sensed that this new work was musically sound, but dramatically feeble. Papacoda's opening eulogy of macaroni, and Annina's entry as a vendor of seafood, singing *Frutti di Mare*, were auspicious beginnings which served to relieve the otherwise extraordinary dullness of the first act, but the intrigue which develops between the Duke, the Senator and the Senator's wife, Barbara (sister of Annina), and the complicated abduction of Barbara which is carried out by Caramello, the Duke's barber, who unwittingly kidnaps and delivers his own fiancée, Annina, to the Duke, soon assumed an all-too-familiar pattern and bored the public. Matters

---

* *Note that this is the only Strauss operetta ever premièred outside of Vienna. Although delighted to be rid of Angelika, masculine pride forbade Strauss's giving the première to one of her former lovers, Max Steiner, director of the Theater-an-der-Wien.*

progressed from bad to worse. Finally, the excellent *Lagunen-walzer* appeared, set to utterly moronic words:

"At night of course all cats are gray,
Then tenderly 'miaouw' they say. . . ."

This was too much; the audience took up the catcall, and the rout started. The operetta momentarily got no further. The words were ridiculous, and the exquisite music of the *Lagoon Waltzes*, the Duke's two charming arias, *Treu sein, das liegt mir nicht* and *Sei mir gegrüsst, du holdes Venetia*, the magnificent finale to Act II, with its 2/4-time chorale work set against the 3/4-time waltz songs of the principals, and the hauntingly lovely serenade, *Komm' in die Gondel*, were not enough to carry the production.

Strauss was entirely to blame. Did he think himself so infallible that he could take a book without reading it, set it to music without proper knowledge of its contents, and hope to make it a successfully integrated work? One can forgive him only in view of his domestic problems. Nevertheless, Richard Specht's accusation is only too just: "To compose a musical comedy without knowing what mood has inspired the songs, without knowing the sequence of the scenes—that is really a depth of indolence which cannot be surpassed."

He might as well have said "insolence"—and the public took it as such from Strauss. Yet *Eine Nacht in Venedig* is not a bad work. Musically, it is well assembled. With many revisions, *A Night in Venice* knew a real success in London in 1944-45, where it played at the Cambridge Theater for over a year. In Germany and Austria, it is still frequently heard and enjoyed; in Germany, it has recently had a considerable success in a new revision by Ferdinand Leitner and Karl Gutheim.

10

ADELE STRAUSS

For the third time in his life, Strauss fell wholly and unreasoningly in love. He could not, by any stretch of charitable imagination, be called a young man. In 1883, Johann Strauss was fifty-eight—not too old for marriage, but surely beyond the age of youthfully impetuous ardor. Yet Strauss fell in love with Adele Deutsch as would a young man. Adele was no Angelika; although still a young woman, there could be no suggestion of a May-September romance. The difference in ages was sufficiently commonplace.

The story of this romance is one of strange coincidence. Years before, when Frau Strauss was still alive, she had had for neighbors in the Hirschenhaus a banker and his son. Although the two families were of the same name, there were no blood ties between the Jewish family of Albert Strauss and the Catholic family of Johann Strauss.

Albert Strauss was a man of unusual culture and taste. As a banker, he possessed a strong sense of material values, yet in the manner of so many of his faith, he also knew how to assess the true, intangible riches of life. He was especially fond of poetry, and admitted a particular preference for Grillparzer, epic bard of the Viennese, and lifelong friend of Franz Schubert. Albert Strauss also loved music. It was therefore to be expected that he should develop a strong friendship with the music-making Strausses.

His son married an extremely attractive and charming young woman, Adele Deutsch. Indeed, to judge by the photographs which still exist, Adele Strauss could, by modern standards, put the overblown beauty of Angelika Diettrich to shame. The marriage of Emil Strauss and Adele was blessed with one child, a daughter, Alice. The father died shortly after her birth, leaving a young widow to face a life filled with little more than the memories of an all-too-brief span of happiness.

The years which Adele spent in the Hirschenhaus as a neighbor of Anna Strauss taught her to understand the whims and eccentricities—and the needs—of Johann Strauss. The years of sorrow through which she had passed had further equipped her for the delicate role of his third wife. However blind he may have been to the failings of his Angelika, he did show excellent judgment when he determined to marry Adele Strauss despite all the obstacles which were set in his path.

He had first to rid himself of Angelika. In view of her infidelities, there was no difficulty in obtaining a divorce. But Johann was Catholic, Adele Jewish. In the Holy Roman Empire their union was forbidden. Strauss refused to allow anything to stand in his path. He left Vienna and established residence in Coburg, capital of the Duchy of Saxony-Coburg-Gotha, and there forswore his Austrian allegiance to become a subject of the Duke. Franz-Josef found it hard indeed to forgive one of his foremost subjects this traitorous transgression. Devout Catholic that he was, he found it even harder to forgive Strauss his conversion to Protestantism.

Johann and Adele were married in Coburg, and soon returned to the Igelgasse palace, where Strauss resumed his work. His marriage to Adele brought him not only a wife, but also a daughter, for Alice Strauss, then still a young girl, became a member of his household. Strauss lavished affection upon her, and it was wholeheartedly returned. He found that his palace and villas ceased to be houses; they became homes.

The diabolical Angelika, who had flaunted her infidelities for five years before all Vienna, now assumed the role of the martyred wife, parading up and down the Igelgasse before the Strauss palace and the door of the villa at Schönau, whence she followed the Waltz King and his family. She fooled no one. An injunction was granted Strauss by the courts, and the second Frau Strauss was soon dissuaded by the police from pursuing her ridiculous picketing.

It had taken the years of shelter, care and loving attention showered upon Johann by Jetty to produce the iridescent music of *Die Fledermaus*. The cankerous years with Angelika had only produced shriveled deformities which had done much to hurt his prestige as an operettist. It took all the understanding, consideration and loving kindness of which Adele was capable to rehabilitate the drooping spirits of this man, and make him again feel his powers. Angelika had, by his own confession, made him feel old. Yet after his death, Adele said, "I never felt that I had married an old man." It was true. She never thought of Strauss in terms of actual years; she measured him by the eternal youthfulness of his music. And if his music had been threatened by a few crow's-feet and a double chin during the tyrannical reign of Angelika, it flowered once more and regained its youth under the benign sun of Adele's cheerful personality.

Jetty had given him *Die Fledermaus*. It was Adele who gave him *Der Zigeunerbaron*.

While on a visit to Budapest, where Strauss was to conduct the first performance of his *Lustige Krieg*, he and Adele, at her suggestion, paid a visit to the great Hungarian novelist, Maurus Jokai. Jokai was the Homer of his people; in novels and short stories, he told of the old days and the new. His tales dealt with the simple rustic and the sophisticated city dweller, the happy and the downcast, the great and the small—all Hungarians.

Jokai told them the story of his newest book, a novel *Saffi*. It enchanted Strauss; he felt that he had at last found a book equal to his music. He sensed, too, the timeliness of the story. Although the action occurs in the middle 1700's, the atmosphere was of Strauss's present. It had not been long since confiscation of Hungarian estates by the Austrian Emperor, banishment, return from exile, câched treasure and wasted lands had been the topics of the day.

The establishment of the Dual Monarchy, whereby Franz-Josef ruled Hungary not as Emperor of Austria, but as King of Hungary, had focused attention upon this colorful country. In the realm of music, the Hungarians had been publicized by Franz Liszt, with his *Hungarian Rhapsodies,* by Hector Berlioz, with his orchestration of the *Rakocsy March,* and by Johannes Brahms, with his *Hungarian Dances.* Josef Joachim, perhaps the leading violinist of the day, was himself an Hungarian. The fiery compulsion of gypsy music had spread through European café-concerts, from Vienna to Paris, London and Berlin—wherever the *Zigeuner* had carried his magic fiddle and cymbalom.

Strauss insisted that he must have *Saffi* for an opera. Jokai consented, with reservations. He would not, he said, write the libretto—he knew too little about stage technique—but he would select a man whom they could both trust to handle the book carefully. This man was an Hungarian journalist, Ignaz Schnitzer.

Schnitzer was a godsend. He went further than either Jo-kai or Strauss had dared to hope. He seemed to have been

born with an intuitive knowledge of what makes "good theater." He pruned Jokai's book of every unnecessary trace of
the fantasy-atmosphere of Hungarian fairy-tales with which
it had been surcharged. As for Strauss, Schnitzer was emphatic in advising *him* not to make too early a use of Hungarian musical forms. For the initial appearance of Sandor
Barinkay, returning from Austria to claim his ancestral lands,
Strauss intended to use the Hungarian czardas; it was Schnitzer who pointed out the error of this, and suggested that it
would be more appropriate to substitute the international
waltz. It is to Schnitzer, therefore, that we are indebted for
Barinkay's entrance song, *Als flotter Geist,* with its accompanying waltz refrain, *Ja, das alles auf Ehr'.*

Strauss was determined to produce this time a comic opera
in which words and music would be properly correlated. He
felt that in *Saffi* he had found a story of unusual value, worthy
of a great comic opera, and he did not mean to waste his
opportunity. To aid Strauss, Schnitzer suggested that they
first exhaustively discuss each scene, with an eye to text and
music. Strauss might then write whatever music he wished,
in the mood of the scene. He would then set the lyrics to fit

Strauss's music. Nothing could have been more ideal than this highly unorthodox system. The result is an opera where words, music and mood are well fused into a living whole, rather than a chain of unrelated numbers.

In contrast to the lightning-like manner in which Strauss penned *Die Fledermaus* is the slow, painstaking fashion in which he wrote *Der Zigeunerbaron*. It was not that the master was losing his touch; far from it, as the world was soon to learn. There had simply been too many failures, due, as Strauss knew all too well, to a carelessness on his part in relating music to libretto. Strauss had written to Paul Lindau, in connection with the failure of *Eine Nacht in Venedig*, a confession of the most damning sort:

"The style of the libretto is such that with the sincerest intentions in the world I could find no inspiration in it. It is a scatterbrained affair, without the least trace of action. I never saw the libretto dialogue, but only the words of the songs. Consequently, I put too much nobility into some parts of it, and that did not suit the work as a whole. There is no part of this book where a noble interpretation will fit. At the final rehearsal, when I learnt the complete story in its correct sequence, I was utterly horrified."

It is impossible to fathom why Strauss could have been so foolish and imprudent. "Down with dialogue," Rossini once said. Was Strauss of a like mind? Hardly; the lyric stage had progressed too far since the days of Rossini, and comic opera is of necessity too dependent upon the contents of its libretto.

Determined not to repeat his earlier follies, Strauss took two years to write *Der Zigeunerbaron*. It was not until October 24th, 1885, that it was given its first performance at the Theater-an-der-Wien, despite the appeals of Steiner for an earlier date. Adele never forgot the night which preceded that opening, when Strauss, in an agony of nerves, paced back and forth across their bedroom, drenched in nervous perspiration.

Strauss had reason to be anxious. The fiasco of *Eine Nacht in Venedig* was still fresh. The Viennese were shaking their heads dubiously: Could Strauss write another *Die Fledermaus*? Had he not burnt himself out? There was a sense of anxiety and uncertainty as Strauss entered the pit to lead the orchestra in the Overture. The opening section, dark and richly colored, with its traces of *Zigeunerlied*, excited and delighted the audience. It was at once apparent that here was a deeper, more musicianly Strauss than Vienna had hitherto known. Yet still the audience seemed to wait for something. Then came the *Tempo di Vals*, the unforgettable fragment of the *Schatzwalzer*. There was a stir and a sigh throughout the hall. God's in his Heaven, all's well with the world....

THE story of *Der Zigeunerbaron* remains fresh today, after a lapse of over half a century, as satisfying a play as it was on the evening when it was introduced to Vienna. Eschewed were the mistaken identities of conventional comic opera; there is nothing to this tale which requires the coöperative imagination of the audience. The action opens before the ruined ancestral home of the Barinkays, in the Hungary of the middle Eighteenth Century. The family was exiled from Hungary, after participating in an unsuccessful revolution against the domination of Austria, and the lands are now a *Zigeuner* encampment. Upon this scene arrives Sandor Barinkay to claim his paternal estate. The order of banishment has been lifted, and Sandor, son of the lord who was driven from his home, has been allowed to return. His entrance song is a brilliant recitation of his past life and travels. In this, Schnitzer's words set a Viennese parallel for the type of patter song in which Gilbert excelled. Sandor meets his neigh-bor, the hog-breeder Zsupan, and his lovely daughter Arsena. Sandor falls in love with her and asks for her hand. Arsena refuses him—she will not, she says haughtily, marry anyone who is not at least a Baron. Actually, she is in love with Ottokar, the son of her governess.

Incensed, Sandor joins the gypsies who have made his ruined home their camp, and is chosen their leader—a Gypsy Baron. He returns to Arsena and proposes once more, re-marking that she may now wed a "Baron." Then, as Arsena still appears reluctant, he takes the gypsy girl Saffi, daughter of old Czipra, and leaves with her, while a spurned Arsena vows revenge.

The second act opens with Czipra, Saffi and Sandor stand-ing, the following morning, before the ruins of the old Bar-inkay Castle on the banks of the Temes River. Saffi says she has dreamt that the câched fortune of the Barinkays, hidden when they fled, may be found under a certain stone in the wall of the castle. Sandor is inclined to laugh the dream away, but he is persuaded by Czipra to make a search. Behold! there lies the treasure! This is the *Treasure Waltz,* a Trio as spark-ling as the gems themselves:

"Ha! see, it winks,
It sings, it rings!
Feel how it tingles!
Hear how it jingles!"

Upon this scene arrive Ottokar, Zsupan, Ottokar's mother, Mirabella, and Arsena, followed by Homonay, who is seek' ing recruits for the Austrian Army in its war with Spain. He presses Ottokar and Zsupan into service, much against their will. They complain of Sandor's affront to Arsena, and insist that he be drafted, too. Homonay laughs and compli' ments Sandor on his excellent choice. He inquires who mar' ried them. The reply startles everyone, for it seems they were married most informally by "that cathedral priest, the bull' finch wise," while the nightingale sang her song and the storks looked on as witnesses. This duet, *"Who tied the knot?"*, is one of the most exquisite moments in the entire book. The music is high among Strauss's most sensuous and caressing melodies, the voices floating warmly over a liquid *arpeggio* accompaniment. When Strauss sent the music to Schnitzer, he wrote, "Please give me a great many I's and A's; I have noticed that singers are very fond of these vowels." Schnit' zer took him at his word, and returned the music with this text to the refrain:

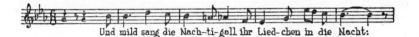
Und mild sang die Nach-ti-gall ihr Lied-chen in die Nacht:

"Und mild sang die Nachtigall ihr Liedchen in die Nacht: die Liebe, die Liebe, ist eine Himmelsmacht."

"And gently sang the nightingale her tune through the night, Our love, our love, is blessed with Heaven's might."

Now trouble develops. It seems that the câche was illegal, and the pardon may be withdrawn. Temporary settlement is reached when Sandor gives Homonay the treasure in trust, and joins the army to fight the war in Spain.

The third act opens in a public square in Vienna, as the conquering army makes its triumphant return. Zsupan enters, bedecked with loot, and wearing a girdle of stolen watches. Amusing as this is, it is based on fact; watches were prize loot during the wars of the Eighteenth Century, and still are today. Russian veterans of World War II wore wrist watches up to their elbows. Augereau, a Napoleonic general, came back to Paris from an Italian campaign so bedecked with watches that even calloused Bonaparte was scandalized.

Yet for all his Falstaffian gusto, Zsupan cut a poor figure during the campaign, while Sandor returns covered not with loot, but with glory. He is now, in truth, a Baron, for the Emperor has ennobled him in reward for his valor. Homonay has returned him the treasure; he now possesses riches and honors. Only Saffi is lacking, and she, too, appears. Here another surprise awaits; Czipra admits that Saffi is not her child, but the abducted daughter of the last Turkish Pasha to rule Hungary. Sandor and Saffi are wedded in proper style, and the curtain falls. . . .

THE night of the opening was the evening before Strauss's sixtieth birthday. *Der Zigeunerbaron* was a magnificent birthday gift, which the Viennese finished off in grand style. They sobbed and cheered throughout the production; the timeliness of the story and the charm of the music had them bordering on hysteria. Every number had to be repeated. Never in Vienna had there been such a furor over a lyric work. What Franz-Josef had tried to do for forty years, Strauss achieved that night—he made the Dual Monarchy one.

With the success of *Der Zigeunerbaron* came renewed confidence and vigor. In a rush, Strauss published the *Wiener
Frauen Waltzes,* Op. 423, and the *Adelen Waltzes,* Op. 424,
dedicated to his wife. These were followed by three works
inspired by his last Russian tour: the *An der Wolga Polka-
Mazurka,* Op. 425, the *Russischer Marsch,* Op. 426, and the
Reiter Marsch, Op. 428.

11

THE LAST YEARS

As WITH every other important composer of light opera, it was perhaps inevitable that Strauss should eventually attempt something of a more serious nature. Jacques Offenbach, having built a life's reputation on such effervescent works as *Orphée aux Enfers, La Belle Hélène,* and *La Vie Parisienne,* felt, in his declining years, the need to leave behind him something of a more ambitious nature, and he wrote *The Tales of Hoffman.*

So did Strauss eventually turn to serious opera. Had he spent a lifetime in the search, he could hardly have found a subject less suited to his talents. He turned to a work of the Seventeenth Century writer, von Grimmelshausen, *Simplizius Simplicissimus,* which antedates *Faust* as the most lugubrious work in German literature. It was young Viktor Léon who made the stage adaptation, the same Viktor Léon who was, years later, to write the delightful book for Lehár's *The Merry Widow,* and who was destined, still many more years in the future, to die miserably in abject poverty in a Vienna crushed beneath the weight of anti-Semitic Nazi ideologies.

Grimmelshausen's story, the point of departure from which Léon expanded his libretto, is of medieval simplicity. A young boy, Simplizius, is brought up in the depths of a forest by an old hermit. Because mankind is motivated by malice and greed which engender wars, the hermit rears the lad as a simple animal, knowing none of his own kind. During the Thirty Years' War, troops reach the hermitage and chance upon the boy, who, never having known any man save the hermit, takes them for devils. Despite the old man's pleas and the terrible fright of the boy, they take Simplizius along to guide them through the forest and back to "civilization." Once in the outer world, his innocence stripped from him, there is nothing left for him to do but to join his fellowmen and become man and murderer like his brothers.

Such was Grimmelshausen's story, a fable and a parable, with its proper place in literature. Such a story was not even remotely suited for the lyric stage, and Léon knew it. He planned to alter the plot to fit, without realizing that no amount of alteration would do. Nor do his changes and additions show that he possessed the ability to handle that world of half-fantasy, half-reality which had made Grimmelshausen's tale so enduring. In Léon's libretto, the original story forms the basis for the first act only (or, as Strauss described it, the Prologue). In the two acts which follow, Simplizius's life and adventures take him through the old, hackneyed routine of the operetta stage: war, confusion of identities, the usual love intrigues with a vivandière's daughter, whom he eventually marries, and the rest of the conventional folderol.

Strauss came by the libretto to *Simplizius* through odd circumstances. Unable to trust his own judgment in such matters, he must always follow another's lead. When he heard that Viktor Léon had written *Simplizius* for Zamara, he must, perforce, command him to withdraw that book from Zamara and give it to him. It mattered not at all to Strauss that Zamara had almost completed his version of the play, and that a tentative date for the first performance had already been set. Strauss was the Waltz King.

The manner in which he took over a book which another composer had in work was not without precedent. Some years before, Offenbach had set his heart upon obtaining the rights to *Les Contes d'Hoffman*. Almost destitute after years of the greatest luxury, forgotten in the city that had once rocked with laughter to his great offenbachiades, he believed that at last he had found the book which would place him among the immortals. Years before, he had set his heart upon breaking into the sacrosanct purlieus of the Opéra-Comique; always this stronghold of conservatism had resisted his assaults. Because of this, he turned to and perfected the *opéra-bouffe,* which he presented in his own little theater, the Bouffes-Parisiens. This style of operetta, based on the Italian *buffa,* had satire for its keynote; its existence depended upon caricaturing some aspect of contemporary life. Offenbach had mocked the Opéra-Comique itself; in *La Grande-Duchesse de Gérolstein* he had satirized the theatrical and unsound life of the court of the Second Empire—nothing was safe from his scalpel pen. Then, with the debacle of the Second Empire, Offenbach's rule passed; the public associated him too closely with the political regime which had just been overthrown, and considered him no longer in tune with the times. He desperately wanted *Les Contes d'Hoffman* to recoup his fortunes. Another composer had done considerable work on a version of his own, but with great generosity he consented to abandon all rights to the story and turned it over to Offenbach, who was finally able to invade the Opéra-Comique with this work. He did not live to see this triumph, but he was able to attend the rehearsals, finding satisfaction in the knowledge that he had fulfilled a lifelong ambition. Yet, ironically, his best music is still that of the offenbachiades.

Any chronicler of Strauss's life must perforce make obeisance to the French master for the debt which Strauss owes him in the field of light opera. Without Offenbach's *La Vie Parisienne*, Strauss's *Die Fledermaus* might not have been written. It does not matter which comic opera or which composer is greater (they took different lines and are, in many respects, not to be compared); the pioneering of Offenbach was all-important, and his music does not deserve the comparative oblivion which today is its fate in Anglo-Saxon lands.

Strauss, then, was only following Offenbach's lead when he demanded that Léon withdraw *Simplizius* from Zamara in order to give it to him. He set to work at once on what was to be "grand opera." Like Offenbach, Strauss hoped to achieve one triumph in that field. He was to fail; he did not realize that to be supreme in one field of art, whether light or serious, popular or recondite, is in itself the greatest assurance of immortality. And Strauss lacked Offenbach's pressing reason; he was at the pinnacle of his fame those last years when he was fêted at one jubilee after another.

He was not unaware that he had blundered, only the matter had gone too far for him to be able to withdraw. During the rehearsals at the Theater-an-der-Wien, and up to the moment when the curtain went up on December 17th, 1887, he resisted Steiner's requests to have him designate the new work as anything but a Prologue and Two Acts. At least, in this designation, he was completely honest, for there is no possible relation between the sober first act and the nonsensical two which follow. Small wonder that instead of enjoying a long run, as had been hoped, *Simplizius* was withdrawn after only thirty performances. Although it had been accepted for St. Petersburg and for Munich, Strauss himself asked that the productions be cancelled. He did not wish to injure a prestige reëstablished with *Der Zigeunerbaron*. All that remains today are the *Donauweibchen Waltzes*. Op. 427.

In 1888, Franz-Josef was fifty-eight. Forty years had elapsed since the day when, at eighteen, he had mounted the throne left vacant by the abdication of Ferdinand. There were still many years to pass before he became that legendary figure which haunted the Hofburg during the tragic days of World War I, yet already he had become Austria's beloved *der alter Kaiser*. Gone were the days of bad blood provoked by the Revolution of 1848, and laid to rest were most of the spectres of internal strife. Hungary had autonomy; even Bohemia was on the verge of being granted some measure of self-government. What if the minor provinces were dissatisfied? The death of Franz-Ferdinand at Sarajevo was still in the nebulous future.

In the place of the young and impulsive Emperor whose unbending, autocratic measures had at first made him unpopular with his people, Austria now knew an Emperor saddened and softened by innumerable blows of Fate. He had found himself, despite intensive schooling, an unsuccessful militarist who had lost, on the fields of Sadowa, Austria's age-old domination over the Teutonic peoples to the rapidly growing power of Prussia. He had seen an idyllic love curdled by court intrigue, to the point where his beautiful Empress, now a stranger to him, was more frequently to be found at Capri or in Hungary, in the company of Count Andrassy, than in the Hofburg which she found so hostile. He had lost his only son, the Archduke Rudolf, whose death at Mayerling, instead of causing a *rapprochement,* had only served to estrange even further the Imperial couple. He said of himself in confidence, to certain of his aides, "Gentlemen, my hand is unlucky. . . ."

Forty years of rule by a man who had become an honored and admired figure was ample cause for Austria to indulge in one of the many jubilees which she was to tender through-

ADELE STRAUSS
Autographed to Professor Fritz Lange, eminent Viennese musicologist,
who collaborated with her on a book on her husband, Johann II.

FRANZ LEHÁR

Photograph presented to the author's mother on the occasion of the
first performance of his musical comedy *Frühling*.

out these years with impartiality to Franz-Josef and Johann Strauss.

As befitted the man who was Königlich und Kaiserlich Hofballmusikdirektor, Strauss wrote the music for his Emperor's jubilee. He did not content himself with one composition; he wrote two. The *Kaiser-Jubiläum Waltzes*, Op. 434, were written expressly for the ceremonies, but it was with another composition, three opus numbers later, that Schani paid heartfelt tribute to his sovereign, when he produced the *Kaiserwalzer*.

The *Kaiserwalzer* is Strauss's most symphonic waltz; danceable though it may be, this is but an adjunct to its primary purpose as concert music. The French writer Guillaume Ritter said that "it was the most beautiful flower that the incredible tree of Strauss music had produced in seventy-five years."

A 4/4 rhythm, in rapid Austrian march tempo, establishes the mood, *piano*. Then appears the march proper, fifty measures long. It is writing that might have come directly from Mozart; it possesses all his style and spirit, the characteristics of his orchestration, even to the placement of the trills. Masterly stroke of craftsmanship that it is, it is perhaps the most vivid proof of Strauss's affinity to the genius of Salzburg. It creates the scene; this is indubitably Austrian. Crisp and clean, it is also discreet:

Another antique episode follows. Exciting by virtue of its simple style, it is kin to the famous *Rondo alla turca* of the *Piano Sonata in A Major*:

A swell in the orchestra presages the presence of the principal waltz theme, but this is overwhelmed by a *forte* reappear-
ance of the march. And then, at the moment when the *forte*
threatens to develop into a *fortissimo,* it vanishes, and the
oboe enters, *piano,* hesitantly. It is a moment of awe and reverence. The violins take flight, soaring with Mendelssohnian
grace. Then, gently, an unexpected Wagnerian chord in-
trudes. Thus the years have flown; what began with Mozart
concludes with Wagner:

It is only after these preliminaries that Strauss allows his
waltz to appear. It is a waltz of tenderness, respect, friendliness and love—an open, unabashed declaration of loyalty. Its
reiterated notes on the lower G give it solidity and strength;
it is an affection that is fundamental and deep-rooted:

The inevitable Ländler makes its appearance. Indeed, why
not? The waltz is cosmopolitan, the Ländler, Austrian:

The military must have its moment as well, for it might be said of the Emperor that he was born with his spurs on. Yet this is also the people themselves, with its lack of subtlety and its accent on the first beat:

Finally, when the tumult and the shouting, the pomp and circumstance, the pageantry and parades have had their say, there remains still the steady current of affection, in this Schubertian phrase:

It sounds in the supremely masculine voice of the violoncello, through which threads a recollection of the first waltz in the light tones of the flute. At the last, everything is brought to a brilliant conclusion by a flourish of trumpets and a few final chords.

AFTER the Jubilee came another opera, *Ritter Pasman,* produced at the Hofoperntheater on New Year's Day, 1892. At last Johann Strauss invaded the holy precincts of the Imperial Opera, and this with a serious opera written on a rococo theme of almost medieval gallantry. The story is weak and undramatic, and although Strauss wove about it one of his most cunning scores, the work of an experienced hand, it met with a lukewarm reception. It was Strauss whom the audience applauded, not *Ritter Pasman*.

If this opera did not establish him in the Hofoperntheater, his ultimate goal, *Die Fledermaus* eventually did. This came about during the spectacular tenure of Gustav Mahler as Generalintendant of the Court Opera. This magnificent conductor and composer recognized in Strauss's finer works not only the essence of what is truly Viennese, and therefore deserving of recognition by Vienna's greatest musical theater, but also something more important—a quality of genius worthy of measure against other operas presented in the Imperial Opera. Mahler's production of *Die Fledermaus,* so history tells us, set a standard for the performance of this work approximated only by such masters of the musical stage as Bruno Walter and Max Reinhardt.

Of *Ritter Pasman,* only a few ballet sequences caught the public's fancy; even these are forgotten today.

It was during these years that a deep friendship grew and strengthened between Strauss and Brahms, brought about to some extent by the homelike atmosphere which Adele infused into the Igelgasse palace and the country villas which Strauss possessed. Between the Hamburg and Vienna musician (the former himself virtually a Viennese in his later years) there existed the greatest possible respect. The story of Brahms and the autograph fan of Alice Strauss, related elsewhere in these pages, is a classic. Less known is Brahms' comment to a friend recently arrived from Hamburg. "First of all," he said, "you must go to the Volksgarten on Friday evening, where Johann Strauss will conduct his waltzes. *There* is a master of the orchestra; such a master that one never loses a single tone of whatever instrument!" His admiration was such that Geiringer states, in his biography of Brahms, that the master never missed a performance of *Die Fledermaus* if he could help it.

Brahms, conscious of the occasionally opaque pages in his orchestral works, could not fail to be impressed by the lucidity of the Strauss pen. A true classicist among the Romantics, especially in his adherence to form and the traditional orchestra, Brahms revered Mozart among composers, a reverence shared by Strauss. Brahms felt that he had found a counterpart to Mozart's limpid orchestral technique in the writing of the Waltz King. Those who have exhaustively compared *Die Fledermaus* with *Figaro* will appreciate the reasons for Brahms' belief.

Photographs exist of Brahms and Strauss in the garden of the Bad Ischl villa. Here are two old men, each a great master of music, the one the antithesis of the other, each deeply respectful of the other's worth. One is now no longer stocky; he is definitely paunchy, with a patriarchal beard halfway down his chest. One can almost visualize the music in the man—solid, real, and with an epic quality; gruff and brusque, yet full of warmth and overflowing with inner sentiment.

The other had not greatly changed; indeed, he resembles more the Strauss of the late '40's than he does the Strauss of the '70's. Gone are the Dundreary whiskers that flamed in profusion from his cheeks; all that remains is a well-waxed and groomed mustache, not unlike that which he sported in his early years before the public. Neither in the mustache nor in the generous mane of hair can one find a single strand of silver—Strauss would never have been so untrue to his music and to his Vienna. They wished him to remain young, and remain young he did. During his Golden Jubilee, in 1894, the correspondent of an English newspaper wrote home, "The pains he takes to remain the Johann Strauss of yore, with jet-black hair and faultlessly black mustache, is not vanity but a compliment to the Viennese."

The deep friendship between the two composers resulted in a waltz dedicated to Brahms, a tribute from the butterfly to the bear. Thoroughly mature Strauss, expertly contrived, it nonetheless lacks that intangible catalyst which makes his great works immortal. This is the *Seid Umschlungen, Millionen!,* Op. 443. The title is derived from the text to Schiller's *Ode to Joy,* which Beethoven made immortal in his *Ninth Symphony.* It was, therefore, a compliment to the man whose *First Symphony* had been lightly, inappropriately, and yet not uncomplimentarily, called "Beethoven's Tenth."

A waltz more in the usual vein is the next opus, *Märchen aus dem Orient,* dedicated to the Sultan Abdul Hamid of Persia. Here is the familiar style, perhaps more pleasing to an oriental potentate with limited knowledge of occidental music. It is an amazing page, breathing again the spirit of the young Strauss of yesteryear, enamored of Olga Smirnitzki. It hardly seems the product of a septuagenarian. It has youth, passion, abandon. It is another *Serail-Tänze,* written for a Sultan, with the finesse of maturity added to the enthusiasm and imagination of youth.

Age had not altered Strauss's awareness of the life about him. As in years past he had brought forth the *Telegrafische Depeschen,* so did he now write a *Durchs Telephon Polka,* Op. 439. Acknowledegment of Vienna's new position as a leading commercial and industrial city appears in his *Gross Wien Waltzes,* Op. 440. Another significant title occurs in Op. 449—the *Neue Pizzicato Polka.* The first and more widely known *Pizzicato Polka* stemmed from a happier period. For this composition, without opus number, was the joint product of collaboration between Schani and his brother Pepi. Whatever the difficulties and misunderstandings between Johann and Eduard—and they were legion—there was never anything but the closest communion between Johann and Josef. This composition, one of four which these two brothers wrote jointly, is the only one which is generally known. Its piquant melody and intriguing rhythms are so delicious, and yet so distinguished, that the work is perhaps the finest example of the polka form. It is, of course, danceable, but is still properly a concert work:

The three compositions by the two brothers which followed *Pizzicato* consist of two quadrilles and a *Vaterländischer March*. There are also two works which resulted from the joint efforts of all three brothers: *Schützen Quadrille,* and *Trifolien Waltzes.* This last title is an allusion to the triumvirate of composers.

Ritter Pasman was succeeded by *Fürstin Ninetta,* as poor a story as anything Strauss had previously misguidedly attempted. Yet it had its success, which was enhanced at the first performance at the Theater-an-der-Wien on January 10th, 1893, by the attendance of so august a personage as the Emperor himself. The stage mistress presented herself at the Imperial Box, and in a most distracted manner inquired whether His Imperial Majesty proposed to stay for any length of time, and did he prefer to have her send for Strauss immediately? Franz-Josef replied that he had no intention of leaving, nor did he; he remained through to the end. When Strauss came to pay his respects after the performance, the old monarch said, "Really, I did not wish to leave—I have enjoyed myself tremendously. It is strange—your music ages as little as you do. You have not changed at all, although it is many years now that I have known you. I must felicitate you on your opera." Layman though the Emperor was, he had placed his finger unerringly upon the reason for the operetta's even seasonal success when he said, "Your music ages as little as you do." Strauss's operettas have disappeared only because of lack of substance in the libretti.

Jabuka followed *Fürstin Ninetta* at the Theater-an-der-Wien, opening October 12th, 1894. It gained momentary prominence because the date of its opening coincided with the Strauss Jubilee. It was during the course of this famous celebration that Franz-Josef is reputed to have said to Strauss, "It is you who are the true Emperor of Austria-Hungary!" Flattering words, tailored for the occasion, they may also have sprung spontaneously from a heart embittered by a half-century of internal strife, national and personal.

OCTOBER 12th, 1894. As Strauss looked down the long corridor of the years to that day, exactly fifty years before, when posters announcing his first concert were displayed, he must have felt aged and sad indeed. When age looks backward on its youth, it must do so with regret. When the old age of Strauss looked back on the youth of Strauss, it was sadder still. For Strauss was, of necessity, the personification of youth—his music vibrates with it—and he must have bitterly resented the "whips and scorns of Time" which left his eternally youthful spirit clothed in the febrile framework of age.

Strauss's day was, however, not yet done. *Jabuka* had its moment, and gave way to his sixteenth and penultimate stage work, *Waldmeister*. Weaker in story, if possible, than even its immediate predecessors, it was an unsuitable choice. Essentially a *petit-bourgeois* plot, its locale a small village whose inhabitants become mysteriously inebriated, it fitted Strauss's patrician melodies poorly. A Leo Fall, or another composer of humbler style, might have done better with it, for this very reason. It is probable that Strauss was attracted to the plot by his success with the intoxication scenes from *Die Fledermaus*. What he did not consider was that the intoxication of *Die Fledermaus* is that of the *haut monde* on an Elysian plane, whereas that of *Waldmeister* is little more than the common drunkeness of a village brawl. *Waldmeister* opened on December 14th, 1895, at the Theater-an-der-Wien. Like the operettas which immediately preceded it, and the final operetta which followed, it had a seasonal success. It was the success of novelty, not that of merit. Yet one could hardly ask for lovelier music, and were the score to be adapted by competent hands to a book of merit today, *Waldmeister* could still know the acclaim it never had.

Die Göttin der Vernünft was Strauss's last bow on the lyric stage. It would be pleasant to record that with his ultimate stage work he produced another great comic opera; unfortunately, nothing could be further from the truth. If anything, this was the weakest link in the entire chain. The tunes were still young, still fresh, still spontaneously gay. But youth and gaiety do not suit a story of tumbrils, guillotines, and the other paraphernalia of the French Revolution. It was once more the old story of music mismated to plot.

This is indeed the one great artistic failing of Strauss—the great flaw in a musician whose taste was otherwise impeccable. One can excuse it by saying that such haphazard selection of libretti was commonplace in that day (as indeed it was). But such an excuse places Strauss on a level with all his contemporaries—Lortzing, von Suppé, Millöcker and the others—whereas an analysis of his stage works shows, on the musical side, a sense of balance, a craftsmanship, which raises him to heights to which his colleagues and imitators never even aspired. Indeed, in the matter of scoring alone, it is not heresy to compare his clear-toned scores to the elegant Eighteenth Century school of Mozart.

Die Göttin der Vernünft was first heard on March 13th, 1897, at the Theater-an-der-Wien. Much has been made of the fact that Johannes Brahms, gravely ill, attended a concert by the Vienna Philharmonic on March 7th of that year. Those who were present describe Brahms as shrunken, feeble, and suffering acutely from the cancer which was rapidly ending his life. That concert has often been described as the last public appearance which he made, but this is not correct. He made still another, for he was in a box throughout the entire opening performance of Strauss's last operetta. His attendants tried to persuade him to leave, but nothing would induce him to do so until the last curtain had fallen, Strauss had taken his bows on the stage, and had then paid him a visit in his box. It was, so far as is known, the last meeting of the two old friends. Brahms died three weeks later, on April 3rd, 1897.

Strauss now felt increasingly the weight of his advancing years. Yet such was the spirit of the man that he would not retire, but continued to compose. The works from this period which have reached his catalogue are few, and their titles glance nostalgically towards the past. Typical is the *Klänge aus der Raimundzeit,* Op. 479.

It was Hanslick who provided the impetus for Strauss's final major work. Remembering the ballet sequence of *Ritter Pasman,* he urged Strauss to write a work for the Imperial Ballet. At once the question of a story arose. Strauss was wary of approaching a form which would be completely new to him without a story that would not only be choreographically suitable, but would also suit his warm, sentimental style. Finally it was decided to open a public contest for the story, and a board of judges was selected which included Hanslick, Strauss and Gustav Mahler. Mahler was equally eager for a Strauss ballet; perhaps he felt that, freed from tasteless texts and stupid libretti, Strauss's music would be even more striking than in a *Die Fledermaus.*

When the stories submitted were examined, the prize went to a piece called *Aschenbrödel (Cinderella)*, a modernization of the classic story. It had been anonymously submitted, and the prize money was collected by an attorney; rumor at once had it that the story was the work of an Austrian Archduke. Strauss liked the book, and entertained great hopes for it, but one cannot lay great faith in his opinion. Significantly, Mahler was considerably less optimistic, and rightly so. A story similar to that which the Ballet Russe de Monte Carlo set to his music in *Le Beau Danube Bleu* would have been preferable. His music demands a story which scintillates; a saccharine romance of the naïve simplicity of Cinderella was not for him. Strauss set aside an orchestral fantasia on which he had been working, which he had tentatively named *Traumbilder,* and prepared to begin work on the new ballet.

He never finished it. On May 22nd, 1899, he conducted the Overture to an afternoon performance of *Die Fledermaus,* and then found himself so bathed in perspiration that he had to relinquish the baton to an assistant and leave the theater. He returned to the Iglegasse, and found awaiting him Bösendorfer, the famous Viennese piano manufacturer, and Leschetitzky, the internationally-known piano teacher; they had come to play cards with him. It was a lovely, warm afternoon, but Strauss, feeling chilled, insisted on playing indoors. When his friends had gone, he retired, feeling still somewhat indisposed, to his study, where he nonetheless insisted on orchestrating some scenes of *Aschenbrödel* until the early hours of the morning. Two days later, in the Prater, he was stopped for his autograph by a number of young people, and stood amongst them, chatting pleasantly, oblivious to the chill breeze which came flowing down from the mountains. He was taken with a cold, and the next day he was confined to his bed. Acute bronchial catarrh set in, and this developed into double pneumonia. Doctors and specialists were called in; every expert care was given, but it was obvious that a crisis must develop. On the night of June 1st, he suddenly sat up in bed and sang the song which his old teacher, Josef Drexler, had written for Raimund's *Maiden from the Fairy World*:

> "Too soon its glory will dissolve in night!
> Brother dear, O brother dear!
> Our parting is so near, so near!"

On the night of June 3rd, his mind cleared, and he woke to find Adele at his bedside. She said to him, "Sleep, my dear." "Oh, that I shall, whatever happens," he replied. Early in the afternoon, his face marked with the faintest trace of a smile, he passed away.

It was an hour later when Vienna heard the news. Eduard Kremser was conducting the Strauss Orchestra in the Volksgarten. They were playing a lively galop when a messenger pressed into his hand a note bearing word of the master's

death. Abruptly, he stopped the orchestra, and without announcement began the haunting, nostalgic introduction to
An der schönen, blauen Donau, muted and pianissimo. Everyone understood—all Vienna knew of Strauss's illness. Heads
bowed, the audience paid homage to the Waltz King with
their tears.

On June 6th, 1899, Johann Strauss was buried in the
Central Cemetery in Vienna. The funeral began early in the
afternoon from the Igelgasse palace. It took a course which
led past all those musical centers over which Strauss had
reigned for years: the Theater-an-der-Wien, the Hofoperntheater, the Musikvereinsaal, and those great dance halls
which still remained. Thousands of people lined its passage.
Describing the scene, which he witnessed as a child, H. E.
Jacob said, "It was as if the gardens of Vienna were being
carried out to the Central Cemetery."

Aware of it or not, Vienna had double reason to mourn;
it was bidding adieu not only to one of its greatest and most
characteristic geniuses, but to an entire epoch as well. The
Strauss reign was ending. Josef had died; Eduard might be
a gifted conductor, but his talents in composition were inferior to those of younger men, led by Franz Lehár. The
younger composers were writing music in the Viennese tradition, it is true, but music tinged with cynicism. Gone were
the gay old days of pink champagne, gone was the era of
Hapsburg brilliance, gone in fact was the Romantic Era. It
was a century that died, not a man.

A few days after the funeral, the Gesellschaft der Musikfreunde gave a memorial performance of Brahms' *Deutsches
Requiem* in Strauss's honor.

There was but one discordant note—the much-remarked-
upon absence of the widow of Josef Strauss. Because no thematic material was found among Josef's effects after his death,

Eduard had foolishly and jealously accused Johann (fortunately in private) of having pilfered his brother's store of melodies. Did Karoline Strauss believe this? It would have been most foolish. What could such an accusation mean, leveled against a man who had proven, long before Josef's death, that he was a bottomless well of melody, when the accusation stemmed from a man who had to pilfer regularly from other composers for his melodic material? Surely it was evident that this accusation was jealously founded, especially when one considers that the styles of the two brothers were quite different.

A few years later, the famous Strauss memorial was erected in the Stadtpark, near the little bandstand which has so often resounded to his melodies. This was brought about by the efforts of a committee headed, in Vienna, by Princess Rosa Croy-Sternberg, Rudolf Ritter von Lewicki, Max Kalbeck, Siegfried Löwy, and Felix Weingartner, and, in England, by Professor Granville Bantock, Sir Edward Elgar, and Sir Alexander Mackenzie. But no memorial of stone and bronze can compare with his music in perpetuating the world fame of Johann Strauss, the Waltz King.

BOOK III

THE END
OF A DYNASTY

1

JOSEF STRAUSS

IF THE younger Johann Strauss sorely taxed the hairtrigger patience of his stubborn father in his own stubborn determination to become a professional musician, young Josef was his father's delight in his ready acquiescence to all that the elder Johann wished for him.

It was not an act of passive submission; Pepi was by nature shy and retiring. The merciless limelight of public acclaim which beat upon his father repelled him, and made him satisfied to accede to the elder Strauss's wish that he study for some other profession. Although he never acquired Johann's proficiency as a violinist, and was always more at ease on a piano bench, he loved music with equal passion, and was every bit as fine a musician as his brother. But whereas Schani spent every waking moment in dreams of his own orchestra, Pepi's retiring nature led him to consider music as an art for home enjoyment. He did not consider the atmosphere of the concert hall conducive to true musical enjoyment, either from the standpoint of the performer or of the listener. He was known to have made many disparaging remarks about conductors in general and dance conductors in particular, with especial emphasis on the ebb-state of their mental level.

The Revolution of 1848 found Pepi still a student at the Wiener Hoch-Schule; he left school to join a student regiment and shoulder a gun. His uniform, in which he took great pride, nearly caused the death of his mother, his younger brother and his sisters. All were at home when Jellacic's victorious army of Poles, loaned to the Austrian Emperor by the Czar, entered Vienna and began to search homes for rebels. The Hirschenhaus received a visit in due time. Had it not been for the ingenuity of Anna Strauss, who hid the uniform and two rifles (one belonged to Johann) out of sight in the chimney flue, where the search-party failed to look, all of them would have been summarily shot. When life resumed its habitual routine under Austria's new Emperor, Josef doffed his regimental dress for the more pacific uniform of a Hoch-Schule classman. He received his diploma as engineer and architect, and was thoroughly happy in his work, finding in music nothing more than a relaxing avocation.

If he repudiated music as a career for himself, he did take tremendous pride in Schani's activities. Unlike his elder brother, who slept soundly through the night preceding his début, Pepi tossed and turned, agonized with fears that his beloved brother would not be well received. Holding little Edi by the hand, he followed in the wake of those who escorted Schani home in triumph, with his heart and mind so in the stars that in later years he could give no coherent account of how he made the journey from the Dommayerbau to the Hirschenhaus.

But for chance, he would never have become a professional musician. As with his father before him, Schani fell prey to the terrific pace which this life demanded of him. It was inhuman: an afternoon rehearsal, time for a little work in composition (not merely the tune itself, but the complete orchestration!), a snatch of supper, the evening's concert or ball, perhaps a bit more composition before all-too-few hours of sleep, and, *da capo,* the whole schedule over again. And into this routine must be found time to squeeze visits to publishers, interviews with the press, and the myriad other details which plague all celebrities. The amazing thing is that he withstood this grueling pace as long as he did. It finally took its toll; without warning, he suffered a complete nervous collapse. Further work in any form was out of the question. Relaxation, a change of scenery, regular meals and hours, new stimuli; these were the order of the day.

However simple it might be for a doctor to make this sane prescription, there could be no cure until Schani knew someone competent could be persuaded to take over the orchestra and lead it through the engagements which had been made for months ahead. There was only Josef to whom he could turn. Pepi was now a young man of twenty-five, soundly educated in music, and equipped, as Schani realized better than Pepi himself, with great talent in composition. Edi was still too young—only seventeen. It was one thing for his eldest brother to have made his own début at a mere nineteen. Schani had then been directing an unknown orchestra; the Strauss Orchestra was a different matter. It already knew twenty-eight years of unbroken existence, nor was it any longer a small group of less than twenty players, such as that with which both father and son had made their starts. In 1852, it counted some fifty regular players and a reserve force four times that number; as such, it was equal to most symphony orchestras of the day. In quality, discipline, and proficiency, it could hold its own with any contemporary group. Such an orchestra was not to be placed in the hands of a young man of seventeen, even though he was a Strauss. Johann and his mother knew this, as did Josef. Yet he persisted in making difficulties, even though he knew he must finally give in. He made one condition: as soon as circumstances would permit, Schani was to return to his orchestra, and Pepi to his draughtsman's board.

Josef was justly proud of his reputation as engineer and architect. Upon graduation from the Polytechnik School, he had entered the services of the Municipal Architect. Eventually he went into business for himself; the following year he built, at Trunau, a large waterworks, and he was later appointed Chief Engineer of a spinning-factory. He was an inventor as well, taking out patents on various mechanical devices, one of which was a street-cleaning machine which was put to use by the city of Vienna.

Josef was securely established in his profession. He was naturally loath to exchange this charted existence for the uncertainties of a musician's life. Finally, there existed another genuine difficulty—he was not a violinist. Today this would mean nothing; a dance leader may play any instrument, or none at all, and the symphonic conductor is expected to use only a baton. But conducting with a baton was still a novelty in that day; a practice which was still young in symphonic performance, it was unknown in the dance world. Josef's argument was that he did not have time to fill the gaps of his musical education, that he could not give up his work for six or eight months. Sometimes he would say that he did not have the talent; then Schani, lying pale against the sheets, would look up at him and comment, "You are the most talented of us all!" Human nature being what it is, it was this argument which finally won Josef over.

Together with his aunt, Josephine Weber, Schani left for the quiet resort town of Neuhaus-Cilli, and later for livelier Bad Gastein, while Pepi threw himself into studies in a headlong effort to prepare himself for his new duties. Never having attempted composition, he concentrated on this and on theory, which he studied with Professor Doleschal, one of

Schani's old teachers. He even took violin lessons from old Amon, yet Pepi never brought himself to conduct with the violin, and adopted the baton. On the stand, when he made his début on July 23rd, 1853, Josef appeared restrained in his movements, and a little *gauche*. Yet far from displeasing a public accustomed to the exuberance of the two Johanns, he attracted them by contrast. As a conductor, he was most successful, and to him must go the credit for first introducing to the dance orchestra that technique of conducting which hitherto had been limited to symphonic bodies. Even Schani, in later years, modeled his manner on the stand after that of his favorite brother, at the last abandoning the violin entirely for the baton.

If Josef made the adjustment to the role of conductor without great trouble, he rebelled for some time against composition, which came to him with extreme difficulty. There is evidence of this in his first published work, which he called *Die Ersten und Letzten* (*The First and Last*). Of the ten compositions which followed, only one is a waltz; six polkas and three quadrilles, which he no doubt found simpler to write, make up the balance. With his Opus 12, a comic hint of weakening resistance appears, for this waltz is called *Die Ersten nach dem Letzten* (*The First after the Last*). By the time Schani had recovered, Pepi had thrown himself into a life of music with complete enthusiasm, and gone were all his plans for becoming a great architect. It was Schani who first perceived it. He saw history repeating itself; once more there would be not one, but two Strausses. This pleased him, for there would not be the rivalry and coldness which had existed between father and son, but a warm understanding between two brothers who, although completely different in character, had grown up together in the bonds of a deep affection.

What ensued is almost past understanding. Suddenly, from

this diffident man who had complained about the writing of one composition, there gushed a geyser of music. One after another the compositions came, as facilely as though Josef's fecund brother had composed them. Schani had stated only the bare truth when he said that Josef's talent was great. With the elder Johann, composition had been the outgrowth of a determination to succeed in a chosen field; in the younger Johann, composition was a necessary function of life, as natural and inevitable as eating or sleeping. In Josef, composition resulted involuntarily, against the man's own intentions. Yet in the comparatively short life granted him, he wrote as much music as either his father or Eduard, and often of a quality equal to that of his more illustrious brother Johann. There has been nowhere in the Stauss family such a confusion of identities as between Johann and Josef; one continually find's Josef's *Dorfschwalben, Dynamiden, Delirien, Flattergeister* and *Sphärenklänge* Waltzes appearing on programs under his brother's name.

The photographs of Josef at this period reveal a young man bearing a closer resemblance to Liszt than he does to any member of his own family. Beneath long hair, parted in the middle and flowing down along the cheeks almost to the neck, two large and serious eyes gaze upon the world with an expression of sorrow that borders on disenchantment. Josef was the idealist par excellence; the edges of everyday life must have laid their mark upon him. He was as antisocial as a Viennese could be; a strange attitude for one of the leading citizens of a city noted for its warmth and friendliness. He was an introvert, seeking quiet and solitude, in a family of exuberant extroverts. His character finds voice in a long letter, written to his father when he was still in his teens, which reveals amazing maturity of thought. The elder Strauss at this time wished to make an army officer of him. Josef appealed to his father to recognize how unsuited he was to a military life. Two paragraphs vividly reveal the introspective nature that was Josef Strauss.

"Leave me where I am; leave me as I am. Do not seek to tear me from a life that may bring me joy, a life full of satisfaction. Do not cast me into that rough, inconstant world which destroys all feeling for humanity, a world for which I am not fitted, to which I was not born.

"I do not wish to learn to kill people, do not want to be honored by high military rank for having hunted human beings; I want to be useful to mankind as a human being, and to the State as a citizen. If I can do this, then I shall give innermost thanks and live my days in peace and happiness."*

Josef's service in the student regiment may seem at odd variance with his words. In fact it was no more than a projection of them into actual practice. Against any encroachment on the rights of free speech, thought, or action, within the bounds of democratic propriety, he was willing and ready to fight. He was the exemplary citizen, the true democrat, peaceful in all his ways, but willing to sacrifice life itself in the protection of those common rights which give life its meaning.

Josef's melancholy countenance finds its parallel in his

---

* Lassen Sie mich doch, wo ich bin; lassen Sie mich, was ich bin. Entreissen Sie mich nicht einem Leben, das mir mannigfältige Freuden bringen kann, einem Leben voll Zufriedenheit, einem Stande, der auch die Achtung sich gewinnen macht. Stossen Sie mich nicht in jenes unstäte, rauhe, allen Sinn für Menschliche zerstörende Treiben hinaus, zu dem ich nicht tauge, zu dem ich nicht geboren bin.

Ich will nicht Menschen tödten lernen, will nicht durch Jädgemachen auf Menschleben ausgezeichnet werden mit einem militärisch höheren Rang, ich will den Menschen nützen als Mensch und dem Staat als Bürger. Kann ich das, dann sagt mir mein Inneres Dank dafür und ich werde in Ruhe meine Tage verleben und glücklich sein.

music. Where his father and brother wrote music of incomparable lightness and gaiety, shot through and through with sunlight and laughter, Josef wrote music in a minor key. There are moments when his music could be as cheerful as anything by the Johanns, as in *Dorfschwalben,* but in the main it reflects his dark and reticent nature.

Josef married in 1857, six years before Schani's marriage to Jetty in 1863. His bride was Karoline Pruckmayr, a Viennese girl of middle-class family. On March 27th, 1863, their only child was born—a daughter, named Karoline for her mother. This marriage was blessed with joy throughout its entire course; simple, forthright, *Bürgerlich,* and filled with a rich sense of full living. Unlike Johann, who quit the family circle to establish his own home in a fashionable suburb whose rarefied air knew nothing of the *bonhommie* of the Hirschenhaus, Josef brought his bride to that old building, taking an apartment next to that which his mother still maintained.

One of the difficulties facing a biographer of Josef Strauss is the paucity of interesting material dealing with his life. It has been said that in biography the happiest life is the dullest. So with Josef Strauss; what remains today is largely the bare statement of a life lived at an even tenor, and a straightforward chronicle of the music which he composed.

2

MUSIC OF THE SPHERES

Dorfschwalben aus Österreich is to Josef what *An der schön-en, blauen Donau* is to Johann. Both are atmospheric impres-sions of the Austria the brothers loved so deeply, and each marks the beginning of the best period in its composer's life.

The introductory measures to *Dorfschwalben* are of a pas-toral character, a *mise-en-scène*. With the first waltz, the swallows appear, winging their way in a characteristic swoop-ing flight which the music suggests superbly:

Then, as happens when swallows fly low between build-ings and trees, the flight becomes erratic; the birds turn and flash in and out through sunlight and shade. Note the swooping effect of the last three notes of this phrase, marked "A," and the chirruping effect of the grace notes which be-gin it:

The second half of the first waltz introduces a Ländler, that primitive form of the elegant waltz, as a delineation of the village itself:

The swallows reappear in the opening of the second waltz, flitting rapidly up and down in their peculiarly rhythmic flight:

The third waltz introduces a second Ländler, heavily accented on the first beat. The fourth is a melody in broken thirds, such as is typical of Tyrolean folk tunes. A fifth waltz follows, with prominent *arpeggios,* and then the *coda* begins, recapitulating the waltzes and effecting a return to the introductory measures as a means of rounding off the whole.

Another fine waltz appeared shortly after *Dorfschwalben.* Although not the equal of its predecessor, it is still insufficiently known today. This is the *Geheimne Anziehungskräfte,* more simply known as the *Dynamiden Waltzes,* Op. 173. With its tender opening melody, delicate and without the sensuality that lies in Johann's themes, it is reminiscent of Schubert—indeed, Josef has been termed "the Schubert of the Waltz." His long, beautifully balanced melodies are un-

like any which his father or Eduard wrote, nor are they often like Johann's; they contain an elegiac strain which is
unique.

One of Josef's most magical scores is that to the *Sphärenklänge,* Op. 235. It is quite unlike any other set of waltzes,
and to its individual tones no better title could have been fitted. It opens with an introduction for harp and *tremolo*
strings, *lento.* The harp continues its liquid *arpeggios* into the
first waltz, while the strings lead with the theme:

A variation is heard, in the manner of Johann's *Morgenblätter* and *Accelerationen:*

A lively passage, *staccato,* and then the second waltz appears. In it is this gay moment, as lively as anything by Johann:

Then the third waltz, a typical Strauss theme, common to all the family:

The fourth waltz offers this amazing and wonderful thought, almost a variation on the first waltz:

The usual recapitulation completes the work.

THE *Aquarellen Waltzes*, Op. 258, are yet another of Josef Strauss's fine waltz sets. The introduction, of filmy tex-ture, and reminiscent of Johann's opening measures to *Wo die Zitronen blüh'n*, gives way to an energetic, exuberant waltz, suggesting the styles of the elder Johann and Eduard; this, in turn, is replaced by the tender melody whose uptwists of phrasing cast yet another glance at Johann. But the lan-guorous waltz which follows, with its subtle tinge of melan-choly, could belong only to Josef. Even the succeeding gay moments are solely his; their style partakes almost of the bal-let. Exclusively Josef's, too, is the handling in waltz-time of the melody of the introduction. The waltzes close with a final return of the opening waltz-theme, and an enlarged working of the introduction.

It was at this time that Anna Strauss passed away. Although Johann was grief-stricken, it was still Josef who felt her loss most keenly. Johann had basked in the adulation of the successful, eldest child; Josef, less glamorous, quiet and retiring, almost taken for granted by his mother, had loved her the more deeply, perhaps, in part, because of her calm acceptance of him, certainly because of the ties which had bound them together in the Hirschenhaus. Only once had he been near to leaving the old building; this was when he was making his last Russian tour. At the height of the tour, Eduard, in a moment of pique because he had never had an opportunity to take the orchestra through Russia, suddenly decided to make a tour of his own, leaving unfulfilled the engagements which the Strausses had made in Vienna, and imperiling Josef's venture by establishing competition against it from within. It was under these circumstances that Josef wrote his wife that she was to leave the Hirschenhaus, and make a home for them elsewhere, unless Eduard immediately abandoned his plan. Nervous and hypersensitive like his father, Josef had had enough of the internal strife in which Eduard had for so long been the principal protagonist. Although he was extremely fond of his younger brother, he felt he could no longer endure the petty squabbles which Eduard constantly fostered. At the insistence of Johann and Karoline, Eduard finally capitulated, and Josef's threatened move never took place. . . .

ON APRIL 17th, 1870, Josef Strauss gave his final concert of the season in Vienna in the hall of the Gesellschaft der Musikfreunde, preparatory to his departure for a tour of Poland. He gave the following program:

Overture to the Opera *Jeanne d'Arc*	BALFE
Pro und Contra, Polka	E. STRAUSS
Nilflüten, Waltzes	JOS. STRAUSS
Romance and Chorus from *L' Africana*	MEYERBEER
Die Emanzipierte, Polka-Mazurka	JOS. STRAUSS
Aria from the *Missa Solemnis*	ROSSINI
Neu Wien, Waltzes	JOH. STRAUSS II
Egyptischer Marsch	JOH. STRAUSS II
Frauenwürde, Waltzes	JOS. STRAUSS
Banditten, Quadrille	E. STRAUSS
Moment Musical	SCHUBERT
Heitere Mut, Polka-Française	JOS. STRAUSS
Stempelfrei, Polka-Française	E. STRAUSS

Fatigued, Josef bade the enthusiastic audience farewell. Arrived in Warsaw, difficulties arose at once. A number of the musicians had been delayed and could not enter Poland to take part in the concert. Josef wired in haste for replacements, culled from the list of musicians which the Strausses kept under contract. These men arrived promptly, and with extra rehearsals it was possible to begin the concerts on the appointed day. For three days, all went well.

During the rehearsals for the fourth concert, a violinist failed repeatedly to make his entrance in a certain passage correctly. After several attempts, during which Josef's nerves seemed to be roused to an unusual state of tension, it was decided to cut the passage and effect an entrance further on. During the concert, the violinist forgot the change and threw his section into confusion; some attempted to follow his lead, others followed instructions and made the later entrance. Unable to control the growing confusion, and seemingly without proper control over himself, Josef fainted and, rolling across the platform, fell down a short flight of steps into the hall. Bleeding profusely from nose and mouth, and with a bad wound in the back of his head, he was pronounced to be suffering from a severe concussion. Johann immediately entrained for Warsaw. When he arrived, Josef was fully conscious, but still in danger, although a gradual improvement had begun to take place.

Meanwhile a new contract had been drawn up on July 9th, whereby Johann and Josef together leased the Schweizertals from Wlodowsky, the proprietor, until the first of September, for the sum of three thousand rubles. There was at no time any thought that Josef himself would be sufficiently recovered to conduct; his condition, which had shown marked improvement after the first shock, was retrogressing, and the doctors now feared that some as yet undetermined ailment was responsible for his prostration.

At first Johann conducted in his brother's stead. But his anxiety and his other duties made it impossible for him to continue, and he was succeeded first by Gustav Carlberg, and later by Philip Fahrbach, who directed the concerts until the close of the Warsaw engagement. Meanwhile, laboring under great difficulties, for travel in 1870 was not the simple matter of railroad and airline timetables which it is today, Johann and Karoline brought the now-dying Josef back to Vienna.

When he was examined by a trio of specialists, their concerted opinion was that his condition was the result of the bursting of an old brain tumor. There was nothing they could do, no hope that they could give. A few days later, on July 22nd, Josef found relief from his torture, and breathed his last. He was only forty-three years old—two years younger than his father had been when he died in 1849.

A strange legend grew out of his death. As he lay ill in Warsaw, it was rumored that he had been brutally beaten by

Cossack officers for having refused to play a composition they had requested. This story, still current today, has persisted because it is founded on a half-truth. As Josef was conducting in the Schweizertals, four Russian lieutenants, each with a lively *demimondaine* on his arm, were attempting to enter the hall through the adjoining garden. Having no tickets, they sought to force an entrance. Since the concert had already begun, the ticket collector, Strouza, refused them admittance, and warned that he would call the police if they were not quiet. Incensed, one of the lieutenants struck Strouza over the head with his sword. When the police arrived, the officers and their friends had escaped, and Strouza was lying in a pool of blood.

The coincidence between the names Strauss and Strouza, the similarity between their wounds, and inaccurate newspaper reporting, gave rise to the story which has persisted to this day. It was lent credence by a population filled with hatred for their Russian overlords. The Russian nobility, for years the hosts and staunch friends of the Strausses during their Russian tours, found themselves in a most embarrassing situation. The Grand Duke Constantine, the Governor of Poland, was most distressed of all—a noted amateur musician, he had even, on occasion, played in the Strauss Orchestra at Pavlovsk under Johann's baton. At the express request of the Grand Duke and Johann, the Austrian Consul General in Warsaw officially denied the veracity of the rumors, but they would not die. The temper of oppressed peoples, Polish and Russian, saw to that.

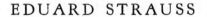

3

EDUARD STRAUSS

LIKE Johann, Eduard had been drawn to music from his earliest days, but whereas Johann was impelled by an irresistible creative urge, Eduard was attracted by the fame and glamor attached to the position of conductor of so famous an orchestra as that of his illustrious brother. Again, whereas Johann, at the first opportunity, withdrew from regular direction of the orchestra in order to compose, Eduard took to writing with little grace. He wrote because he had to; because original compositions were demanded of a dance orchestra leader by the waltzing world of the day, as a measure of his ability. Melody was not native to him, and although he wrote some music of genuine loveliness, such as his *Doctrinen Waltzes,* he was often compelled to resort to the timeworn device of drawing upon other men's works for melodic material. When we raise a hue and cry today because our dance music is pilfered from Chopin, Tchaikovsky, Grieg or Schubert, we forget that a precedent had been set well over a century ago. Waltz composers before Lanner were adapting the tunes of Mozart, Haydn, and even Lully and Rameau, to waltz rhythm. Of the first twenty-five of Eduard's published works, no fewer than six are based upon the melodies of other composers. Typical are the *Liederkranz Quadrille,* Op. 23, on melodies from Schubert's songs, and the *Vie Parisienne Quadrille,* Op. 24, on themes from Offenbach's operetta.

In the years of their youth, Josef's influence upon Eduard is not to be underestimated. Josef, firm in his distaste for the adulation given waltz conductors, was able to persuade his young brother to set aside all thought of a musical career. It was at first decided, therefore, that Edi would train for the diplomatic service. There could hardly have been a better choice for him, and, had he chosen this field, he would surely have been most successful. Tactful, suave, gifted with that rare ability to smooth over the most difficult moments, and persuasive to an unusual degree, he would have made a mark in the world of international diplomacy. As it was, these traits stood him in good stead when he came to direct the Strauss Orchestra, for he was able to draw more from the men than his brothers or his father before him.

At the Gymnasium and later at the Hoch-Schule, he followed a course of study which was designed to prepare him for his chosen career. As with Josef, whose ideas he slavishly copied, music became for him an important avocation. He developed into an excellent pianist, and even studied harp with Zamara.

Two events diverted him from the diplomatic service. The first was Schani's illness, which occasioned a complete change in Josef's attitude towards music. As a result, the love of music which Eduard felt in common with his whole family, no longer repressed, led him to devote himself exclusively to the art. The second event was Schani's retirement from the orchestra in favor of Josef. This meant that someone else would have to share the duties of direction, which were now too arduous for one man. Eduard prepared himself for this by studying composition with Gottfried von Preyer.

His training completed, Eduard made his début as conductor of one of the Strauss orchestras on February 5th, 1859, appearing for the first time in the Dianasaal. Two other orchestras played in the same hall that night, alternating with one another, one under Johann, the other under Josef. As the final work of the evening, all three orchestras joined in playing a galop, simultaneously.

It was apparent from the first that in Eduard the orchestra had found its natural leader. Had Johann tried, he might have achieved more than his young brother, for the men worshiped his genius and perceived the lack of it in Eduard. The younger man, conscious of the limitations of his creative gifts, bent his energies to conducting. With Johann, the orchestra was of importance only because of its earning power, which had made it, for a long time, the main support of the family, and because it was the medium whereby the world might hear his compositions. With Eduard, the orchestra was *le tout pour tout;* all began and ended with it, and compositions were merely the means of allowing it to be heard.

Eduard's popularity with the Viennese rivaled that of Johann, and even surpassed that of the somber Josef before his death. Indeed, his popularity grew to such proportions that Johann repeatedly introduced himself to strangers by saying, "I am Edi's brother." As Johann withdrew from public appearances, the burden of directing the orchestra after Josef's death rested exclusively with Eduard. It was he whom the Viennese knew best as conductor in the last three decades of the Nineteenth Century, but their deepest affection was still reserved for their never-aging Johann. It was this unvoiced preference for Johann, the ten-year difference in age between the brothers, and the galling knowledge that in the last analysis it was Schani who was the greatest, that made Eduard so unnaturally envious.

Josef's death brought Eduard yet another honor, for the post of Königlich und Kaiserlich Hofballmusikdirektor again became vacant. In one sense, it carried a special honor, for

Eduard was the fourth Strauss to be given this mark of distinction. Since Lanner's death, it had passed directly from one member of the Strauss family to the next. No wonder that the Viennese said that the Strausses ruled Austria-Hungary jointly with the Hapsburgs!

Under Eduard's persuasive but inexorable training, the orchestra reached a level of proficiency which it had never previously known. Composers and critics of the time commented on its amazing virtuosity. The music critic of the *Berliner Börse-Kurrier* compared the Berlin Philharmonic to the Strauss Orchestra, to the latter's advantage. Meyerbeer was lavish in his praise, as was Richard Wagner. Praise from Wagner was especially significant, for he was one of the first of the modern dynasty of conductors; it was he who first established many of the fundamentals by which the modern conductor is guided. Whatever his fantastic instructions on how to conduct some works, there is no question but that, like Berlioz, he exerted a tremendous influence on the performance of symphonic music as we hear it today.

It was in 1873 that the ill will between the two brothers, engendered solely by Eduard's jealousy, flared for the first time into open conflict. This was provoked by the question of what orchestras were to be used in the concerts of the Vienna International Exhibition. Eduard knew that all musical honors would devolve upon Johann, and he hoped that the musical directorate of the Exhibition (which included Johann) would engage the Strauss Orchestra for Johann to conduct. Eduard was enraged that, when the Langenbach Orchestra was selected, Johann made little or no effort to influence a change in favor of his own musicians. Eduard's anger was purely selfish. Of course, the engagement of the orchestra would have meant an increase in the family's income, but this was merely the excuse for Eduard's spleen;

his real motive was that he knew Johann had no intention of directing all the scheduled concerts. Therefore, if the Strauss Orchestra were engaged, Eduard would automatically have a prominent part in the concerts.

Johann constantly fought this ill will. For years he denied its existence, and it was not until he was an old man that he finally mentioned it in a letter. "You always look on the gloomy side of things—you are ever thinking that I mean to harm you. Will you finally stop letting off steam in this foolish way—how old must you be before you can understand that your brother is not your enemy? You are old—I am ten years older; if we live for a thousand years, you will ever have some cause for complaint. At times our relationship has been endangered by your personal ambition, and still I have never denied the fraternal feeling which I have always had for you. *Au fond du coeur,* I have always remained the same to you as I was at the start of your musical career. Therefore, dear Eduard, put an end to these reproaches that I have acted in an unfraternal manner. If you care to think very far back, you will change your mind."

If Eduard chewed his fingernails in '72 and '73 because of Johann's fabulous success on his American tour, and his important position at the Exhibition, he found an opportunity to sate his vanity and ambition in 1885, when he brought the Strauss Orchestra to London to direct the musical activities at the South Kensington Exposition. During the course of his duties there, he was introduced to Queen Victoria. Faced with this handsome, dynamic man, the aging Queen recalled that distant day when his father had officiated at her Coronation festivities. "You remind me of your father," she said. "It seems like yesterday that he played at my Coronation Ball. I remember the pieces; could you play some of them?"

Honors and decorations from many lands came to him; he was Commander, Knight, and Officer of at least a dozen orders of the different sovereigns of Europe.

Queen Victoria had not been wrong when she said that Eduard reminded her of his father. The two were much alike in temperament; this is reflected in their music. It is typified in the younger man's *Doctrinen Waltzes,* Op. 79, which resembles the father's music in a number of respects, notably in the characteristic rhythm of the first waltz. Like the waltzes of the father, it is jerky and short-breathed, its thematic material thinly related to that which follows. It is a waltz of charm and considerable grace, but it never aspires to that integrated homogeneity which elevates the best waltzes of Johann from the ballroom to the concert hall.

EDUARD's marriage in 1864 gave him two sons. His first-born he named Johann, in memory of his father; the second, Josef, for his brother, then still alive. Johann III, the selfsame Johann who directed the various recordings listed at the end of this book, was born on February 16th, 1866. His younger brother, Josef II, who was born two and a half years later, on September 20th, 1868, took little part in the world of music.

Eduard's family life was not unlike that of the first Johann, especially with regard to his sons. Differences were frequent, and grew more violent with the passing years, as both sons showed an interest in music. With the example of his own father before him, it is strange that Eduard, for the third time in Strauss history, should have opposed a musical life for his sons. Alter the course of musical events, he could not. One son made no name in music, perhaps because of his father's efforts, but the other had his way. . . .

{ 234 }

It SHOULD NOT be assumed that the concerts of the Strauss
Orchestra were devoted only to the compositions of the
Strausses. From the first, long ago in the days of Johann the
Elder, the concerts of the orchestra (a different matter from
dance soirées) were noted for the inclusion of music by von
Weber, Beethoven, Mozart, Gluck—even Bach. It should
be remembered that the first performance in Vienna of Wagner's "impossible" music to *Tristan und Isolde* was at a
Strauss Orchestra Volksgarten concert under Johann II. Under Johann II, Josef and Eduard, these concerts retained the
music of the old masters, and added to them many of the
works of the great Romantics. A typical program is this one,
given in Munich under Eduard:

I

Overture to the opera *If I Were King*	ADAM
Doctrinen Waltzes, Op. 79	E. STRAUSS
Suite from the opera *Carmen*	BIZET
Wildfeuer Polka	J. STRAUSS II

II

Operetta Potpourri	SCHMID
On Wings of Song—arr. E. Strauss	MENDELSSOHN
Serenade	SCHUBERT
G'schichten aus dem Wiener Wald—Waltzes	
	J. STRAUSS II

III

Les Colombes—Entr'Acte	GOUNOD
Alpenrose—Polka-Mazurka	JOS. STRAUSS
Goldelse—Gavotte—arr. E. Strauss	FUCHS
Mit Dampf!—Schnellpolka	E. STRAUSS

It was at this time that the phonograph first entered the history of the Strausses. During a visit to Europe, in the course of which he had made a number of recordings on his new invention, Thomas A. Edison arrived in Vienna. What took place was recounted by the Vienna correspondent of the *London Daily News*.

"It was Mr. Edison's express desire to have some of Strauss's waltzes, as being among the most characteristic products of Vienna, recorded on the phonograph. Accordingly, the phonograph was taken to the music hall yesterday, where Herr Eduard and his famous band were waiting. When the enormous funnel had been adjusted, and everything was waiting, the band struck up *By the Beautiful, Blue Danube*. Musicians and conductor seemed to be fully aware that they were playing not only to the world, but for posterity."

This record, made under primitive conditions and on a machine totally incapable of capturing the commonest nuances of orchestral tone, would be of little interest in terms of listening pleasure today; but as an example of how the Strausses themselves played their own music, it would be of immense value.

4

AMERICA AGAIN

IT WAS in 1890 that Eduard retraced Johann's path across the Atlantic to the rich shores of America, a tour which was brought about through the efforts of Z. Blakely, a former government official who operated an artists' management bureau. Blakely had heard Johann conduct in Boston, and his enthusiasm for the Waltz King's music gave him the idea of bringing to America not only Eduard Strauss (since Johann would, under no condition, consent to another such journey), but the entire Strauss Orchestra as well. Blakely traveled to Germany in the summer of 1889, to meet Eduard and discuss arrangements for the tour.

It was not until Blakely had returned to America and it was almost time for the orchestra to set sail that obstacles appeared. The New York Musicians' Union invoked the Alien Contract Labor Law in order to keep out an orchestra which they knew to be superior to all save two or three American symphony orchestras.

The Alien Contract Labor Law had been enacted in order to keep within bounds the influx of unskilled workers; it was a fantastic insult to invoke it against the Strauss Orchestra. Fortunately, a number of prominent Americans vouched for the quality of the orchestra, and their recommendations later had a large part in voiding the claims of the Musicians' Union. Among those who wrote the State Department in this matter were Chauncey M. Depew, General William M. Sherman, the impresario P. S. Gilmore, and William Steinway.

Henri Watterman, editor of the *Louisville Journal,* published some biting editorial comment on this subject:

"The question properly is this: Are the musicians who have been trained for years by the most celebrated conductors in the world sufficiently skilled in their art to entitle them to rank with actors and lecturers of indifferent ability, who are included in the favorite class and exempt from the law? Strauss's Orchestra is world famous, and has been for more than half a century. What possible construction of the Alien Contract Labor Law could be used against such an organization?"

The State Department eventually reached the only logical conclusion, but its hemming and hawing was mainly responsible for Eduard's decision to employ a makeshift orchestra when he made his final visit to the United States some ten years later. The first tour began in New York in May, 1890. It led a merry chase through no less than seventy-three cities, until the exhausted players and conductor embarked for the relative sanity of Europe's shores.

During the tour, in a strange land where he would be expected to feature not only the Strauss Orchestra, but also the famous Strauss compositions, Eduard's programs contain more Strauss music than was customary in Europe. The opening Boston concert is typical:

I

Der Lustige Krieg—Overture   J. STRAUSS II
Duet from *Der Fliegende Holländer* RICHARD WAGNER
Life in America—Waltzes
(1st Performance; Dedicated to the people of America)
                                                      E. STRAUSS

Chromatique—Galop	FRANZ LISZT
The Phonograph—Polka-Française	E. STRAUSS
Suite from the opera *Carmen*	GEORGES BIZET

II

Overture to the comic opera *Die Fledermaus*

	J. STRAUSS II
Kaiserwalzer	J. STRAUSS II
Barcarolle Orientale	E. STRAUSS
Aus dem schlesischen Bergen—Waltzes	E. STRAUSS
Evening Prayer from *Maiden Songs*	REINECKE
In the Whirl—Schnellpolka	J. STRAUSS

Four thousand miles is admittedly a considerable distance, yet it is surprising that the Americans could have been so completely confused as to the proper identity and chronology of the Strausses. Only eighteen years after Johann had visited America, Blakely issued the following muddled statement in his announcement of the Strauss Orchestra's American tour: ".... the peerless Strauss Orchestra of Vienna, which has been under the leadership of the famous Strauss family of waltz-composers; Joseph the father, and Joseph, Johann and Eduard, the sons, for more than forty years." Among the other errors, the Strauss Orchestra was at this time sixty-six years old, making it older than any American orchestra.

When Eduard returned to Vienna with pockets stuffed with American dollars, he was interviewed by the leading Viennese journalists. Their articles were edited and wired to America by certain correspondents of American newspapers, who in doing so distorted Eduard's original statements to such an extent that they conveyed a meaning not at all complimentary to the United States. The resultant furor placed him in an awkward position. He certainly never made the tactless remarks of which he was accused; trained for a diplomatic career, he would never have given vent to opinions of this sort in a public interview, whether he held them or not. The tempest in a teapot became so annoying that he wrote a long letter to the *Wiener Tageblatt*, recounting his impressions of the United States. This was published on February 3rd, 1891, and was widely circulated throughout America, where it quieted the indignation. Although some of his comments sting, their barbs are tipped with painful honesty, and not with malice, as the following extracts show:

"North America can boast of many good symphony orchestras, especially that of the Philharmonic-Society under Walter Damrosch; of the Metropolitan Opera House under Anton Seidl; and also the Boston Symphony Orchestra under Nikisch.

"The middle-class throng the concert hall, where the workingmen are also represented, particularly on a Sunday, when they express their appreciation of Beethoven, as well as the taking rhythms of the waltz. In Europe this is, sad to say, not always the case. . . .

"But what would the European traveler say if our railway servants behaved as they do in America? Their method is peculiar. They are likely to ask for your ticket by a clap on the shoulder, walk with hands on their hips, hustle through the train, and even seat themselves familiarly beside the passenger.

"One cannot advise travel in Europe too strongly for Mr. Vanderbilt! . . . .

"The temperance towns are highly surprising to a foreigner. . . . the whole place seems to die out at seven o'clock, after the closing of the stores. The teetotaler visits neither the theater nor concerts, and 'twere a sin for one of his children to learn to dance.

"In some cities, such as Springfield, Ohio (not a temperance locality), the Lutheran and Calvinist ministers preached against such concerts, and the congregation listened and allowed this tyranny. . . .

"And now I have perhaps given the readers as good an idea of American life, its customs and manners, as is possible in the small space allotted me. I can only add that America is a land blest by the Almighty; full of natural beauty, and rich in its soil and commerce."

Written at a time when every returning traveler was pleased to describe America as a nation of savages, this is an analysis which is reasonably just and penetrating.

THE fast-flying years were quickly altering the scene about Eduard. He continued to compose, but it was still the end of an era. Nor were these last years happy ones. His family life had gone from bad to worse. At the insistence of his sons, his wife had invested a large part of his fortune in an enterprise which went bankrupt, almost wiping out the savings of a lifetime. Litigation followed recrimination as Eduard brought suit against his sons—it was a most tragic business.

Anxious to forget this sad affair, and in an attempt to recoup his fortune, Eduard sailed for New York on another tour, less than a year after Johann's death in June, 1899. His second tour lacked the glory of the first. He was now an old man, no longer the living embodiment of the virile music which he still conducted so expertly. He did not bring the Strauss Orchestra with him, but only a few of the leading players, recruiting the balance upon his arrival in New York. His group may have succeeded in pleasing a large part of his audience, but it failed to deceive the keen ear of Philip Hale, the famous

Boston music critic. His comments on the orchestra—not its leader—were few but caustic:

"I wonder how many of his band saw Vienna. I wonder how many of the players ever followed his beat in that gay and lighthearted city? I do not say that any of them were snatched suddenly by the manager from the garden-life of Weehawken or Hoboken, but surely the orchestra was one of the species known as 'scratch.'"

In spite of this, Eduard's tour had more than a *succès d'estime*. He was fêted and cheered, and returned to Europe tired but gladdened that the New World still remembered the Strauss Waltz despite its own ragtime. But the strain of regular concerts and the inner strife of the orchestra was too much for him to bear alone. On the return voyage, his leading players had quarreled with him, and he no longer had the strength to maintain the old discipline. It was with infinite sorrow that he disbanded the Strauss Orchestra in 1901, after seventy-seven years of uninterrupted success.

Whatever their differences in life, after Schani's death Eduard paid him a gracious and touching compliment when he published, as the fourth-from-last of his compositions, a "Bouquet of Strauss Waltzes in Chronological Order from 1844 to the Present." They were his final tribute to his great brother and his swan song to Vienna. Shortly thereafter he retired completely, a sad figure of vanished glory. He emerged from time to time through the medium of newsprint to flail anyone who made a misstatement concerning the activities or compositions of the members of his family. He lived wholly in the past, yet he refused to recognize the absolute truths of that past. He denied categorically that Johann I had ever tried to prevent his sons from becoming musicians; he even dared deny that his father had deserted his mother, although a record of the divorce proceedings was still on file in the City Hall.

Before his death, Josef had obliged Eduard to agree that whoever outlived the other would, before his own death, destroy the library of the Strauss Orchestra. The seriousness of this promise can be understood only when it is remembered that the Strauss works were generally published as piano solos, the orchestral versions in almost every instance existing only in manuscript form. This promise had been preying on Eduard's mind for a long time; feeling himself at the end of his years, he believed that he must fulfill the promise he had made his brother. In September of 1907, Eduard asked a manufacturer of stoves for permission to burn a quantity of "waste paper." A date was set for October 22nd. Precisely at two in the afternoon, the ever-dapper Eduard appeared at the factory with a moving van containing a vast quantity of bundles. It was then that the manufacturer realized, to his dismay, that he was in the presence of the combined orchestral libraries, scores and parts, of Johann I, Johann II, Josef and Eduard. The man did his utmost to dissuade Eduard from what he rightly termed criminal folly, but the utter futility of his efforts was soon apparent. Josef had laid his command on Eduard, and Eduard, in his dotage, would obey. He heard the man's entreaties, pondered vacantly for some moments, and replied, "*Das kann ich nicht.*" He seated himself in an armchair, his servant at his elbow. The factory workers then pitched the packages one by one into the flames, waiting only until one lot had been consumed before tossing in the next. Eduard trembled from time to time as he recognized the writing of father or brother upon the yellowed sheets. Occasionally, he would stretch out a hand as though to halt the destruction; then it would fall away again and the holocaust would continue. Still he sat there, until the last sheet, a grey ash, sailed up the flue out of sight. What destruction was there we can realize only when we remember that this cremation of an era lasted a full five hours! Imagine the loss to the world if all the orchestral music of Mozart were to be destroyed, leaving only piano editions of works which were orchestrally conceived. What a loss to posterity! In a like sense, the destruction of the orchestral editions of the writings of Johann I, Josef, and Eduard, together with some of Johann II, is no less great; in robbing us of the heritage and the perspective of a century of light music, this was an act of musical vandalism without par.

It is with this fire that interest in Eduard ends. A lonely figure, he lived on into the era of the languorous but passionate tango, that logical emotional successor to the waltz. Eduard Strauss died three days after Christmas 1916—the Great Waltz had ended....

5

FRANZ LEHAR

In POINT of musical importance, the succession to the Strauss throne fell not to Johann III, but to Franz Lehár. Victor Herbert, who himself might have laid claim to the crown, said of Lehár that "he is the sole heir to the Waltz King's throne."

Franz Lehár was born on April 30th, 1870, in the Hungarian town of Komarom. He showed strong musical aptitude at so early an age that his father, a well-known military bandmaster, began his musical instruction himself. He became proficient on several instruments, learning, in this practical manner, a great deal about instrumental possibilities and combinations which was to serve him in good stead in later years. Indeed, one of the most typical traits of Lehár's orchestration is its rich, sensuous appeal, and its similarity in this sense to the orchestral style of Richard Strauss.

In 1882, Lehár entered the Conservatory at Prague, where he studied violin under Bennewitz and theory under Förster. Three years later, he had the good fortune to attract the attention of Zdenko Fibich, today remembered almost exclusively for his sentimental *Poème*; with Fibich he studied composition after Conservatory hours, while continuing his courses at the school. Two years later, in 1887, Fibich was instrumental in introducing Lehár to Dvořák. The young man submitted two piano sonatas to the famous Bohemian composer, one in G Major, and the other in D Minor. Dvořák was impressed by the promise shown in these early works, and urged Lehár to devote himself exclusively to composition.

In 1888, Lehár left the Conservatory to become first violinist in the Elberfeld theater orchestra. He held this chair for a year, obtaining at first hand experience in the intricacies of operetta technique, but he was unhappy there, finding the work musical drudgery, for the position allowed him little time to compose. He left Elberfeld for Vienna, where he became Assistant Conductor of the Band of the 50th Infantry—the same band of which his father had been Conductor. Two years were spent here, and then Lehár took over the conductorship of another band, retaining the position until 1902. In the meantime, he was busily composing, and in 1896, he completed his first operetta, *Kukushka,* which was given in Leipzig that same year, with little success. Undismayed, he revised it some years later, and again presented it in 1905 as *Tatjana.*

Early in 1902, Lehár became conductor at the Theater-an-der-Wien, that theater which had figured so prominently in the life of the Waltz King. Here, between fine performances of Vienna's greatest light music, given in the tradition of the original performances under the composers' own batons, he completed his first successful operetta, *Wiener Frauen,* which opened in that theater in November, 1902. It created enough of a stir for Lehár to resign from conducting in order to devote himself fully to composition. *Wiener Frauen* traveled to Berlin; the change in locale also brought about a change in name, and in the Prussian capital it was known as *Die Klavierstimme.* Possibly it was feared that the arrogant northern capital would not take kindly to an operetta whose title paid homage to the easy-going rival of the south. Later, to add to the confusion, it was rewritten and presented as *Der Schlüssel zum Paradies.* This is typical of the involved history of many of the Lehár operettas.

Other stage works followed in rapid succession. In 1903, Vienna heard *Der Rastelbinder*. The next year saw the production of two new operettas: *Die Juxheirat* and *Der Göttergatte*. None of these has survived, although isolated arias from *Der Rastelbinder* are sometimes heard on records and radio.

But these early works were merely practice flights for a triumph which came in 1905, when Lehár gave the world *Die Lustige Witwe*. Not since *Die Fledermaus* had any stage work known such a success, nor has any new operetta since produced equaled the world-wide success which it achieved. From its opening in Vienna, on December 30th, 1905, it flashed quickly into other cities on the continent and in England, and then made its way to the New World. Even the Far East fell beneath its spell. In Rome, Naples and Milan, it was heard as *La Vedova Allegra;* in Madrid, Barcelona, Buenos Aires, Valparaiso, Santiago and Havana, as *La Viude Alegre;* in London, New York, Chicago, San Francisco, Sydney and Melbourne, it thrilled audiences to the title of *The Merry Widow.* In Buenos Aires, it had the unusual distinction of playing at seven theaters at the same time, in five languages!

Ask almost any American what he best remembers musically in connection with the first decade of the Twentieth Century, and he will surely say, "Donald Brian and Ethel Jackson in *The Merry Widow*." It invaded every nook and cranny of daily living. Women's clothes were patterned after the styles set by the Merry Widow. The music was to be heard in every café, in every restaurant; the famous waltz even succeeded in sweeping native dances from the floor, and this at a time when dancing the waltz was beginning to be considered old-fashioned. (Fortunately, we are today past that stage!) It was more than a success, it was a conquest. Lehár and his publisher became millionaires almost overnight. The mantle of the Waltz King fell fast upon the new monarch's shoulders.

There is more than a coincidental resemblance between Viktor Léon's book and that which Genée and Haffner wrote for *Die Fledermaus*. In essence, the two stories have much in common. The locale of one is Vienna, the other, Paris. The two cities are alike in their nocturnal gaiety, their effervescent mode of living, their love of elegant and beautiful women. Both are glamour-cities. The setting, then, was substantially the same. In *Die Fledermaus*, everything builds up to the intoxicated bacchanalia of the second-act finale, and thence to the *dénouement* of the third act. In *The Merry Widow*, we have again the second-act ball scenes, floating on a froth of champagne bubbles, and the third-act untangling of the Gordian knot. However, it would be incorrect to suggest that, consciously or otherwise, Léon patterned his book upon the Meilhac-Halévy-Genée-Haffner story which Strauss used.

The story of *The Merry Widow* is much more straightforward, much less involved in the old tradition of confused identities in operetta, than is any of the Strauss repertory.* The setting is the Paris of the early 1900's. Baron Popoff, the Ambassador of the mythical Kingdom of Marsovia, is in a state of near-apoplexy. He has just received word that Sonia, the richest and most beautiful woman in Marsovia, is arriving in Paris on a visit. If she marries a foreigner, her money will pass out of the country and Marsovia will be bankrupt. Popoff's career—indeed, his fortune—depends upon his seeing that, if this lively widow, on her first visit to the enchanting French capital, does marry anyone, that man will be a Marsovian. The Ambassador sends for Prince Danilo, a former fiancé of Sonia, and instructs him to escort her during

---

* *The edition quoted here is one which postdates the original version still in use in German lands; it varies the story in some details, renames a character or two, and is more international in tone than the somewhat naïve 1905 libretto.*

her stay in Paris, and to take care that she engage in no flirtations with anyone who is not a Marsovian. Danilo wishes to
refuse; he has not the courage to see Sonia again, for he rudely
broke his engagement with her at his family's request, because
they were opposed to his marriage to a girl who was then only
a shopkeeper's daughter.

A secondary intrigue is developed between Natalie, the
wife of the Ambassador, and his French secretary, Raoul de St.
Brioche, for the dramatic purpose of keeping the action going
constantly. The Ambassadress, young and beautiful, finds life
more appealing with Raoul than with the aging and admittedly
senile Ambassador.

A ball is held in Sonia's honor. Danilo, entering when the
party is well under way, is asked where he has been, and sings
his delight with the pleasures and the girls of Maxime's.* Sonia's arrival creates a furor, as all the men in the room flock to
her, drawn by her beauty and her wealth. Danilo quickly extri-
cates her from the throng. They dance together, and find that
they are still in love. Here occurs the first of the famous waltz
passages:

Meanwhile Raoul and Natalie have met in the garden and
have gained the privacy of the summerhouse:

---

* The Café Maxime, on the rue Royale, is to this day one of the
finest, most famous and most elegant dining places in Paris.

Sonia discovers Baron Popoff, suspicious of the identity of the occupants of the pavilion, trying to learn who is inside. To save Natalie's honor, Sonia enters the little house through the rear door, and changes places with her. Danilo comes upon the scene just as the Baron, now convinced that his wife is within the locked building, pounds upon the door. Danilo sees Sonia appear with Raoul, and departs in a rage, without allowing anyone time to make an explanation:

"I'm going to Maxime's, and you may go to . . . ."

As in all operettas, it is the third act which sweeps away the clouds and makes everything serene once more. Danilo by now understands what actually happened in the pavilion, but still he will not marry Sonia, for he does not wish to be accused of marrying for money.

Sonia tells him that her husband's Will provides that if she remarries, she loses her money, and Danilo then wastes no time in proposing, whereupon Sonia gleefully explains that of course she will lose her money, since under Marsovian law its title will pass to her husband! Here appears the delightful *Girls, Girls, Girls!*

"You may study her ways as you can,
  But a woman's too much for a man...."

A slender story, to be sure, without the breath of intoxication which lends its special touch of credibility to *Die Fledermaus*. It is operetta; *Die Fledermaus* is comic-opera, and this
distinction should not be forgotten. We tend today to confuse
the two forms; actually, they are not alike.

The *Merry Widow* is full of melodious, appealing songs.
Vilia and the *Ballsirenen Waltzes* are known the world over,
but the rest of the music is equally fine. The delightful can-
can, *Ritantou-Ritantourelle,* suggests Offenbach at his best.
The song of the Ambassadress, *For I am a Dutiful Wife,* is almost as piquant and shameless as the first-act duet of Rosalinde and Eisenstein in *Die Fledermaus. The Merry Widow*
is Franz Lehár's masterwork, full of grace, full of charm, full
of good breeding. *The Merry Widow* is always a lady....

DURING the seasons which followed, Lehár tried to duplicate
the success of his first triumph, but the magic touch always
seemed to elude him. In 1906, there were two productions:
one, the Leipziger revision of his *Wiener Frauen* of 1902, under the title *Der Schlüssel zum Paradies;* the other, *Peter und
Paul reisen ins Schlaraffenland.* The success of this last was
hardly as long as the name. In 1907, he introduced *Mitislav,
der Moderne,* and also a private production of *Edelweiss und
Rosenstock,* which does not appear ever to have been given a
public performance. A year later, Vienna saw *Der Mann mit
den Drei Frauen,* and, some few months later, the considerably
more popular *Das Fürstenkind.*

These operettas were the stepping stones to a second great success, which came in 1909. They did not seem to impair Lehár's reputation—one could even say that they bridged the gap between his first triumph and that of *Der Graf von Luxembourg*, four years later. Vienna exulted over this new operetta, many theatergoers rashly predicting that it would be more popular than *The Merry Widow*. They were wrong, but it is true that *The Count of Luxembourg* holds second place in the popular appraisal of Lehár's stage works.

However, it is significant, both for an evaluation of this work in particular, and all his operettas in general, that Lehár evidences no technical or musical advance over *The Merry Widow*. Indeed, as will later be seen, it can be said that his style never developed, but rather degenerated under impure influences.

The story of *The Count of Luxembourg* has no literary quality; it is the conventional fabric of operetta, and the real merit of the work lies in its excellent music. Armand Brissard, an impecunious painter, shares his quarters, his clothes and his last copper with his equally impecunious friend, René, Count of Luxembourg. (Luxembourg being, in fact, a Grand Duchy, the character remains within the bounds of fiction.) Armand loves Juliette Vermont, and René her friend, Angèle Didier, an opera singer. An old *roué*, a Grand Duke, who wishes to marry Angèle, not caring to wed a commoner, offers René twenty thousand pounds to wed her first and then divorce his "Countess," so that the Grand Duke may maintain the febrile fantasy of marrying a noblewoman. Then, in what is virtually an operetta tradition, identities are confused, and the story bogs down in a mire of minor intrigues. The score contains many excellent numbers: *Day Dreams;* the duet, *Love Breaks Every Bond;* the topical songs, *I am in Love* and *Rootsie-Pootsie;* the old Grand Duke's faltering polka-duet, *I was a Lion in the Salon;* and the delightful quintet, *A Cheque on the Bank of England.* The most effective moment of all is the waltz scene, where René and Angèle dance down a broad flight of steps, a novel idea in those days (before Ziegfeld made stairs a scenic necessity!), and still used today. Reminiscent of the famous waltz scene of *The Merry Widow,* it counted for much in the success of the operetta.

The Count of Luxembourg opened in Vienna in 1909; less than two years later it captivated London, where it began a run of 340 performances at Daly's Theater on May 20th, 1911; this did not equal the phenomenal record of 778 performances of *The Merry Widow* at the same house, but it established it as a permanent repertory work.

Degrees, honors, and decorations continued to shower upon Lehár, as they once had upon Strauss. King Alfonso XIII of Spain conferred upon him Knighthood in the Order of Isabella, while the Shah of Persia made him a Knight of the Sun and the Lion. France made him Officer of the Legion of Honor and Officier de l'Instruction Publique.

One year after *The Count of Luxembourg,* Lehàr wrote *Zigeunerliebe.* Although unknown today in England and America, it is still sometimes performed on the continent because, as McSpadden remarks, "the original book is superior to the American version, which had been cheapened by local quips." The music in some respects recalls that of *Der Zigeunerbaron,* with its free use of the intoxicating czardas and the sensuous and languorous *lassan* of Lehár's native Hungary. It almost enters into the realm of light opera.

Not many months later, a new stage work was produced. This was *Eva,* which is still remembered for its waltzes, frequently heard on light concert programs. *Eva* was followed by *Die Ideale Gattin* in 1913; by *Endlich Allein* in 1914; *Der Sterngucker* in 1917; and *Wo die Lerche singt* in 1918, which was given its première in Budapest. With the exception of the last named, nothing remains of these operettas, born of the war years. In 1920, Paris was given the first performance of *La Mazurka bleu*. Probably the French capital was the only city on the Continent where such an operetta could have been produced. Certainly Vienna in the 1920's, undergoing the death agonies of the Hapsburg dynasty and the birth pangs of a republican government, was no place for mazurkas, blue or otherwise. *Die Tangokönigin* failed when it was produced in Vienna, in 1921. But anything would have failed in that dismal city in the early aftermath of the war. The currency had been inflated beyond all conceivable values, to the point where one American dollar was worth ten thousand kronen. It was a city of destitute, despairing people.

It has always remained true that while a nation endures its blackest moments, it must be cheered and entertained. The boom in entertainment in America and England during the war, and in Germany and Austria after the war, are cases in point. For close to a century, the Strausses had played their enchanting fiddles to ease minds worried by Prussia's rising militarism and Austria's dwindling influence in the Teutonic family of nations. Now it was Lehár's turn to play the Pied Piper. He outdid himself in 1922, in point of numbers. Four new numbers came from his pen that year: a musical comedy, *Frühling;* an operetta in Italian which was produced in Milan as *La Danza delle Libellule;* and two operettas introduced in Vienna, *Frasquita* and *Schön ist die Welt* (The World Is Beautiful). It must have taken a sort of courage to bring an operetta so named into an Austria burdened with poverty and sorrow. Perhaps nowhere save in Vienna could such a play have been produced without affronting the audience. But the desire of the human species to escape is strong, and that of the Viennese is among the strongest. As a matter of fact, the operetta is still frequently performed in Germanic countries, and is considered a repertory work. Two unsuc-cessful works followed: *Die gelbe Jacke* in 1923, and *Cloclo* the year after.

These minor plays were succeeded by the last four of Le-hár's stage works: *Paganini* in 1925, *Friedericke* in 1928, *Das Land des Lächelns* in 1929, and *Giuditta* in 1934. *The Land of Smiles* is another example of Lehár's husbandry with his musical material. Aware that he was not possessed of Strauss's endless melodic fertility, he rarely allowed material which had proved unsuccessful to go so carelessly to its doom. The unsuccessful *Die gelbe Jacke* was reworked, had some numbers changed, and was endowed with a new song which has become world-famous, and so turned into the highly successful *Land of Smiles*. The hit song is none other than *Dein ist mein ganzes Herz* (Yours is my heart alone).

Although none of these last four operettas has ever achieved the international popularity of Lehár's two leading productions, they contain many pages of his finest music. In these works he shows himself, at times, as a serious com-poser, for some scenes tend more to the style of comic opera than operetta. The best of the four is *Das Land des Lächelns*. Although this score lacks the infectiously gay quality of *The Merry Widow*—indeed, it has no happy ending—it has depth, and has earned the approbation of many a fine musi-cian. It is still a standard work, frequently played throughout German-speaking lands.

A comparison between the musical styles evidenced in *The Merry Widow* (1905) and these last four works leads to interesting revelations. One notes a constantly clouding style from the crystal instrumentation of the early great suc-cesses, which are suggestive of the influence of Johann

Strauss, to the overladen and cluttered instrumentation of the last four works, which betray the unhealthy influence of Richard Strauss.

Also, it must be confessed, Lehár's standards of taste did not uphold themselves under the onslaught of 4/4-time fox-trot rhythm in the operetta. The relatively high level of musical taste shown in the waltz-duets of *The Merry Widow* are not to be classed together with the pitiful standards evidenced in, for example, the duet, *Niemand liebt dich so wie ich,* from *Paganini.*

No biography of Franz Lehár would be complete without a parallel mention of Richard Tauber, for he was to Lehár all and more than Girardi was to Johann Strauss, creating many of the leading roles in Lehár operettas. It is also true that, as the finest tenor in Viennese light opera in the Twentieth Century, he earned a reputation as interpreter of many of the roles in Strauss operas, notably Eisenstein in *Die Fledermaus,* and Barinkay in *Der Zigeunerbaron.* It would, however, be doing Tauber an injustice to draw the parallel too closely, for he was a far more finished musician than Girardi. In addition to his stature as a singer (and he was famous also for opera and German *Lieder*), he was also a composer of light symphonic compositions, and conductor of his own music. When, in later years, age betrayed him and his golden voice no longer held its former glory, he continued to utilize his extensive knowledge of the Strauss scores as permanent conductor of the 1945 London production of *Gay Rosalinda* (*Die Fledermaus*).

Tauber's caressing and sensuous voice did not alone account for the respect accorded him. No other singer seemed so completely to understand the technique of Viennese light opera; no other singer had such a sensitive feeling for this music. His death in London on January 8th, 1948, robbed

us of the last great vocal link with the original Strauss tradition. . . .

The chronology of the stage works of Lehár by no means
exhausts the list of his compositions, which range beyond the
confines of that medium. There is an *Ungarische Fantasie,*
Op. 45, for violin and small orchestra. There are also the
Huldigungsouvertüre; the symphonic poem, *Fieber,* dating
from 1916; *Il Guado,* another symphonic poem, scored for
piano and orchestra; the *Vision Overture;* and the *Märchen
aus dem Tausend und Eine Nacht.*

Lehár also composed a song-cycle, *Roman Musical,* set to
poems of Pierre Benoit, and published in Paris in 1937, as
well as a large number of other songs, marches and dance
compositions. Of these last, the best known are the *Gold und
Silber Waltzes,* Op. 79.

In 1938, the armies of Nazi Germany invaded Austria,
and Vienna fell from its once-proud position as cultural ruler
of the Teutonic world to that of a minor vassal. The magnificent Vienna Philharmonic Orchestra, at the time one of the
few great in the world, was "purged," and its high quality
has, to this day, not been recaptured. On January 16th of
that year, it had given a performance of Mahler's *Ninth
Symphony,* under the baton of his great disciple, Bruno
Walter; it was only fitting that it should be to Mahler's *Welt-
schmerz* music that the orchestra sing its swan song. A few
days later, so many of its leading spirits—among them its
fine concertmaster, Professor Arnold Rosé—had been summarily dismissed that it existed in name only. Together with
several of its members, its guiding genius, Bruno Walter, had
fled his beloved Austria and had settled in France, where
honorary citizenship was conferred upon him.

In this world of insanity and disaster, Franz Lehár remained, old and weary, clinging to the shreds of the Vienna which he so dearly loved. Of pure Hungarian stock, no Nazi could hope to call him aught but "Aryan," yet he was obliged to make enormous payments to "certain influential parties," that his "Aryan blood" might be certified. Cowardly? It might have been—for a young man, but who can blame a man of seventy for seeking to retain the roots which grew solidly in his native soil? Strauss at twenty fought for liberty, but who can say what Strauss at seventy would have done?

Soon after the fall of France in 1940, Lehár conducted a performance of *Das Land des Lächelns* in Paris for an audience in Wehrmacht field-gray. It would be interesting to know what Land of Smiles Lehár had in mind as his baton rose and fell in this unhappy Parisian theater. This was early (and yet how late!) in the Nazi conquest of Europe, marked at Hitler's personal request by a special performance of this operetta. Later, the same work served to underscore the Nazi régime's ignominious end and the ensuing misery of the German people, for *Land des Lächelns* was, ironically, the first lyric stage work to be produced by the Frankfurt Civic Theater after the end of World War II. Almost at the same time, it appeared on many other stages throughout the country, as though the nation were invoking the jealous gods of their Valhalla through its title.

The final incident of Lehár's death at his home in Bad Ischl, on October 24th, 1948, seemed almost an anticlimax, for even before World War II began, even before World War I had ended, the period which created him had passed. The Golden Age of Vienna is no more, and with it has passed forever that ebullient atmosphere which excited the talents of the great Viennese school of light music. Just as the enchanting waltz melodies of Ravel's *La Valse* finally dissolve into a rude and relentless cacophony, so has the Viennese Waltz, and the era which it represents, vanished beyond recall into the holocaust of two world wars.

REFERENCE
SECTION

RECORDINGS

This section is designed, first, to serve as a catalogue for both the interested record collector and the student of Straussiana, and, second, to indicate certain recordings which the author considers superlative examples of performance in authentic Strauss tradition.

The following abbreviations are used to identify the various manufacturers and their trade labels:

B.	Brunswick	United States
C.	Columbia	United States, unless otherwise indicated
D.	Decca	United States
DP.	Decca	British, or German Polydor reissued in Great Britain through Decca
G.	Grammophon	Germany
Gr.	Gramophone	European affiliates of British HMV and US Victor, i.e.:
		"La Voix de son Maitre" - France
		"La Voce del Padrone" - Italy
		"Electrola" - Germany
HMV.	His Master's Voice	Great Britain (Victor affiliate)
H.	Homophon	Germany
L.	London	U. S. (English Decca subsidiary)
O.	Odeon	Europe
P.	Parlophone	Europe
PD.	Polydor	Europe
IK.	Imperial-Kristall	Germany
S.	Siemens	Germany (Grammophon associate)
T.	Telefunken	Germany
U.	Ultraphon	Germany
V.	Victor	United States

No attempt has been made to make these lists complete. Their purpose is merely to supply the best recordings of each Strauss composition, and not necessarily all recordings.

Many records listed have been discontinued. They have been retained here either because no other version is known, or because the performance is of sufficient quality and importance to make the recording of value to the student if not to the collector.

Recordings marked with an asterisk (*) are recommended as superior performances, demonstrative of the true Strauss tradition. New long-playing records (33 ⅓ rpm) are indicated by the letters *LP* after the catalogue numbers; these are usually also available in the older 78 rpm discs as well as in 45 rpm.

RECORDINGS OF THE MUSIC OF JOHANN STRAUSS I

DONAULIEDER WALTZES, Op. 127
  *V.   13597   Alwin, Vienna Philharmonic Orch.
  HMV.   C.2338   Krauss, Vienna Philharmonic Orch.

LORELEI-RHEIN-KLÄNGE WALTZES, Op. 154
  PD.   22439   Melichar, Symphony Orch.

RADETZKY MARCH, Op. 228
  C.   12543-D   Leinsdorf, Cleveland Orch.
  C.(Br)   CX-9289   Johann Strauss III and Orchestra
  V.   4127   Blech, Berlin State Opera Orch.

*   *   *   *

RECORDINGS OF THE MUSIC OF JOHANN STRAUSS II

ORCHESTRAL WORKS
  (For waltzes and other music from stage works, see OPERAS)

ACCELERATIONEN WALTZES, Op. 234
  V.   8653   Ormandy, Minneapolis Symphony Orch.
  T.   E.1156   Kleiber, Berlin Philharmonic Orch.
  L.   LLP-10 *LP*   Krips, New Symphony Orch.

AN DER SCHÖNEN, BLAUEN DONAU WALTZES, Op. 314

°V.	13691	Szell, Vienna Philharmonic Orch.
°T.	SK.3150	Krauss, Vienna Philharmonic Orch.
C.	ML-2041 *LP*	Ormandy, Philadelphia Orch.
V.	11-8580	Toscanini, NBC Symphony Orch.
L.	LLP-10 *LP*	Krips, New Symphony Orch.
V.	15425	Stokowski, Philadelphia Orch.

For overall performance, Szell excells all other readings save the stiff competition of Krauss, whose beautifully blurred pastel has the slow tempi demanded by Strauss himself. Both enjoy the direction of the finest orchestra possible for this music. Toscanini's introduction and coda are unmatched, but his waltz beat is unyielding and un-Viennese, his orchestra inferior. Krips, though Viennese in his reading, leans more to the dance- than the concert-hall in his tempi, which are monotonously uniform, and his British orchestra cannot, of itself, supply the missing impulse. The Stokowski atrocity is to be avoided at all costs.

ANNEN POLKA, Op. 117

°HMV.	B.3149	Krauss, Vienna Philharmonic Orch.
V.	10-1207	Fiedler, Boston Pops Orch.

BALLG'SCHICHTEN WALTZES, Op. 150

C.	71028-D	Barlow, CBS Symphony Orch.

BEI UNS Z'HAUS WALTZES, Op. 361

D.	20302	Knappertsbusch, Berlin Symphony Orch.

CHAMPAGNER POLKA, Op. 211

C.	71029-D	Barlow, CBS Symphony Orch.

EGYPTISCHER MARCH, Op. 335

°V.	10-1019	Fiedler, Boston Pops Orch.

ELECTROPHOR POLKA, Op. 297

C.	69756-D	Barlow, CBS Symphony Orch.

EXPLOSIONS POLKA, Op. 43

C.	69756-D	Barlow, CBS Symphony Orch.

FRÜHLINGSTIMMEN WALTZES, Op. 410

°V.	13597	Szell, Vienna Philharmonic Orch.
V.	4387	Fiedler, Boston Pops Orch.
C.	70388-D	Beecham, London Philharmonic Orch.
V.	18060	Ormandy, Philadelphia Orch.

Szell's faster tempo avoids the heavy-handed feeling from which the others suffer, and is more in keeping with the virtuoso piano piece which this originally was. Beecham and Ormandy, in different ways, lack here all feeling for Viennese waltz rhythm. The Fiedler version is good.

FESTIVAL QUADRILLE, Op. 341
    C.   69756-D   Barlow, CBS Symphony Orch.

FREUT EUCH DES LEBENS! WALTZES, Op. 340
    Gr.   EH.119   Knappertsbusch, Berlin State Opera Orch.
    C.   9226   Johann Strauss iii and Orchestra

G'SCHICHTEN AUS DEM WIENER WALD WALTZES, Op. 325
    C.   ML-2041 *LP*   Ormandy, Philadelphia Orch.
    *DP.   LY 6129/30   Melichar, Berlin Philharmonic Orch.
    C.   69562-D   Walter, Symphony Orch.
    C.(Br)   DX.1503   Krips, Philharmonic Orch.
    V.   15425   Stokowski, Philadelphia Orch.

Only Melichar gives the complete waltz with the solo zither introduction (although English Decca, alias London, plans to have Krips record it). Musically, Walter's recording stands mountain-high above all others, but the solo zither passage is given to the strings (an alternative authorized by Strauss) and the recording is prehistoric. The Krips disc is mellifluously recorded and well-played, but hardly exciting. Stokowski's anguished variations on a Strauss theme ought not to be inflicted on one's worst enemy!

IDYLLEN WALTZES, Op. 95
    Gr   EG.2464   Marek Weber and Orchestra

KAISERWALZER, Op. 437
    *V.   13690   Walter, Vienna Philharmonic Orch.
    C.   11854-D   Walter, New York Philharmonic Symphony Orch.
    C.(Br)   LX.1021   von Karajan, Vienna Philharmonic Orch.
    L.   LLP-10 *LP*   Krips, New Symphony Orch.
    V.   12195   Fiedler, Boston Pops Orch.

Asked to name the finest performance of a Strauss waltz on American records, I would unhesitatingly choose the Walter-Vienna Philharmonic version of this waltz. By contrast, the one he has made with the New York Philharmonic is a poor imitation, partly due to inferior recording, partly due to a basic lack of Viennese feeling in the orchestra. In the Victor disc, conductor and orchestra give this waltz the loving care they would bestow on a Beethoven symphony, and the results are to be heard. Von Karajan is too angular to understand the *Gemütlichkeit* of Vienna, but the orchestra helps him along; Fiedler's reading is a bit militant; that of Krips lacks character, although the actual playing is delightful.

KÜNSTLERLEBEN WALTZES, Op. 316
   C.(Br)   LX.1013   von Karajan, Vienna Philharmonic Orch.
  *V.   9992   Kleiber, Vienna Philharmonic Orch.
   V.   12194   Fiedler, Boston Pops Orch.

By process of elimination, Karajan gets the palm here, for it is hard to vote against the superb recording and orchestral performance, but his feeling for Strauss's music is variable, never **great**. Kleiber's exquisite reading, airy and delicate, unfortunately suffers from over-age recording. Fiedler is somewhat heavy-handed here, a fact which is exaggerated and accentuated by the coarse-grained recording accorded him.

LEICHTES BLUT, SCHNELLPOLKA, Op. 319
  *Gr.   EG.1780   Krauss, Vienna Philharmonic Orch.
   V.   10-1026   Fiedler, Boston Pops Orch.

LIEBESLIEDER WALTZES, Op. 114
   V.   (in) DM-907   Krauss, Vienna Philharmonic Orch.
   PD.   15077   Prüwer, Berlin Philharmonic Orch.

MAN LEBT NUR EINMAL WALTZES, Op. 167
   C.   4270-M   Ania Dorfman, piano (arr. Tausig)

MÄRCHEN AUS DEM ORIENT WALTZES, Op. 444
   V.   36181   Marek Weber and Orchestra

MORGENBLÄTTER WALTZES, Op. 279
   V.   11-8217   Krauss, Vienna Philharmonic Orch.

MOTOREN WALTZES, Op. 265
   C.   71027-D   Barlow, CBS Symphony Orch.

NEU WIEN WALTZES, Op. 342
   V.   4478   Fiedler, Boston Pops Orch.

PAROXYSMEN WALTZES, Op. 189
   C.   69757-D   Barlow, CBS Symphony Orch.

PERPETUUM MOBILE, SCHERZO-GALOPP, Op. 257
  *G.   15359-EM   Ludwig, Berlin State Opera Orch.
  *HMV.   B.3149   Krauss, Vienna Philharmonic Orch.
   V.   4435   Fiedler, Boston Pops Orch.
   C.   12543   Leinsdorf, Cleveland Orch.

PERSISCHER MARCH, Op. 289
  *V.   10-1019   Fiedler, Boston Pops Orch.

SÄNGERLUST POLKA, Op. 328
    C.   9371   Johann Strauss III and Orchestra

SANS-SOUCI POLKA, Op. 178
    V.   10-1205   Fiedler, Boston Pops Orch.

SCHNELLPOST POLKA, Op. 159
    C.   71029-D   Barlow, CBS Symphony Orch.

SEID UMSCHLUNGEN, MILLIONEN! WALTZES, Op. 443
    G.   11563-E   German Radio Orch.
    U.   EP.520   Grosz, Berlin Philharmonic Orch.
    D.   25765   Dajos Béla Orch.

SERAIL-TÄNZE WALTZES, Op. 5
    C.   69755-D   Barlow, CBS Symphony Orch.

TELEGRAFISCHE DEPESCHEN WALTZES, Op. 195
    C.   71029-D   Barlow, CBS Symphony Orch.

THERMEN WALTZES, Op. 245
    D.   25765   Dajos Béla Orch.

TRITSCH-TRATSCH POLKA, Op. 214
    *V.   11-9188   Toscanini, NBC Symphony Orch.
    *HMV. C.2687   Szell, Vienna Philharmonic Orch.
    V.   10-1058   Fiedler, Boston Pops Orch.
    C.   ML-4118 *LP*   Carnegie Pops Orch.
    C.   386-M   Orchestre Raymonde, G. Walter
                               (alias W. Goehr, London Symphony Orch.)

ÜBER DONNER UND BLITZ, SCHNELLPOLKA, Op. 324
    *V.   4319   Fiedler, Boston Pops Orch.
    C.   12543   Leinsdorf, Cleveland Orch.

WEIN, WEIB UND GESANG WALTZES, Op. 333
    V.   12192   Fiedler, Boston Pops Orch.
    C.   71210-D   Weingartner, Paris Conservatory Orch.
    T.   E.1206   Kleiber, Berlin Philharmonic Orch.
    C.   ML-2017   Ormandy, Philadelphia Orch.

    Of all these, the best performance of the introduction is by Fiedler; the best performance of the waltzes, by Weingartner.

WIENER BLUT WALTZES, Op. 354
    *C.   11579-D   Reiner, Pittsburgh Symphony Orch.
    V.   12193   Fiedler, Boston Pops Orch.
    C.(Br) L.2270   Walter, Berlin State Opera Orch.
    V.   18060   Ormandy, Philadelphia Orch.

    Reiner's performance far outclasses all others. Fiedler's disc is a poor second-best, Walter's very old, and Ormandy's incomplete and insentient.

WIENER BONBONS WALTZES, Op. 307
> PD.   15030   Melichar and Symphony Orch.
> V.   26514   Marek Weber and Orchestra
> D.   25063   Dajos Béla Orch.

WO DIE ZITRONEN BLÜH'N WALTZES, Op. 364
> *V.   11894   Fiedler, Boston Pops Orch.
> HMV. C.2338   Alwin, Vienna Philharmonic Orch.

An example of what a superb Strauss conductor Fiedler can be when the spirit moves him.

OPERAS and OPERETTAS
(This section contains only the original Strauss operas and operettas. No attempt has been made to catalogue recordings of the many operettas which, since Strauss's death, have been concocted from his tunes, with the sole exception of *Wiener Blut,* for which Strauss personally selected the music to the individual numbers from his old dance tunes, and which was prepared under his supervision. The *première* occurred shortly after his death, in the Carl Theater on October 25th, 1899.)

INDIGO (1871)

INTERMEZZO
> DP.   LY.6130   Melichar, Berlin Philharmonic Orch.
> V.   11910   Blech, Berlin State Opera Orch.

LAUNISCHES GLÜCK
> C.(Br) DF.1477   Charles Kullman, tenor
> D.   20331   Josef Schmidt, tenor
> V.   4411   Miliza Korjus, soprano

The Korjus disc, entitled *There'll Come a Time,* gives an English version of this song as sung by her in the film *The Great Waltz.* The other two are the authentic Strauss song.

INDIGO MARCH, Op. 439
> *V.   10-1020   Fiedler, Boston Pops Orch.

TAUSEND UND EINE NACHT WALTZES, Op. 346
> V.   9990   Krauss, Vienna Philharmonic Orch.
> T.   E.1233   Kleiber, Berlin Philharmonic Orch.
> C.   69563-D   Weingartner, British Symphony Orch.

DIE FLEDERMAUS (1874)

OVERTURE

*V.   13688   Walter, Paris Conservatory Orch.
V.   12-0189   Fiedler, Boston Pops Orch.
T.   SK.3161   Krauss, Vienna Philharmonic Orch.
C.   ML-2041 *LP* Ormandy, Philadelphia Orch.
PD. 68043   von Karajan, Berlin Philharmonic Orch.

"COMPLETE" PERFORMANCE   *Cast*: Hilde Güden, Wilma Lipp,
  L.   LLP-281/2   *LP*   Julius Patzak, Anton Dermota, other soloists and chorus of the Vien-
na State Opera, with the Vienna
Philharmonic Orchestra under Cle-
mens Krauss.

"COMPLETE" PERFORMANCE   *Cast*: Risë Stevens, Patrice Munsel,
  V.   LM-1114 *LP*   Regina Resnik, James Melton, Jan
          or   Peerce, Robert Merrill, Hugh
    DM-1457 (78)   Thompson, Robert Shaw Chorale,
          or   RCA Victor Orchestra under Fritz
    WDM-1457 (45) Reiner.

"COMPLETE" PERFORMANCE   *Cast*: Ljuba Welitch, Lily Pons,
  C.   SL-108   *LP*   Richard Tucker, Charles Kull-
man, John Brownlee, chorus and
orchestra of the Metropolitan Opera, conducted by Eugene Ormandy.

"ABRIDGED" PERFORMANCE   *Cast:* Adele Kern, Else Ruziska,
  DP.   CA.8118/22   Margaret Pfahl, Hertha Klust,
Franz Völker, Willi Domgraf-Fass-
bänder, Waldemar Henke, Eduard Kandle, Leonard Kern, Berlin
State Opera Chorus and Orchestra
under H. Weigert.

A few months ago, it was almost impossible to find a record
of *Die Fledermaus* in the United States, for the Decca-Polydor set is imported (and of 1929 vintage). Today one is faced
by an embarrassing choice. Musically, the London set is one
hundred per cent complete, and an excellent performance—*but
there is no dialogue!* Musical number follows on musical num-

ber with scarcely a break, and this in German, so that despite an admirable libretto and excellent program notes, it is overpowering to listen to this score straight through. The music is simply too much without at least some of the intervening dialogue (as included in the old Decca-Polydor set); this dialogue is as important to the balance of the whole as the dialogue in *Zauberflöte* and *Fidelio*.

The Victor set also has excellent voices, and is sung in understandable English—all it needs, it would seem, to make it perfect. But—alas!—it is not *echt Wienerisch!* One must forgive Melton for lacking *Wiener Schmiss*; indeed, his voice is far too impregnated with the lilt of the typical Irish tenor for one to believe for a moment that he is Eisenstein, boulevardier and man of the world. Risë Stevens is a superb Orlovsky, Munsel a charming Adele, and Mr. Merrill's work likewise deserves only praise. But there is no excuse for an old Austro-Hungarian like Reiner turning in so mannered, so distorted and un-Viennese a performance. I'm sadly afraid it's based on champagne which has gone very flat, a matter which is made clear in the overture alone. And the Victor set also lacks dialogue.

Columbia's newer set, which can also claim to be an authentic Metropolitan version, since Ormandy prepared and conducted the production which now graces that opera house's boards, is several notches better. Ormandy has a distinct flair for everything which is *alt Wien;* as a pure matter of individual taste and preference, I can sometimes question some of his tempi and phrasing, but I can never say that he is at fault in using them. Welitch is a magnificent Rosalinde—the best, I think, on records. Pons makes Adele a distinctly Parisian creation, which Strauss did not mean her to be, but the results are not displeasing, although at moments her intonation is. Tucker is certainly a better Eisenstein than Melton, although also imperfect—neither sounds masculine or choleric enough. And again, there is no dialogue.

The old English Decca-Polydor set, surprisingly good despite its years, is probably unobtainable, and is in German—but it does combine effectively the musical numbers with an intelligent amount of dialogue. It remains my favorite, but in view of its inaccessibility, a choice will probably have to be made among the other sets.

(*In view of the above recordings, only the more important vocal numbers are listed below.*)

TRINKE, LIEBCHEN, TRINKE SCHNELL (Drinking Song)
DP. PO-5002 Else Kochmann, soprano; Franz Völker, tenor

MEIN HERR, WAS DÄCHTEN SIE VON MIR?
HMV. D.1733 Lotte Schöne, soprano
D. 20280 Lotte Lehmann, soprano

MEIN HERR MARQUIS (Laughing Song)
*HMV. E.545 Elisabeth Schumann; Alwin—Vienna Philharmonic
T. E.2571 Erna Sack, soprano
V. 11-8579 Miliza Korjus, soprano
PD. 10169 Erna Berger, soprano

CZARDAS: KLÄNGE DER HEIMAT
C. 3-568 *LP* Ljuba Welitch, soprano; Reiner—Metr. Opera

FINALE, ACT II: IM FEUERSTROM DER REBEN
*D 29015 Lotte Lehmann, Richard Tauber, Karin Branzell, Grete Merrem-Nikisch, Waldemar Stägemann, Berlin State Opera and Chorus, conductor Frieder Weissmann.

Actually begins some bars later at *Herr Chevalier, ich grüsse Sie*, but is otherwise complete. It is one of the finest vocal records of Strauss music, despite poor surfaces and old recording.

TIK-TAK POLKA, Op. 365
V. 10-1205 Fiedler, Boston Pops Orch.

DU UND DU WALTZES, Op. 367
V.(in)DM-907 Kleiber, Vienna Philharmonic Orch.
V. 10-1310 Stokowski, Hollywood Bowl Symphony Orch.
The latter is in a new orchestration by Stokowski, which is as untrue to Strauss as is his distorted phrasing.

CAGLIOSTRO IN WIEN (1875)
CAGLIOSTRO WALTZES, Op. 370
V. 4479 . Fiedler, Boston Pops Orch.

PRINZ METHUSALEM (1877)
ORCHESTRAL SELECTIONS
Gr. EG.2487 Marek Weber and Orchestra
O SCHÖNER MAI WALTZES, Op. 375
PD. 24364 Melichar, Berlin Philharmonic Orch.

O KOMM, O KOMM, HERZLIEBCHEN MEIN
  D.   20308   Vera Schwarz, soprano; Wiessmann and Orch.

DER LUSTIGE KRIEG (1881)
ORCHESTRAL SELECTIONS
  Gr.   EH.334   Marek Weber and Orchestra
OVERTURE
  PD.   47424   Melichar, Berlin State Opera Orch.
  Gr.   EG.463   Viebig, Berlin State Opera Orch.
NUR FÜR NATUR
  Gr.   EG.3385   Marcel Wittrisch, tenor
  PD.   90061   Julius Patzak, tenor
KUSS WALTZES, Op. 400
  D.   20304   Knappertsbusch, Berlin Symphony Orch.
  C.   9224   Johann Strauss III and Orchestra

DAS SPITZENTUCH DER KÖNIGIN (1880)
OVERTURE
  V.   36138   Dol Dauber Salon Orch.
DU MÄRCHENSTADT IM DONAUTHAL
  H.   4122   Hans-Heinz Bollmann, tenor
ICH BIN JA EIN REITER
  H.   4122   Hans-Heinz Bollmann, tenor
ROSEN AUS DEM SÜDEN WALTZES, Op. 388
  V.   11-8986   Fiedler, Boston Pops Orch.
  C.   ML-4116 *LP*   Reiner, Pittsburgh Symphony Orch.
  C.   69561-D   Walter, Berlin State Opera Orch.
  L.   LLP-10 *LP*   Krips, New Symphony Orch.
  V.   6647   Stock, Chicago Symphony Orch.

EINE NACHT IN VENEDIG (1883)
ORCHESTRAL SELECTIONS
  V.   36093   Marek Weber and Orchestra
OVERTURE
  °PD.   57314   Leitner, Nollendorfplatz Theater Orch.
  HMV.   B.2547   Viebig, Berlin State Opera Orch.

Ferdinand Leitner, in 1949 Music Director of the Württemberg State Orchestra, and the arranger of a new version of this

operetta, made this recording when he first conducted the operetta at the Nollendorfplatz Theater in Berlin. The reading is excellent; the score, the original.

HÖR MICH, ANNINA! and KOMM' IN DIE GONDEL

Gr.	EH.2166	Marcel Wittrisch, tenor; Lotte Schöne, soprano
Gr.	EG.2545	Marcel Wittrisch, tenor
V.	16184	John Charles Thomas, baritone

All listings save the first give only *Komm' in die Gondel*. Thomas
sings an English version titled *Love Can Be Dreamed*, as interpolated in an American production of *Gypsy Baron*.

VERSÄUME NICHT DIE STUNDE

Gr.	AM.2330	Wanda Achsel, soprano

TREU SEIN, DAS LIEGT MIR NICHT

O.	8069	Richard Tauber, tenor
Gr.	EG.2167	Marcel Wittrisch, tenor
PD.	21043	Franz Völker, tenor

SEI MIR GEGRÜSST, DU HOLDES VENETIA!

O.	8069	Richard Tauber, tenor
Gr.	EG.2167	Marcel Wittrisch, tenor
PD.	21043	Franz Völker, tenor

LAGUNEN WALTZES, Op. 411

V.	4480	Fiedler, Boston Pops Orch.

DIE ZIGEUNERBARON (1885)

OVERTURE

C.	ML-2041 *LP*	Ormandy, Philadelphia Orch.
*V.	13689	Walter, London Symphony Orch.
C.(Br)	LX.1009	von Karajan, Vienna Philharmonic Orch.
V.	12-0188	Fiedler, Boston Pops Orch.

ALS FLOTTER GEIST and JA, DAS ALLES AUF EHR'!

D.	20394	Richard Tauber, tenor
V.	16184	John Charles Thomas, baritone
C.(Ger)	DF.1477	Charles Kullman, tenor

Tauber's performance is superlatively Viennese, but an extremely old recording. Thomas has no understanding of the
proper style, and he indulges in extraneous vocal tricks which
are pure virtuoso nonsense. He sings in English.

SO ELEND UND SO TREU

*C.	3-568 *LP*	Ljuba Welitch, soprano; Reiner—Metr. Opera

ACT I: ER IST BARON!

D.   29013   Lotte Lehmann, Karin Branzell, Richard Tauber, Grete Merrem-Nikisch, Waldemar Stägemann, Berlin State Opera Chorus and Orchestra, conductor Frieder Weissmann.

In effect a heavily abridged version of the Finale, with many cuts.

MEIN AUG' BEWACHT - Trio

PD.   27072   E. Kochmann, E. Bassth, F. Völker

HA SEHT, ES WINKT! - Trio

DP.   PO.5002   E. Kochmann, E. Bassth, F. Völker

WER UNS GETRAUT? - Duet

*D.   25775   Richard Tauber, Carlotta Vanconti-Tauber.

*P.   R.1257   Emmy Bettendorf, H. E. Groh—Berlin State Opera Orch. and Chorus.

V.   4411   Miliza Korjus, soprano

The Korjus disc is titled *One Day When We Were Young*, setting the refrain of this duet to English lyrics from the film *The Great Waltz*.

WERBELIED—CZARDAS: *Hier die Hand—Wir alle wollen lustig sein.*

PD.   27072   Franz Völker, chorus and orchestra

FINALE, ACT III: EIN FÜRSTENKIND

*D.   29013   Lotte Lehmann, Karin Branzell, Grete Merrem-Nikisch, Waldemar Stägemann, Richard Tauber, H. Lange, Berlin State Opera Chorus and Orchestra, conductor Frieder Weissmann.

Although they both provide superlative singing (despite sandpaper surfaces), these records do not have the high quality of the Finale to *Die Fledermaus*, recorded by the same artists, for both of the *Zigeunerbaron* finales have been heavily cut.

ACT III: ENTRANCE MARCH: *Hurrah! der Schlacht mit gemacht!*

*V.   10-1020   Fiedler, Boston Pops Orch.

Incomplete in that the choral parts are omitted, this is nonetheless a crackerjack performance.

SCHATZ WALTZES, Op. 418

V.   9991   Blech, Berlin State Opera Orch.

C.   11800-D   Reiner, Pittsburgh Symphony Orch.

SIMPLIZIUS (1887)

DONAUWEIBCHEN WALTZES, Op. 427

   P.   R.1804   Knappertsbusch, Berlin Symphony Orch.

RITTER PASMAN (1892)

CZARDAS

   G.   15359-EM Ludwig, Berlin State Opera Orch.

DER WALDMEISTER (1895)

OVERTURE

   G.   15373-EM Melichar, Berlin State Opera Orch.

   *V.   36391   Viennese Waltz Orch.

The Viennese Waltz Orchestra disc is not, strictly speaking, the overture, for a number of other Strauss tunes have been interpolated as a middle section. It is, however, a superlative performance by one of the best-known symphony orchestras in Europe.

WIENER BLUT (Posth.: 1899)

GRÜSS GOTT - Duet

   D.   25296   Adele Kern, soprano; Alfred Strauss, tenor

ENTRANCE ARIA OF THE DUCHESS

   G.   27144-EM   E. Kochmann, soprano

WIENER BLUT (*Du süsses Zuckertäuberl mein*)

   Gr.   EG.2545   Marcel Wittrisch, tenor.

MISCELLANEOUS WORKS

LE BEAU DANUBE - Ballet Suite (arr. Désormière)

   V.   M-414   Dorati, London Philharmonic Orch.

Désormière arranged this ballet suite for Serge Diaghilev's Ballet Russe from scraps of tunes by more than one of the Strausses and even Lanner, although the music of the Waltz King predominates, climaxed, of course, by the *Blue Danube* itself. Many fragments can be identified; there is a trace of Lanner's *Schönbrunner*, as well as Johann's *Cagliostro, Neu Wien*, and *Morgenblätter Waltzes*. Most of the excerpts, however, are from the many now-forgotten dance pieces. Désormière re-orchestrated many of these to fit a symphony orchestra, but always tastefully, and Strauss would have been the last to complain. The performance is sparkling, the recording very good.

GRADUATION BALL - Ballet Suite (arr. Dorati)
> V.   DM.-1180   Dorati, Dallas Symphony Orch.

   Like the suite above, this was also originally prepared for the Ballet Russe in 1940 from little-known Strauss fragments. The comment above holds basically true here, in all respects.

RECORDINGS OF THE MUSIC OF
JOHANN II and JOSEF STRAUSS

PIZZICATO POLKA (no opus no.)
> °HMV. C.2687   Szell, Vienna Philharmonic Orch.
> V.   1757   Ormandy, Minneapolis Symphony Orch.
> V.   10-1206   Fiedler, Boston Pops Orch.

   The Fiedler disc, in every other sense a fine performance, gets my veto for using an orchestration (possibly from Strauss for dance orchestras?) which clouds the *pizzicati* with other instruments.

RECORDINGS OF THE MUSIC OF JOSEF STRAUSS

AQUARELLEN WALTZES, Op. 258
V.   8867   Ormandy, Minneapolis Symphony Orch.

DELIRIEN WALTZES, Op. 212
DP.   LY.6023   Melichar, Berlin State Opera Orch.

DORFSCHWALBEN AUS ÖSTERREICH WALTZES, Op. 164
*V.   9993   Kleiber, Vienna Philharmonic Orch.
*T.   E.1422   Kleiber, Berlin Philharmonic Orch.
PD.   15204   Melichar, Berlin Philharmonic Orch.
V.   11-9189   Fiedler, Boston Pops Orch.

DYNAMIDEN (*Geheimne Anziehungskräfte*) WALTZES, Op. 173
D.   25766   Dajos Béla Orch.

FEUERFEST POLKA, Op. 269
D.   20243   Johann Strauss III and Orchestra

FLATTERGEISTER WALTZES, Op. 62
D.   25766   Dajos Béla Orch.

FRAUENHERZ POLKA, Op. 166
G.   11563-E   Deutschlandsenders Orch.

DIE GUTEN, ALTEN ZEITEN WALTZES, Op. 26
PD.   27174   Ilja Livschakoff Orch.

JOCKEY GALOP, Op. 278
P.   R.298   Edith Lorand Orch.

DIE LIBELLE POLKA, Op. 204
V.   22513   Bourdon, Victor Concert Orch.

MARIENKLÄNGE WALTZES, Op. 214
V.   24370   Marek Weber and Orchestra
D.   25063   Dajos Béla Orch.

MEIN LEBENSLAUF IST LIEB UND LUST! WALTZES, Op. 235
Gr.   EH.696   Marek Weber and Orchestra
D.   20303   Odeon Orchestra

{ 277 }

SPHÄRENKLÄNGE WALTZES, Op. 235
　°DP.　K.1924　　Kleiber, London Philharmonic Orch.
　C.　　12579-D　Leinsdorf, Cleveland Orch.
　V.　　12-0068　Fiedler, Boston Pops Orch.
　HMV. C.2195　　Krauss, Vienna Philharmonic Orch.

Most Kleiber recordings of Strauss are old; this is a new record-ing of 1948, apparently part of a series being made competitively in England by Decca and HMV. Unfortunately, most in the series have been recorded by Krips or Karajan, neither an ideal Strauss interpreter. Kleiber definitely is. Leinsdorf may be Austrian, but he is still not at home in this music. Fiedler is somewhat heavy-handed, and the resonance of his orchestra in Symphony Hall a bit weighty for this music. Neither he nor Leinsdorf senses the elegiac strain perceived by Kleiber, and, to some extent, by Krauss, whose recording is, however, rather old.

TRANSAKTIONEN WALTZES, Op. 184
　Gr.　EH.687　　Marek Weber and Orchestra

WIENER KINDER WALTZES, Op. 61
　D.　　20303　　Dajos Béla Orch.

RECORDINGS OF THE MUSIC OF
EDUARD STRAUSS

BAHN FREI GALOPP, Op. 45
　°V.　　10-1207　Fiedler, Boston Pops Orch.
　C.　　12543　　Leinsdorf, Cleveland Orch.
　D.　　20245　　Johann Strauss III and Orchestra

The history of the Fiedler disc is amusing; he heard the Strauss recording at my home and expressed a wish to get the parts so as to do it in a Pops concert. By good chance, I was able to find a piano edition of the piece in a secondhand bookstore—from this and the record, Frank Bodge made the orchestration, an excellent one. The sole variant seems the conception of this as a race-track number (gallop?) as indicated by the opening trumpet solo, a Bodge addition. Piccolo overtones in the original Strauss indicate that the conductor's father considered "Free Track" to have railway significance.

DOCTRINEN WALTZES, Op. 79
   V.   12428   Fiedler, Boston Pops Orch.

LEUCHTKÄFERL'N WALTZES, Op. 161
   Gr.   EG.2464   Marek Weber and Orchestra

RECORDINGS OF THE MUSIC OF JOHANN STRAUSS III

DICHTERLIEBE WALTZES, Op. 38
   V.   4477   Fiedler, Boston Pops Orch.

A CATALOGUE BY OPUS NUMBERS OF THE COMPOSITIONS OF

JOHANN STRAUSS I	JOSEF STRAUSS
JOHANN STRAUSS II	EDUARD STRAUSS

JOHANN STRAUSS I

1 Täuberlin — Walzer
2 Döblinger Reunion — Walzer
3 Wiener Karneval — Walzer
4 Kettenbrücke — Walzer No. 1
5 Gesellschafts — Walzer
6 Wiener Launen — Walzer
7 Alpenkönig — Galopp
8 Champagner — Polka
9 Seufzer — Galopp
10 Tempête — Polstertänze und Galoppade
11 Walzer à la Paganini
12 Krapfen-Wald'l — Walzer
13 Trompeten — Walzer
14 Champagner — Walzer
15 Erinnerungs — Walzer
16 Fort nach einander! — Walzer
17 Gesellschafts — Galopp
18 Lustlager — Walzer
19 Kettenbrücke — Walzer No. 2
20 Chinesen — Galopp
21 Karolinen und Kettenbrücke — Galopp
22 Es ist nur ein Wein! — Walzer
23 Josefstädter Tänze
24 Hietzinger Reunion — Walzer
25 Der unzusammenhängende Zusammenhang — Potpourri
26 Frohsinn im Gebirge — Walzer
27 Erinnerungs — Galopp
28 Hirten — Galopp
29 Wettrennen-und Wilhelm-Tell — Galopp
30 Sperlsfest — Walzer
31 Des Verfassers beste Laune — Charmant Walzer
32 Cotillion on *La Muette de Portici* by Auber
33 Benefiz — Walzer
34 Gute Meinung für die Tanzlust — Walzer
35 Einzugs — Galopp
36 Ungarische — Galopp

37 Wiener Tags Belustigung —
Potpourri
38 Souvenir de Baden —
Walzer
39 Wiener Tivoli-Rutsch —
Walzer
40 Wiener Damen — Walzer
41 Fra Diavolo — Cotillion
42 Sperl — Galopp
43 Der Raub der Sabinerinnen
— Walzer
44 Contre-Tänze
45 Tivoli-Freudenfest —
Walzer
46 Musikalisches Ragoût —
Potpourri
47 Vive la Danse! — Walzer
48 Heiter auch in ernster Zeit!
— Walzer
49 Das Leben ein Tanz, der
Tanz ein Leben — Walzer
50 Cotillion on *Die Unbe-
kannte*
51 Hofball-Tänze
52 Bajaderen — Galopp
53 Bajaderen — Walzer
54 Contre-Tänze
55 Ein Strauss von Strauss —
Potpourri
56 Alexandra — Walzer
57 Zampa — Walzer
58 Mein schönster Tag in
Baden — Walzer
59 Die vier Temperamente —
Walzer
60 Karnevals-Spende —
Walzer
61 Tausendsapperment —
Walzer
62 Zampa-und Montecchi —
Galopp

63 Frohsinn mein Ziel —
Walzer
64 Robert Tänze (from *Robert
le Diable)*
65 Mittel gegen den Schlaf —
Walzer
66 Erinnerung an Pest —
Walzer
67 Erste Walzer-Guirlande
68 Gabriellen — Walzer
69 Fortuna — Galopp
70 Pfennig — Walzer
71 Elisabethen — Walzer
72 Cotillion on *Der Zwei-
kampf*
73 Original — Parademarsch
74 Venetianer Galopp
75 Iris — Walzer
76 Rosa — Walzer
77 Zweite Walzer-Guirlande
78 Erinnerung an Berlin —
Walzer
79 Gedankenstriche — Walzer
80 Huldigungs — Walzer
81 Grazien — Tänze
82 Philomelen — Walzer
83 Merkurs-Flügel —. Walzer
84 Heimatklänge — Walzer
85 Reise — Galopp
86 Ballnacht — Galopp
87 Erinnerung an Deutsch-
land — Walzer
88 Die Nachtwandler —
Walzer
89 Eisenbahn-Lust — Walzer
90 Jugendfeuer — Galopp
91 Krönungs — Walzer
92 Cotillions on *Les Huguenots*
93 Galopp on *Les Huguenots*
94 Künstlerball — Tänze
95 Brüssler Spitzen — Walzer

96 Ball-Raketen — Walzer
97 Cachucha — Galopp
98 Pilger am Rhein — Walzer
99 Bankett — Tänze
100 Der Karneval in Paris — Walzer
101 Paris — Walzer
102 Original — Parademarsch
103 Huldigung der Königin Viktoria — Walzer
104 Boulogner — Galopp
105 Freudengrüsse — Walzer
106 Musikalischer Telegraf — Potpourri
107 Versailler — Galopp
108 Gitana — Galopp
109 Exotische Pflanzen — Walzer
110 Taglioni — Walzer
111 Indianer — Galopp
112 Londoner Saison — Walzer
113 Die Bergmeister — Walzer
114 Furioso — Galopp
115 Rosenblätter — Walzer
116 Wiener Gemüts — Walzer
117 Ghibellinen — Walzer
118 Myrthen — Walzer
119 Tanz-Rezepte — Walzer
120 Cäcilien — Walzer
121 Dritte Walzer-Guirlande
122 Palmzweige — Walzer
123 Amors-Pfeile — Walzer
124 Wiener Karnevals — Quadrille
125 Elektrische Funken — Walzer
126 Erinnerung an Ernst, oder Der Karneval von Venedig
127 Deutsche Lust, oder Donaulieder ohne Texte — Walzer
128 Apollo — Walzer

129 Adelaiden — Walzer
130 Jubel-Quadrille — Walzer
131 Die Wettrennen — Walzer
132 Die Debutanten — Walzer
133 Sperl — Polka
134 Egerien-Tänze — Walzer
135 Die Tanzmeister — Walzer
136 Stadt-und Landleben — Walzer
137 Annen — Polka
138 Mode — Quadrille
139 Die Fantasten — Walzer
140 Musikverein-Tänze — Walzer
141 Die Minnesänger — Walzer
142 Haute-Volée — Quadrille
143 Latonen — Walzer
144 Parademarsch
145 Minos-Klänge — Walzer
146 Die Lustwandler — Walzer
147 Walhalla-Toaste — Walzer
148 Saison — Quadrille
149 Die Dämonen — Walzer
150 Künstlerball-Tänze — Walzer
151 Quadrille zur Namensfeier Kaiser Ferdinands
152 Tanz-Caprizen — Walzer
153 Quadrille zur Namensfeier der Kaiserin Maria Anna
154 Lorelei-Rhein-Klänge — Walzer
155 Bruder Lustig — Walzer
156 Asträa — Tänze
157 Volksgarten — Quadrille
158 Redoute — Quadrille
159 Nur Leben! — Walzer
160 Waldfräulein Hochzeits — Tänze
161 Salon — Polka
162 Orpheus — Quadrille

163 Frohsinns-Salven — Walzer

164 Aurora-Fest-Klänge — Walzer

165 Fest — Quadrille

166 Rosen ohne Dornen — Walzer

167 Wiener Früchteln — Walzer

168 Willkommen-Rufe — Walzer

169 Haimonskinder — Quadrille

170 Masken-Lieder — Walzer

171 Eunomien-Tänze — Walzer

172 Odeon-Tänze — Walzer

173 Marianka — Polka

174 Musen Quadrille

175 Faschings-Possen — Walzer

176 Geheimnisse aus der Wiener Tanzwelt — Walzer

177 Flora — Quadrille

178 Stradella — Quadrille

179 Österreichische Jubelklänge — Walzer

180 Sommernachtsträume — Walzer

181 Heitere Lebensbilder — Walzer

182 Der Landjunker — Walzer

183 Amoretten — Quadrille

184 Concordia — Tänze

185 Sofien — Tänze

186 Moldauklänge — Walzer

187 Konzert Souvenir — Quadrille

188 Österreichischer Festmarsch

189 Die Vortänzer — Walzer

190 Epigonen — Tänze

191 Zigeuner — Quadrille

192 Esmeralda — Marsch

193 Festlieder — Walzer

194 Eldorado — Quadrille

195 Die Unbedeutenden — Walzer

196 Charivari — Quadrille

197 Bouquets — Walzer

198 Ländlich, sittlich — Walzer

199 Neujahrs — Polka

200 Souvenir de Carnaval 1847 — Quadrille

201 Themisklänge — Walzer

202 Eisele-und Beisele-Sprünge — Polka

203 Herztöne — Walzer

204 Helenen — Walzer

205 Triumph — Quadrille

206 Najaden — Quadrille

207 Schwedische Lieder — Walzer

208 Die Schwalben — Walzer

209 Österreichischer Defiliermarsch

210 Kathinka — Polka

211 Quadrille on *Des Teufels Anteil*

212 Marien — Walzer

213 Feldbleameln — Walzer

214 Nador-Kör — Palatinal-Tanz

215 Martha — Quadrille

216 Die Adepten — Walzer

217 Schäfer — Quadrille

218 Tanz-Signale — Walzer

219 Fortuna — Polka

220 Wiener Kreuzen — Polka

221 Nationalgarde — Marsch

222 Äciden — Walzer

223 Marsch der Studentenlegion

224 Amphionklänge — Walzer

225 Äther-Träume — Walzer

226 Freiheits — Marsch

227 Marsch des einigens Deutschlands — Militärmarsch
228 Radetzky — Marsch
229 Quadrille im Militärischen Stil
230 Sorgenbrecher — Walzer
231 Brünner Nationalgarde — Marsch
232 Landesfarben — Walzer
233 Huldigungs — Quadrille
234 Louisen — Quadrille
235 Piefke-und Purfke — Polka
236 Damen-Souvenir — Polka
237 Des Wanderers Lebewohl — Walzer
238 Alice — Polka
239 Frederica — Polka
240 Two Marches for the Spanish Noble Guard
241 Die Friedensboten — Walzer
242 Soldatenlieder — Walzer
243 Almacks — Quadrille
244 Jellacic — Marsch
245 Wiener Jubelmarsch
246 Wiener Stadt — Garde-marsch
247 Deutsche Jubellaute — Walzer
248 Quadrille without title
249 Exeter — Polka
250 Fliegende Blätter — Pot-pourri
251 Melodische Tändeleien — Fantasy on Willmer's *Pompa di Festa*

JOHANN STRAUSS II

1 Sinngedichte — Walzer
2 Débût Quadrille
3 Herzenslust — Polka
4 Gunstwerber — Walzer
5 Serail-Tänze — Walzer
6 Entheren Quadrille
7 Die jungen Wiener — Walzer
8 Patriotenmarsch
9 Amazonen Quadrille
10 Liebesbrunnen Quadrille
11 Faschingslieder — Walzer
12 Jugendträume — Walzer
13 Czechenpolka
14 Serben Quadrille
15 Sträusschen Walzer
16 Elfen Quadrille
17 Jux — Polka
18 Berglieder — Walzer
19 Dämonen Quadrille
20 Austria Marsch
21 Lindgesänge — Walzer
22 Die Österreicher — Walzer
23 Pester Czardas
24 Zigeunerin Quadrille
25 Zeitgeister Quadrille
26 Fiedler Polka
27 Die Sanguiniker Walzer
28 Hopfer Polka
29 Odeon Quadrille
30 Die Zillerthaler — Walzer im Ländlerstil
31 Quadrille on motifs from Balfe's *The Siege of Rochelle*

32 Irenen — Walzer
33 Alexander — Quadrille
34 Die Jovialen Walzer
35 Architekten-Ball Tänze
36 Industrie — Quadrille
37 Wilhelminen — Quadrille
38 Bachus — Polka
39 Slaven — Quadrille
40 Quadrille on motifs from Boisselot's *La Reine de Lyons*
41 Sängerfahrten — Walzer
42 Wildrosen — Walzer
43 Explosions — Polka
44 Fest — Quadrille
45 Erste Tänze — Walzer
46 Martha — Quadrille
47 Dorfg'schichten — Walzer
48 Seladon — Quadrille
49 Fest — Marsch
50 Klänge aus der Malachei — Walzer
51 Marien — Quadrille on Rumanian Themes
52 Freiheitslieder — Walzer
53 Annika — Quadrille
54 Revolutions — Marsch
55 Burschenlieder — Walzer
56 Studenten Marsch
57 Ligourianer-Seufzer — Scherz-polka
58 Brünner-Nationalgarde Marsch
59 Quadrille on motifs from Halévy's *Lightning*
60 Seisselheibe Polka
61 Neue Steirischen Tänze
62 Einheitsklänge — Walzer
63 Sans-Souci — Quadrille
64 Fantasiebilder — Walzer
65 Nikolai — Quadrille on Russian Themes
66 D'Woaldbuama — Walzer im Ländlerstil
67 Kaiser Franz-Josef Marsch
68 Äolstäne — Walzer
69 Triumph Marsch
70 Die Gemütlichen — Walzer
71 Künstler — Quadrille
72 Scherzo — Polka
73 Frohsinnspender — Polka
74 Lava-Ströme — Walzer
75 Soften — Quadrille
76 Attaque — Quadrille
77 Wiener Garnisons Marsch
78 Heiligenstädter-Rendezvous — Polka
79 Marien-Tänze — Walzer
80 Herski-Holki — Polka
81 Luisen-Sympathie-Klänge — Walzer
82 Johanniskäferln — Walzer
83 Ottingen — Reitermarsch
84 Warschauer — Polka
85 Heimatskinder — Walzer
86 Bonvivant Quadrille
87 Aurora-Balltänze — Walzer
88 Slavenball — Quadrille
89 Hirtenspiele — Walzer
90 Orakelsprüche — Walzer
91 Hermann — Polka
92 Maskenfest — Quadrille
93 Kaiser-Jäger Marsch
94 Rhadamantus-Klänge — Walzer
95 Idyllen — Walzer
96 Viribus Unitis — Walzer
97 Sambrinn — Tänze
98 Promenade Quadrille
99 Frauenkäferln — Walzer

100   Böslauer — Polka
101   Mephistos Höllenrufe
        — Walzer
102   Albion — Polka
103   Vivat — Quadrille
104   Windsor-Klänge — Walzer
105   5 Paragraphen aus der
        Walzer-Bodex
106   Harmonie — Polka
107   Grossfürsten — Marsch
108   Die Unzertrennlichen
        — Walzer
109   Tête-à-Tête — Quadrille
110   Electro-Magnetische
        — Polka
111   Blumen — Polka
112   Melodie Quadrille nach
        Verdi
113   Sachsen-Kürassier Marsch
114   Liebeslieder Walzer
115   Wiener-Jubelgrüsse Marsch
116   Hofball — Quadrille
117   Annen — Polka
118   Lockvögel — Walzer
119   Volkssänger — Waltzer
120   Nocturne — Quadrille
121   Zehner — Polka
122   Indra — Quadrille
123   Satanella — Quadrille
124   Satanella — Polka
125   Phoenix-Schwingen Walzer
126   Jubel Marsch
127   Freudengrüsse — Polka
128   Solonsprüche — Walzer
129   Motor — Quadrille
130   Äsculap — Polka
131   Wiener-Punsch-Lieder
        — Walzer
132   Veilchen — Polka
133   Karussel Marsch
134   Tanzi-Bai Polka

135   Bouquet Quadrille
136   Vermählungs-Toaste
        — Walzer
137   Neuhauser — Polka
138   Pepita — Polka
139   Kron Marsch
140   Knallkügeln — Walzer
141   Wellen und Wogen —
        Walzer
142   Wiedersehen — Polka
143   Schneeglöckchen — Walzer
144   La Viennoise — Polka-
        Mazurka
145   Bürgerball — Polka
146   Novellen — Walzer
147   Musen — Polka
148   Schallwellen — Walzer
149   Erzherzog Wilhelm-Gene-
        sungsmarsch
150   Ballg'schichten — Walzer
151   Elisen — Polka
152   Karnevals-Spektakel —
        Quadrille
153   Nordstern — Quadrille
154   Myrthen-Kränze — Walzer
155   Haute-Volée — Polka
156   Napoleon Marsch
157   Nachtfalter Walzer
158   Alliance Marsch
159   Schnellpost — Polka
160   Ella — Polka
161   Panacea-Klänge — Walzer
162   Souvenir — Polka
163   Glossen — Walzer
164   Sirenen — Walzer
165   Aurora — Polka
166—Handels-Elite — Quadrille
167   Man Lebt Nur Einmal
        — Walzer
168   Leopoldstädter Polka
169   Bijouterie — Quadrille

170   Nachtveilchen — Polka-
  Mazurka
171   Freuden-Salven — Walzer
172—Gedanken auf den Alpen
  — Walzer
173   Marie Taglioni — Polka
174   Le Papillon — Polka-
  Mazurka
175   Erhöhte Pulse — Walzer
176   Armenball — Polka
177   Juristenball — Tänze
178   Sans-Souci — Polka
179   Abschiedsrufe — Walzer
180   Libellen — Walzer
181   Grossfürstin Alexandra
  — Walzer
182   L'Inconnue — Polka-
  Mazurka
183   Krönungsmarsch
184   Krönungslieder — Walzer
185   Strellna-Terrassen —
  Quadrille
186   Demi Fortune — Polka-
  Française
187   Une Bagatelle — Polka-
  Française
188   Herzel — Polka
189   Paroxysmens Walzer
190   Etwas Kleines — Polka-
  Française
191   Controversen — Walzer
192   Wien, mein Sinn — Walzer
193   Phänomene — Walzer
194   La Berceuse — Quadrille
195   Telegrafische Depeschen
  — Walzer
196   Olga — Polka-Française
197   Spleen — Polka-Mazurka
198   Alexandrinen — Polka-
  Française
199   Le Beau Monde — Quadrille

200   Souvenir de Nice — Walzer
201   Künstler Quadrille
202   L'Enfantillâge —Polka-
  Française
203   Helenen — Polka
204   Vibrationen — Walzer
205   Die Extravaganten —
  Walzer
206   Concordia — Polka-Mazurka
207   Cycloden — Walzer
208   Juxbrüder — Walzer
209   Spiralen — Walzer
210   Abschied von St. Petersburg
  — Walzer
211   Champagner — Polka
212   Fürst Bariatinsky Marsch
213   Bonbons — Polka-Française
214   Tritsch-Tratsch — Polka
215   Gedankenflug — Walzer
216   Hell und Voll — Walzer
217   La Favorita — Polka-
  Française
218   Irrlichter — Walzer
219   Auroraball — Polka-
  Française
220   Deutsche Walzer
221   Promotionen — Walzer
222   Nachtigall — Polka
223   Schwungräder — Walzer
224   Dinorah — Quadrille
225   Grüsse an Wien — Polka-
  Française
226   Der Kobold — Polka-
  Mazurka
227   Reise-Abenteuer — Walzer
228   Niko — Polka
229   Jäger — Polka-Française
230   Kammerball — Polka-
  Française
231   Drolerie — Polka-Française
232   Lebenswecker — Walzer

233 Sentenzen — Walzer
234 Accelerationen — Walzer
235 Immer heiterer — Walzer
236 Orpheus — Quadrille
237 Taubenpost — Polka-
Française
238 Die Pariserin — Polka-
Française
239 Polka-Mazurka champêtre
240 Maskenzug — Polka-
Française
241 Fantasieblümchen — Polka
Française
242 Bijoux — Polka-Française
243 Romanze
244 Diabolin — Polka-Française
245 Thermen — Walzer
246 Rokonhangok-Sympathie
Polka-Française
247 Grillenbanner — Walzer
248 Camelien — Polka
249 Hesperus — Polka-Française
250 Wahlstimmer — Walzer
251 Klangfiguren — Walzer
252 Dividenden — Walzer
253 Schwärmereien — Walzer
254 Neue Melodien — Quadrille
255 St. Petersburg — Quadrille
256 Veilchen — Walzer
257 Perpetuum Mobile — Scherzo-Galopp
258 Secunden — Polka-Française
259 Chansonetten — Quadrille
260 Furioso — Polka quasi
Galopp
261 Die ersten Kuren — Walzer
262 Kolonnen — Walzer
263 Studenten — Polka-Française
264 Patronessen — Walzer
265 Motoren — Walzer

266 Luzifer — Polka
267 Konkurenzen — Walzer
268 Wiener Chronik — Walzer
269 Demolierer — Polka-
Française
270 Karnevals-Botschafter
— Walzer
271 Bluette — Polka-Française
272 Quadrille on motifs from
Verdi's *Un Ballo in Maschera*
273 Leitartikel — Walzer
274 Patrioten — Polka
275 Lieder — Quadrille
276 Bauern — Polka-Française
277 Invitation à la Polka-
Mazurka
278 Neues Leben — Polka-
Française
279 Morgenblätter — Walzer
280 Juristenball — Schnellpolka
281 Vergnügungszug — Schnellpolka
282 Gut Bürgerlich — Polka-
Française
283 Saison — Quadrille
284 Deutsche Krieger — Marsch
285 Studentenlust — Walzer
286 Patronessen — Polka-
Française
287 Verbrüderungsmarsch
288 Neva — Polka-Française
289 Persischer Marsch
290 Quadrille sur des airs
français
291 'S giebt nur a Kaiserstadt,
's giebt nur a Wien — Schnellpolka
292 Aus den Bergen — Walzer
293 Feuilleton — Walzer
294 Prozesspolka — Schnellpolka
295 Bürgersinn — Walzer

296 Episode — Polka-Française
297 Electrophor — Schnellpolka
298 Hofballtänze — Walzer
299 Quadrille on motifs from
Meyerbeer's *L'Africaine*
300 Flugschriften — Walzer
301 Kreuzfidel — Polka-
Française
302 Der Zeitlose — Polka-
Française
303 Bal Champêtre — Quadrille
304 Kinderspiele — Polka-
Française
305 Damenspende — Polka-
Française
306 Bürgerweisen — Walzer
307 Wiener Bonbons — Walzer
308 Par Force — Schnellpolka
309 Sylphen — Polka-Française
310 Tändelei — Polka-Mazurka
311 Express — Schnellpolka
312 Feen-Märchen — Walzer
313 Wildfeuer — Polka-
Française
314 An der schönen, blauen
Donau — Walzer
315 Lob der Frauen — Polka-
Mazurka
316 Künstlerleben — Walzer
317 Postillon d'Amour — Polka-
Française
318 Telegramme — Walzer
319 Leichtes Blut — Schnellpolka
320 Figaropolka — Polka-
Française
321 Die Publicisten — Walzer
322 Stadt und Land — Polka-
Mazurka
323 Ein Herz, ein Sinn — Polka-
Mazurka

324 Über Donner und Blitz
— Schnellpolka
325 G'Schichten aus dem
Wiener Wald — Walzer
326 Freikugeln — Schnellpolka
327 Quadrille on themes from
Auber's *Le Premier jour de
Bonheur*
328 Sängerlust — Polka
329 Erinnerungen an Covent
Garden — Walzer on English
motifs
330 Fata Morgana — Polka-
Mazurka
331 Illustrationen — Walzer
332 Eiljen a Magyar — Schnellpolka
333 Wein, Weib und Gesang
— Walzer
334 Königslieder — Walzer
335 Egyptischer Marsch
336 Im Krapfenwald — Polka-
Française
337 Von der Börse — Polka-
Française
338 Slovakiana — Polka on
Russian melodies
339 Louischen — Polka-
Française
340 Freut euch des Lebens!
— Walzer
341 Festival — Quadrille
on English motifs
342 Neu-Wien — Walzer
343 Shawl — Polka-Française
(*Indigo*)
344 Indigo — Quadrille (*Indigo*)
345 Auf freiem Fusse —
Mazurka (*Indigo*)
346 Tausend und Eine Nacht
— Walzer (*Indigo*)

347 Aus der Heimat — Polka-Mazurka

348 Im Sturmschritt — Schnellpolka

349 Indigo Marsch (*Indigo*)

350 Lustiger Rath — Polka-Française

351 Die Bajadere — Schnellpolka

352 Russische Marsch-Fantasie

353 Russische Marsch-Fantasie

354 Wienerblut — Walzer

355 Im Russischen Dorfe — Fantasie

356 Vom Donaustrande — Schnellpolka

357 Karnevalsbilder — Walzer

358 Nimm sie hin — Polka-Française

359 Grüsse aus Österreich — Polka-Française

360 Rotunde — Quadrille

361 Bei uns z'Haus — Walzer

362 Die Fledermaus — Overture (*Fledermaus*)

363 Fledermaus — Quadrille (*Fledermaus*)

364 Wo die Zitronen blüh'n — Walzer

365 Tik-Tak — Schnellpolka (*Fledermaus*)

366 An der Moldau — Polka-Française (*Fledermaus*)

367 Du und Du — Walzer (*Fledermaus*)

368 Glücklich ist, wer vergisst — Polka-Française (*Fledermaus*)

369 Cagliostro Quadrille (*Cagliostro in Wien*)

370 Cagliostro — Walzer (*Cagliostro in Wien*)

371 Hoch Österreich! — Marsch (*Cagliostro in Wien*)

372 Bitte schön — Polka-Française (*Cagliostro in Wien*)

373 Auf der Jagd — Schnellpolka (*Cagliostro in Wien*)

374 Licht und Schatten — Polka-Mazurka (*Cagliostro in Wien*)

375 O schöner Mai — Walzer (*Prinz Methusalem*)

376 Methusalem Quadrille (*Prinz Methusalem*)

377 I-Tipferl — Polka-Française (*Prinz Methusalem*)

378 Bareditter Galopp

379 Kriegers Liebchen — Polka-Mazurka (*Prinz Methusalem*)

380 Ballsträusschen — Schnellpolka (*Prinz Methusalem*)

381 Kennst Du mich? — Walzer (*Prinz Methusalem*)

382 Pariser Polka-Française (*Prinz Methusalem*)

383 Nur fort! — Schnellpolka (*Prinz Methusalem*)

384 Opern-Maskenball — Quadrille (*Prinz Methusalem*)

385 Waldine — Polka-Mazurka

386 Frisch heran — Schnellpolka

387 In's Centrum — Walzer

388 Rosen aus dem Süden — Walzer (*Spitzentuch der Königin*)

389 Bürschenwanderung — Polka-Française (*Spitzentuch der Königin*)

390 Nordseebilder — Walzer
(*Spitzentuch der Königin*)

391 Gavotte der Königin
(*Spitzentuch der Königin*)

392 Spitzentuch Quadrille
(*Spitzentuch der Königin*)

393 Stürmisch in Lieb' und
Tanz — Schnellpolka
(*Spitzentuch der Königin*)

394 Liebchen, schwing Dich
— Polka-Mazurka
(*Spitzentuch der Königin*)

395 Myrthenblüten — Walzer

396 Jubelfest Marsch

397 Der Lustige Krieg —
Marsch (*Der Lustige Krieg*)

398 Frisch ins Feld — Marsch
(*Der Lustige Krieg*)

399 Was sich liebt, neckt sich
— Polka-Française (*Der Lustige Krieg*)

400 Kuss — Walzer (*Der Lustige Krieg*)

401 Der Klügere gibt nach —
Polka-Mazurka (*Der Lustige Krieg*)

402 Quadrille (*Der Lustige Krieg*)

403 Entweder, oder! — Schnellpolka (*Der Lustige Krieg*)

404 Violetta — Polka-Française
(*Der Lustige Krieg*)

405 Nord und Süd — Polka-Mazurka (*Der Lustige Krieg*)

406 Matador — Marsch
(*Das Spitzentuch der Königin*)

407 Italienischer March
(*Der Lustige Krieg*)

408 Habsburg Hoch! — Marsch
(*Der Lustige Krieg*)

409 Rasch in der That —
Schnellpolka

410 Frühlingstimmen — Walzer

411 Lagunen — Walzer (*Eine Nacht in Venedig*)

412 Papacoda — Polka-Française (*Eine Nacht in Venedig*)

413 So ängstlich sind wir nicht
— Galopp (*Eine Nacht in Venedig*)

414 Die Tauben von San Marco
— Polka-Française (*Eine Nacht in Venedig*)

415 Annina — Polka-Mazurka
(*Eine Nacht in Venedig*)

416 Quadrille (*Eine Nacht in Venedig*)

417 Bratschau — Polka (*Eine Nacht in Venedig*)

418 Schatz Walzer (*Der Zigeunerbaron*)

419 Kriegs-Abenteuer — Galopp
(*Der Zigeunerbaron*)

420 Die Wahrsagerin — Polka
Mazurka (*Der Zigeunerbaron*)

421 Husaren — Polka (*Der Zigeunerbaron*)

422 Zigeunerbaron — Quadrille
(*Der Zigeunerbaron*)

423 Wiener Frauen — Walzer

424 Adelen — Walzer

425 An der Wolga — Polka-Mazurka

426 Russischer Marsch

427 Donauweibchen — Walzer
(*Simplizius*)

428 Reitermarsch

429 Quadrille (*Simplizius*)

430 Soldatenspiel — Polka-Française (*Simplizius*)

431 Lagerlust — Polka-Française (*Simplizius*)
432 Mutig voran! — Schnell-polka (*Simplizius*)
433 Spanischer Marsch
434 Kaiser-Jubiläum — Jubel-Walzer
435 Sinnen und Minnen — Walzer
436 Auf zum Tanze — Schnell-polka
437 Kaiserwalzer
438 Rathausball-Tänze — Walzer
439 Durchs Telephon — Polka
440 Gross-Wien — Walzer
441 Ritter Pasman — Piano Arrangement
442 Unparteiische Kritiken — Polka-Mazurka
443 Seid Umschlungen, Million-en! — Walzer
444 Märchen aus dem Orient — Walzer
445 Ninetta — Walzer
and
Herzenkönigin — Polka-Française (*Fürstin Ninetta*)
446 Ninetta — Quadrille (*Fürstin Ninetta*)
447 Ninetta — Marsch (*Fürstin Ninetta*)
448 Diplomaten — Polka
449 Neue Pizzicato Polka
450 Ninetta — Galopp (*Fürstin Ninetta*)
451 Übersprungen
452 Festmarsch
453 Hochzeitsreigen — Walzer
454 Auf dem Tanzboden

455 Ich bin dir gut — Walzer (*Jabuka*)
456 Zivio! — Marsch (*Jabuka*)
457 Höh'! — Schnellpolka (*Jabuka*)
458 Tänze mit dem Besenstiel — Polka-Française (*Jabuka*)
459 Sonnenblume — Polka-Mazurka (*Jabuka*)
460 Jabuka Quadrille (*Jabuka*)
461 Gartenlaube — Walzer
462 Klug Gretelein — Walzer
463 Trau, schau, wem! — Walzer
464 Herjemineh — Polka-Française (*Waldmeister*)
465 Liebe und Ehe — Polka-Mazurka (*Waldmeister*)
466 Klipp-Klapp — Galopp (*Waldmeister*)
467 Es war so wunderbar — Marsch (*Waldmeister*)
468 Waldmeister — Quadrille (*Waldmeister*)
469 Hochzeits — Praeludium
470 Deutschmeisterjubiläums-marsch
471 Heut' ist Heut' — Walzer (*Die Göttin der Vernunft*)
472 Nur nicht mucken — Polka-Française (*Die Göttin der Vernunft*)
473 Wo unsere Fahne weht — Marsch (*Die Göttin der Vernunft*)
474 Husarenlied (*Die Göttin der Vernunft*)
475 Solowalzer (*Die Göttin der Vernunft*)
476 Potpourri on motifs from *Die Göttin der Vernunft*

477   An der Elbe — Walzer
478   Aufs Korn! — Bundesschüt-
     zenmarsch

479   Klänge aus der Raimund-
     szeit

UNPUBLISHED WORKS
(Incomplete)

Aschenbrödel — Ballet
Traumbilder — Orchestral
   Fantasia
Overture Comique

Josefinen-Tänze (Piano 4-hands)
Graduale
Romulus, Operetta
   (Act 1 complete)

OPERAS AND OPERETTAS BY JOHANN STRAUSS II

Die Lustigen Weiber von Wien		Never Produced
Indigo	February 10th, 1871	Theater-an-der-Wien
Karneval in Rom	March 1st, 1873	Theater-an-der-Wien
Die Fledermaus	April 5th, 1874	Theater-an-der-Wien
Cagliostro in Wien	February 27th, 1875	Theater-an-der-Wien
Prinz Methusalem	January 3rd, 1877	Carl Theater
Blindekuh	December 18th, 1878	Theater-an-der-Wien
Das Spitzentuch der Königin	October 1st, 1880	Theater-an-der-Wien
Der Lustige Krieg	November 25th, 1881	Theater-an-der-Wien
Eine Nacht in Venedig	October 3rd, 1883	Friedrich-Wilhem-strasse Theater, Berlin
Der Zigeunerbaron	October 24th, 1885	Theater-an-der-Wien
Simplizius	December 17th, 1887	Theater-an-der-Wien
Ritter Pasman	January 1st, 1892	Hofoperntheater, Wien
Fürstin Ninetta	January 10th, 1893	Theater-an-der-Wien
Jabuka	October 12th, 1894	Theater-an-der-Wien
Waldmeister	December 4th, 1895	Theater-an-der-Wien
Die Göttin der Vernunft	March 13th, 1897	Theater-an-der-Wien
Wiener Blut	October 25th, 1899	Carl Theater

Posthumous Revisions of Unsuccessful Strauss Operettas:

Gräfin Pepi (combination: Simplizius, Blindekuh)		
	July 5th, 1902	Vienna
1001 Nights (Indigo)	June, 1906	Vienna

JOSEF STRAUSS

1 Die Ersten und Letzten — Walzer
2 Vergiss mein nicht — Polka-Mazurka
3 Sturmquadrille
4 Mille fleurs — Polka
5 Flinserln — Walzer
6 Tarantel — Polka
7 Vielliebchen — Polka-Mazurka
8 Bacchanten — Quadrille
9 Punsch — Polka
10 Bauern — Polka-Mazurka
11 Rendezvous — Quadrille
12 Die Ersten nach dem Letzten — Walzer
13 Wiener Polka
14 Avantgarde — Marsch
15 Titi — Polka
16 Die Vorgeiger — Walzer
17 Maiblümchen — Polka-Mazurka
18 Wiegenlieder — Walzer
19 Lustlager — Polka
20 Schottischer Tanz
21 Policinello — Quadrille
22 Sehnsuchts — Polka-Mazurka
23 Joujou — Polka
24 Armee Marsch
25 Kadi — Quadrille
26 Die guten, alten Zeiten — Walzer
27 Jucker Polka
28 Sylphide — Polka-Française
29 Die Veteranen — Walzer
30 Ball-Silhouetten — Walzer
31 Herzbleameln — Polka-Mazurka
32 Dioscuren — Quadrille
33 Masken — Polka
34 Mairosen — Walzer
35 Une Pensée — Polka-Mazurka
36 Lichtenstein — Marsch
37 Psikos — Quadrille
38 Gedenke mein — Polka
39 Perlen der Liebe — Walzer
40 La Simplicité — Polka-Française
41 Wallonen — Marsch
42 La Chevalrêsque — Polka-Mazurka
43 Steeple-Chase — Polka
44 Fünf Kleebladln — Walzer
45 Parade — Quadrille
46 Musen — Quadrille
47 Frauenblätter — Walzer
48 Harlekin — Polka
49 Die Amazone — Polka-Mazurka
50 Nymphen — Polka-Française
51 Zeitbilder — Walzer
52 Matrosen — Polka
53 Defilier Marsch
54 Flora — Polka-Mazurka
55 Bonbon — Polka-Mazurka

56 Liebesgrüsse — Walzer
57 Moullinet — Polka-Française
58 Bivouâc — Quadrille
59 Kronprinzen Marsch
60 Laxenburger — Polka
61 Wiener Kinder — Walzer
62 Flattergeister — Walzer
63 Waldröslein — Polka-
Mazurka
64 Lanciers — Quadrille
65 Caprice — Quadrille
66 Wintermärchen — Walzer
67 Minerva — Polka-Mazurka
68 Soll und Haben — Walzer
69 Saus und Braus — Polka
70 Die Kokette — Polka-
Française
71 Schwert und Leier —
Walzer
72 Amanda — Polka-Mazurka
73 Sympathie — Polka-Mazurka
74 Elfen — Polka
75 Sturm — Polka
76 Adamira — Polka
77 Die Naive — Polka-
Française
78 Gurli — Polka
79 Waldbleameln — Ländler
80 Stegreif — Quadrille
81 Cupide — Polka-Française
82 Euterpe — Polka-Française
83 Figaro — Polka-Française
84 Cyclopen — Polka
85 Die Zufälligen Walzer
86 Erzherzog Karl — Marsch
87 Heldengedichte — Walzer
88 Immergrün — Polka-
Mazurka
89 Mignon — Polka-Française
90 Grüsse an München —
Polka-Française

91 Lustschwärmer — Walzer
92 Turner — Quadrille
93 Tag und Nacht — Polka
94 Bellona — Polka
95 Diana — Polka-Française
96 Sternschnuppen — Walzer
97 Débardeurs — Quadrille
98 Schabernak — Schnellpolka
99 Zephir — Polka-Française
100 Die Kosende — Polka-
Mazurka
101 Flammen — Walzer
102 Maskengeheimnisse —
Walzer
103 Fortunio-Magellone-
Daphnis — Quadrille
104 Aus dem Wiener Wald —
Polka-Mazurka
105 Phönix Marsch
106 Blitz — Schnellpolka
107 Dornbacher Rendezvous —
Polka-Française
108 Wiener Bonmots — Walzer
109 Die Soubrette — Schnellpolka
110 Die Schwebende — Polka-
Mazurka
111 Die Sonderlinge — Walzer
112 Faust Quadrille
113 Irenen — Polka-Française
114 Zeisserln — Walzer
115 Folichon — Quadrille
116 Hesperus-Ball Tänze
117 Die Lachtaube — Polka-
Mazurka
118 Amazonen — Quadrille
119 Amaranth — Polka-
Française
120 Tanzinterpellanten —
Walzer
121 Winterlust — Schnellpolka

122 Lieb' und Wein — Polka-Française
123 Angelika — Polka-Française
124 Glückskinder — Walzer
125 Seraphinen — Polka-Française
126 Neue Weltbürger — Walzer
127 Vorwarts! — Schnellpolka
128 Freudengrüsse — Walzer
129 Brennende Liebe — Polka-Mazurka
130 Touristen — Quadrille
131 Musenklänge — Walzer
132 Günstige Prognosen — Walzer
133 Auf Ferienreisen! — Schnellpolka
134 Patti — Polka-Française
135 Künstler-Caprice — Polka-Française
136 Sturmlauf-Turner — Schnellpolka
137 Sofien — Quadrille
138 Erzherzog Viktor Marsch
139 Normen — Walzer
140 Souvenir — Polka-Française
141 Streichmagnete — Walzer
142 Ausstellungs — Festmarsch
143 Associationen — Walzer
144 Die Schwätzerin — Polka-Mazurka
145 Capriole — Schnellpolka
146 Deutscher Unions — Marsch
147 Amouretten — Polka-Française
148 Edelweiss — Polka-Mazurka
149 Deutsche Sympathien — Walzer
150 Wiener Couplets — Walzer
151 Fantasiebilder — Walzer

152 Rudolfsheimer — Schnellpolka
153 Petitionen — Walzer
154 Lebensgeister — Polka-Française
155 Die Gazelle — Polka-Mazurka
156 Die Clienten — Walzer
157 Heroldquadrille
158 Die Industriellen — Walzer
159 Gablenz Marsch
160 Abendstern — Polka-Française
161 Pêle-mêle — Schnellpolka
162 Die Zeitgenossen — Walzer
163 Idylle — Polka-Mazurka
164 Dorfschwalben aus Österreich — Walzer
165 Fashion — Polka
166 Frauenherz — Polka-Mazurka
167 Arabella — Polka
168 *Les Géorgiennes,* Offenbach Operetta — Quadrille
169 Turner Quadrille
170 Sport — Polka
171 Einzugsmarsch
172 Herztöne — Walzer
173 Geheimne Anziehungskräfte (Dynamiden) — Walzer
174 Actionen — Walzer
175 Colosseum — Quadrille
176 Combinationen — Walzer
177 Frisch auf! — Polka-Mazurka
178 Gedenkblätter — Walzer
179 Schlaraffen — Polka-Française
180 Causerie — Polka-Française

181 Springinsfeld — Schnellpolka
182 Mailust — Polka-Française
183 Stiefmütterchen — Polka-
Mazurka
184 Transaktionen — Walzer
185 Verliebte Augen — Polka-
Française
186 Prinz Eugen Marsch
187 Flick und Flock — Quadrille
on themes from Hertel Ballets
188 Bouquet — Schnellpolka
189 Heilmethoden — Walzer
190 Pauline — Polka-Mazurka
191 Deutsche Grüsse — Walzer
192 Die Spinnerin — Polka-
Française
193 Forever — Schnellpolka
194 Expens-Noten — Walzer
195 Thalia — Polka-Mazurka
196 Les Bergers — Quadrille on
Offenbach themes
197 Helenen — Walzer
198 Vereinslieder — Walzer
199 Benedik — Walzer
200 Carrière — Schnellpolka
201 Wilde Rosen — Polka-
Mazurka
202 Die Marketenderin —
Polka-Française
203 Schwalbenpost — Schnellpolka
204 Die Libelle — Polka-
Mazurka
205 Genien — Polka-Française
206 Blaubart — Quadrille on
Offenbach operettas
207 Friedenspalmen — Walzer
208 Etiquette — Polka
Française
209 Pariser Quadrille

210 Schwarzenberg Monument
Marsch
211 Farewell — Schnellpolka
212 Delirien — Walzer
213 Theater — Quadrille
214 Marienklänge — Walzer
215 Arm in Arm — Polka-
Mazurka
216 Jocus — Polka
217 Gnomen — Polka-Française
218 Wiener Leben — Polka-
Française
219 Allerlei — Schnellpolka
220 Hesperus — Ländler
221 Die Windsbraut — Schnellpolka
222 Studententräume — Walzer
223 Quadrille on themes from
*La Grande-Dûchesse de Gérol-
stein*, Offenbach
224 Quadrille on themes from
Crispino e la Comare, Ricci
225 Ungarischer Krönungsmarsch
226 Krönungslieder
227 Die Tänzerin — Polka-
Française
228 Viktoria — Polka-Française
229 Nachtschatten — Polka-
Mazurka
230 Im Fluge — Schnellpolka
231 In der Heimat — Polka-
Mazurka
232 Herbstrosen — Walzer
233 Lock — Polka-Française
234 Tanzadressen — Walzer
235 Sphärenklänge — Walzer
236 Dithyrambe — Polka-
Mazurka
237 Gallopin — Schnellpolka

238 Tanzregulator — Polka-Française

239 Wiener Stimmen — Walzer

240 Eingesendet — Schnellpolka

241 Extempore — Polka-Française

242 Hochzeitsklänge — Walzer

243 Disputationen — Walzer

244 Margherita — Polka-Française

245 Plappermäulchen — Schnellpolka

246 Quadrille on themes from *Genoveva*, Offenbach

247 Eile mit Weile — Schnellpolka

248 Die Sirene — Polka-Mazurka

249 Wiener Fresken — Walzer

250 Schützenmarsch

251 Die Galante — Polka-Mazurka

252 Buchstaben — Polka-Française

253 Freigeister — Schnellpolka

254 Ernst und Humor — Walzer

255 Ungarischer Krönungsmarsch

256 Périchole — Quadrille

257 Concordia — Polka

258 Aquarellen — Walzer

259 Vélocipède — Schnellpolka

260 Consortien — Walzer

261 Eislauf — Schnellpolka

262 Neckerei — Polka-Mazurka

263 Mein Lebenslauf ist Lieb' und Lust! — Walzer

264 Frohsinn — Schnellpolka

265 Toto — Quadrille on Offenbach operettas

266 Die tanzende Muse — Polka-Mazurka

267 Die Nasswalderin — Polka-Mazurka

268 Andrassy Marsch

269 Feuerfest — Schnellpolka

270 Aus der Ferne — Polka-Mazurka

271 Ohne Sorgen — Schnellpolka

272 Frohes Leben — Walzer

273 En Passant — Polka

274 Künstlergrüsse — Polka

275 Nilfluthen — Walzer

276 Kakadu — Quadrille

277 Frauenwürde — Walzer

278 Jockey — Galopp

279 Hesperusbahnen — Walzer

280 Tanzprioritäten — Walzer

281 Heiterer Muth — Polka

282 Die Emancipierte — Polka-Mazurka

283 Rudolfsklänge — Walzer

EDUARD STRAUSS

1 Ideal — Polka-Française
2 Die Kandidaten — Walzer
3 Sonette — Polka-Française
4 Gut heil! — Turnermarsch
5 Eldorado — Polka-Française
6 ?
7 Mannschaft an Bord — Quadrille on operetta by Zaytz
8 Karnevalsgrüsse — Polka-Mazurka
9 Iris — Polka-Française
10 Fitzliputzli — Quadrille on operetta by Zaytz
11 Lebenslust — Schnellpolka
12 Maskenfavorite — Polka-Française
13 Die Evolvirende — Polka-Française
14 Quadrille on Offenbach's La Belle Hélène
15 Quadrille on Offenbach's Gascoletto
16 Paragraphen — Polka-Française
17 Grüsse an die Heimat — Polka-Française
18 Die Hesperiden — Walzer
19 Dornröschen — Polka-Mazurka
20 Die Gazelle — Schnellpolka
21 Colibri — Polka-Française
22 Piroutte — Polka-Française

23 Liederkranz — Quadrille on Schubert songs
24 Quadrille on Offenbach's La Vie Parisienne
25 Apollo — Polka-Française
26 Memoiren einer Ballnacht — Walzer
27 Herz an Herz — Polka-Mazurka
28 Kreuz und Quer — Schnellpolka
29 Fleurette — Polka
30 Tanz-Parole — Polka
31 Wiener Stereoscopen — Walzer
32 Karnevals-Blume — Polka-Mazurka
33 Studentenliebchen — Polka-Mazurka
34 Die Ballkönigin — Polka-Française
35 Nachtrag — Polka-Française
36 Harmonie — Polka-Française
37 Wunderblümchen — Polka Française
38 Jugendlust — Polka-Française
39 Freie Gedanken — Walzer
40 Devise — Polka-Française
41 Wiener Genrebilder — Walzer
42 Thauperl — Polka

43 Froh durch die ganze
Welt! — Schnellpolka
44 Lanciermarsch
45 Bahn frei! — Schnellpolka-
Galopp
46 Vom Tage — Polka-
Mazurka
47 In Künstlerkreisen — Polka-
Française
48 Studentenstreiche — Polka-
Française
49 Sardanapal-Ballet — Quadrille
50 Sängerliebchen — Polka-
Française
51 Pegasussprünger — Polka-
Française
52 Flüchtige Skizzen —
Walzer
53 Über Stock und Stein —
Schnellpolka
54 Die Viene — Polka-Française
55 Eisblume — Polka-Mazurka
56 Stempelfrei — Polka-Française
57 Banditenquadrille — Quadrille on themes by Offenbach
58 Pro und Contra — Polka-
Française
59 Echo aus unseren Bergen —
Polka-Française
60 Con amore — Polka-Française
61 Lilienkränze — Walzer
62 Schattenquadrille — Quadrille on themes by Offenbach
63 La Gloire du Brésil —
Marche Triomphâle
64 Flott — Schnellpolka
65 Deutsche Herzen — Walzer

66 Serenade — Polka-Mazurka
67 Von der Aula — Polka-
Française
68 Academische Bürger —
Walzer
69 Mit der Feder! — Polka-
Mazurka
70 Mit Dampf! — Schnell-
polka
71 Trapezuntquadrille — Quadrille on themes by Offenbach
72 Hypothesenwalzer
73 Auf und davon! — Schnellpolka
74 Fusionen — Walzer
75 Fesche Geister — Walzer
76 Herzblättchen — Polka-
Française
77 Goldfischlein — Polka-
Mazurka
78 Bruder Studio — Polka-
Française
79 Doctrinen — Walzer
80 Ehret die Frauen — Walzer
81 Weicht aus! — Schnellpolka
82 Ballpromessen — Walzer
83 Amors Grüsse — Polka-
Française
84 Liebeszauber — Polka-
Française
85 Soldatengrüsse — Polka-
Française
86 Eine neue Welt! — Schnellpolka
87 Myrthensträusschen —
Walzer
88 Huldigungen — Walzer
89 Colombine — Polka-
Mazurka
90 Manuscripte — Walzer

91 Pilger — Quadrille on *The Pilgrims* by M. Wolf

92 Quadrille on themes from *Le Corsair Noir* by Offenbach

93 Lustig im Kreise — Schnellpolka

94 Javotte — Quadrille from the operetta *Javotte* by Émile Jonas

95 Unter eigenem Dache — Polka-Française

96 Pest-Ofener Eissport — Galopp

97 Interpretationen — Walzer

98 Ein Stück Wien — Polka-Française

99 Mädchenlaune — Polka-Mazurka

100 Nach kurzer Rast — Schnellpolka

101 Studentenball-Tänze — Walzer

102 Ein Jahr freiwillig — Polka-Française

103 Expositionen — Walzer

104 Stimmen aus dem Publikum — Walzer

105 Goldchignon — Quadrille from the Jonas operetta

106 Laut und traut — Polka-Mazurka

107 Wiener Weltausstellungsmarsch

108 Wo man lacht und lebt — Schnellpolka

109 Kaiser Franz-Josefs Jubiläum Marsch

110 Angot — Quadrille from *Ma'mselle Angot*, Lecocq

111 Theorien Walzer

112 Ohne Aufenthalt — Schnellpolka

113 Aulalieder — Walzer

114 Die Hochquelle — Polka-Mazurka

115 Flottes Leben — Polka-Française

116 Die Abonnenten — Polka-Française

117 Der König hat's gesagt — Quadrille on *Le Roi l'a dit,* Delibes

118 In Lieb' entbrannt — Polka-Française

119 Augensprache — Polka-Française

120 Weyprecht-Payer Marsch

121 Unter der Enns — Schnellpolka

122 Giroflé — Quadrille on themes from Lecocq operettas

123 Giroflé-Girofla — Walzer on themes from Lecocq operettas

124 Fidele Burschen — Walzer

125 Tour und retour — Polka-Française

126 Aus dem Rechtsleben — Walzer

127 Alpenrose — Polka-Mazurka

128 Kleine Chronik — Schnellpolka

129 Märzveilchen — Polka-Française

130 Bessere Zeiten — Walzer

131 Herz und Welt — Polka-Mazurka

132 Knall und Fall — Schnellpolka

133 Fantasie über neuere Deutsche Lieder

134   Carmen — Quadrille on themes from Bizet's opera
135   Aus Lieb' zu ihr! — Polka-Française
136   Fatinitza — Quadrille on themes from von Suppé's operetta
137   Verdichte Walzer
138   Über Feld und Wiese — Schnellpolka
139   Blümchen-Tausendschön — Polka
140   Von Land zu Land — Polka-Française
141   Aus der Studienzeit — Walzer
142   Aus der Visur — Polka-Française
143   Consequenzen — Walzer
144   Gruss an Prag — Polka-Française
145   Schön Rotraut — Polka-Mazurka
146   Souvenir de Bade — Schnellpolka
147   Fatinitza — Walzer on themes from von Suppé's operetta
148   Graziella — Quadrille on themes from Lecocq's opera
149   Dr. Piccolo — Quadrille on themes from Lecocq's operetta
150   Das Leben ist doch schön — Walzer
151   Seekadett — Quadrille on theme's from Genée's operetta
152   Treuliebchen — Polka-Française
153   Mit frohem Muth und heiter'm Sinn — Walzer
154   Brausteufelchen — Galopp

155   Märchen aus der Heimat — Walzer
156   Ballade — Polka-Mazurka
157   Schneesternchen — Polka-Française
158   Geflügelte Worte — Walzer
159   Saat und Ernte — Schnellpolka
160   Liebesbotschaft — Polka-Mazurka
161   Leuchtkäferln — Walzer
162   Opern-Soirée — Polka-Française
163   Teufels — Quadrille on themes from von Suppé's *Der Teufel aus Erden*
164   Nuetzt das freie Leben! — Walzer
165   Telephon — Polka-Française
166   Reiselust — Polka-Française
167   Ball-Chronik — Walzer
168   Ausser Rand und Band — Schnellpolka
169   Mossröschen — Polka-Française
170   Traumgebilde — Walzer
171   Gruss an Stockholm — Polka-Française
172   Wien über Alles — Schnellpolka
173   Herzblättchen — Quadrille on themes from von Suppé's operettas
174   Mit der Strömung — Polka-Mazurka
175   Boccaccio — Walzer on themes from von Suppé's operetta
176   Poésie und Prosa — Polka-Mazurka
177   Lustfahrten — Walzer

178 Rundgesänge — Walzer
179 Pfeilschnell — Schnellpolka
180 Boccaccio — Quadrille on themes from von Suppé's operetta
181 En miniature — Polka-Mazurka
182 Souvenir de Dresde — Polka-Française
183 Un petit rien
184 Térpsichore — Polka-Française
185 Feuerfunken — Walzer
186 Hectograph — Schnellpolka
187 Still und bewegt — Polka-Française
188 Freie Lieder — Walzer
189 Originalbericht — Polka-Française
190 Juanita — Walzer
191 Juanita — Quadrille
192 Fleur roumaine — Polka-Française
193 Nisida — Walzer on themes from Genée's operetta
194 Herzen's-Telegraf — Polka-Mazurka
195 Bemooste Haupter — Walzer
196 Passe partout — Schnell-polka
197 Je pense à toi — Polka-Française
198 Glockensignale — Walzer
199 Probenummer — Walzer
200 Krone und Schleier — Walzer
201 Mit zartem Kolorit — Polka-Mazurka
202 Wo Lust und Freude wohnen

203 Faschingsbrief — Polka-Française
204 Schneewittchen — Polka-Mazurka
205 Lebende Blumen — Walzer
206 Lustig und durstig — Schnellpolka
207 Heitere Weisen — Walzer
208 Die Träumerin — Polka-Mazurka
209 Quadrille on themes from Der kleine Prinz, by A. Müller, Jr.
210 Jugendfeuer — Schnellpolka
211 Österreichs Völker-Treue Marsch
212 Bettelstudent — Quadrille on themes from Millöcker's operetta
213 Karnevalstudien — Walzer
214 Vergnügungsanzeiger — Polka-Française
215 Nixenreigen — Polka-Mazurka
216 Glühlichter — Walzer
217 Witzblitz — Galopp
218 Gemütswelle — Polka-Mazurka
219 Quadrille on themes from Die Afrikareise by von Suppé
220 Jubelfanfaren — Walzer
221 Mit chic — Galopp
222 Quadrille on themes from Gasparone by Millöcker
223 Chère amie — Polka-Française
224 Bei Sing-Sang und Bech-erklang — Walzer
225 Organ für Tanzlustige Polka-Française

226 Schmeichelkätzchen —
Polka-Mazurka
227 Lustige G'schichten —
Walzer
228 Mit Vergnügen — **Galopp**
229 Gruss an Budapest —
Polka-Française
230 Mein Lieblingsblümchen
Polka-Mazurka
231 Im Flug mit ihr — Schnellpolka
232 Landeskinder — Walzer
233 Grüsse an der Aula —
Walzer
234 Kunstnotiz — Polka-
Française
235 Liebeszeichen — Polka-
Mazurka
236 Stelldichein — Polka-
Française
237 Wiener Dialekt — Walzer
238 Ohne Bremse — Schnellpolka
239 ?
240 Don Césâr — Quadrille on
themes from Dellinger's operetta
241 Um die Wette — Galopp
242 Widmungsblätter — Walzer
243 Sprühfeuer — Schnellpolka
244 Denksprüche — Walzer
245 Lyra — Polka-Française
246 Der Rose Erwachen —
Polka-Mazurka
247 Tagesrapport — Polka-
Française
248 Zeitvertreib — Galopp
249 Freudensalven — Walzer
250 Centifolie — Polka-Mazurka
251 Wer tanzt mir? — Galopp
252 Heimische Klänge — Walzer

253 Karnevals-Bulletin — Polka-
Française
254 Blauäuglein — Polka-
Française
255 Für lustige Leut' — Walzer
256 In Banden der Leibe —
Polka-Mazurka
257 Flüchtiger als Wind und
Welle — Galopp
258 Blumensprache — Polka-
Mazurka
259 Mit Extrapost — Galopp
260 Aus den schlesischen
Bergen — Polka-Mazurka
261 Als ich dich sah: Es war'
vor langen Jahren — Song with
Piano Accompaniment
262 O schöne Jugendzeit —
Polka-Française
263 ?
264 ?
265 ?
266 ?
267 ?
268 ?
269 ?
270 ?
271 ?
272 Myrthenzauber — Walzer
273 ?
274 ?
275 ?
276 ?
277 ?
278 ?
279 ?
280 ?
281 ?
282 ?
283 ?
284 ?

285 ?
286 ?
287 ?
288 ?
289 ?
290 Hochzeitslieder — Walzer
291 Wiener Type — Polka
     Française

292 Bouquet of Strauss Waltzes
     in Chronological Order from
     1844 to the Present
293 Tanz-Candidaten — Walzer
294 Aus dem Künstler-Album —
     Polka Française
295 Die Jubilanten — Walzer

WORKS WRITTEN JOINTLY BY JOHANN AND JOSEF STRAUSS:

Pizzicato Polka
Hinter den Kulissen — **Quadrille**
Vaterländischer Marsch
Monstre — **Quadrille**

WORKS WRITTEN JOINTLY BY JOHANN, JOSEF AND EDUARD STRAUSS:

Trifolien — Walzer
Schützen — Quadrille

BIBLIOGRAPHY

BOOKS

(In German)

Ludwig Eisenberg	*Johann Strauss, ein Lebensbild*
Ernst Decsey	*Johann Strauss, ein Wiener Buch*
R. F. von Prochaska	*Johann Strauss*
Richard Specht	*Johann Strauss*
F. Lange	*Johann Strauss*
K. Kobald	*Johann Strauss*
Siegfried Löwy	*Rund um Johann Strauss*
Ignaz Schnitzer	*Meister Johann* (2 vols.)
H. Sündermann	*Johann Strauss, ein Vollender*
M. Kronberg	*Johann Strauss*
W. Jaspert	*Johann Strauss, sein Leben, sein Werk, seine Zeit*
Adele Strauss	*Johann Strauss schreibt Briefe* (Letters of Johann Strauss)
K. Hushke	*Unsere Tonmeister untereinander*, Vol. V
A. Witeschnik	*Die Dynastie Strauss*
Eduard Strauss	*Erinnerungen*
Max Herzig	*Viribus Unitis — Das Buch vom Kaiser*

(In English)

H. E. Jacob	*Johann Strauss, Father and Son*
Ada B. Alcott	*The Waltz Kings of Old Vienna*
David Ewen	*Musical Vienna*
Karl Geiringer	*Brahms, his Life and Work*
Bertita Harding	*The Golden Fleece*
S. Kracauer	*Orpheus in Paris* (The Life and Times of Offenbach)

ARTICLES

(In German)

As Others See Us, by Eduard Strauss
A Glance at the New World, by E. Strauss   *Wiener Tageblatt,*
                                              February 3rd, 1891

(In English)

Johann Strauss, a Biography   *Musical Times,* 1901
Johann Strauss and his Influence   *Musical Times,* 1894
Eduard Strauss in Boston, clippings of 1890   File, Boston Public
                                              Library

CATALOGUES, ETC.

(In German)
Chr. Flamme   *Verzeichnis sämtlicher Kompositionen von
                       Johann Strauss* (**Vater**), *Johann Strauss* (**Sohn**),
                       Josef Strauss und Eduard Strauss

(In French)
Riemann   *Dictionnaire de Musique*

(In English)
Baker   *Biographical Dictionary of Muscians*
J. W. McSpadden   *Light Opera and Musical Comedy*
R. D. Darrell   *The Gramophone Shop Encyclopedia
                       of Recorded Music* — 1936 Edition
George Leslie   *The Gramophone Shop Encyclopedia
                       of Recorded Music* — 1942 Edition
Boston Public Library: Programs — World's Peace Jubilee
                       and International Music Festival,
                       June 17th — July 4th, 1872.
                       Jubilee Sheet, June 17th, 1872,
                       Boston *Transcript*
McMillan   *Encyclopedia of Music and Musicians*

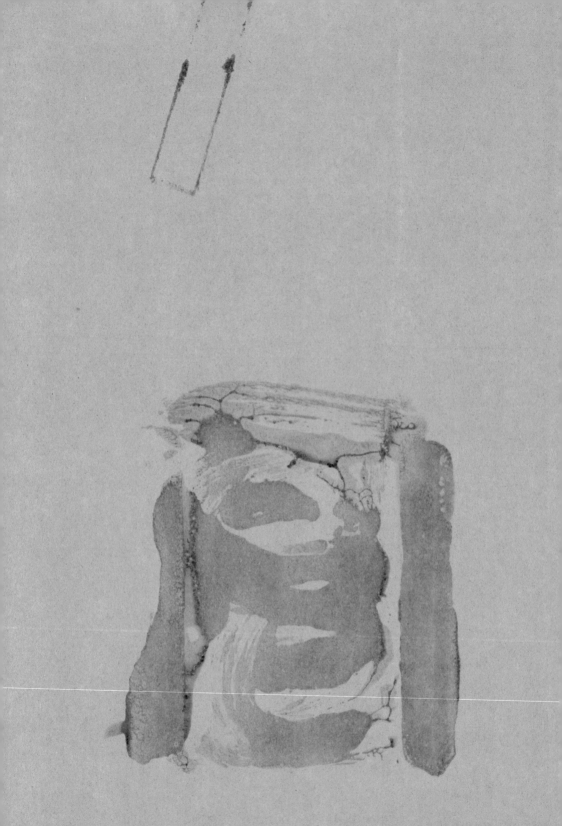